Korean Atrocity!

Korean Atrocity!

Forgotten War Crimes
1950 – 1953

Philip D. Chinnery

Airlife
England

Copyright © 2000 Philip D. Chinnery

First published in the UK in 2000
by Airlife Publishing Ltd

British Library Cataloguing-in-Publication Data
A catalogue record for this book
is available from the British Library

ISBN 1 84037 103 X

Typeset by Phoenix Typesetting, Ilkley, West Yorkshire.
Printed in England by Biddles Ltd, www.biddles.co.uk

Airlife Publishing Ltd

101 Longden Road, Shrewsbury, SY3 9EB England.

E-mail: airlife@airlifebooks.com
Website: www.airlifebooks.com

The author would like to thank the following for their help with his research:

Graham Bailey, Lofty Large and Reverend Sam Davies of the Glosters; Derek Kinne of the 'Fighting Fifth Fusiliers'; Henry O'Kane, George Hobson and Lt Robin Bruford-Davies of the Royal Ulster Rifles; Steve Kiba and Roland Parks who experienced Chinese 'hospitality' north of the Yalu River; Ed Slater and Shorty Estabrook, both Death March survivors; Artilleryman Oscar Cortez; Frank Kestner who survived the fighting at the infamous Chosin Reservoir. Terry McDaniel and Jimmy Montoya from the Namwon Bunch; Harry Gennaro of the 8th Cavalry; Search and Recovery Team Leader Tom Sechrest; James Prewitt. The doctors' side of the story was told by Sidney Esensten, William Shadish, Douglas Patchett and the late Gene Lam. The story of Walter Bray was related courtesy of his daughter Lillian. Thank you also to Michael Baldwin, Robert Dumas and the other family members who still wait for news of the fate of their loved ones. May their patience be rewarded one day.

PREFACE

While newspapers have recently been full of stories concerning the treatment of Albanian civilians at the hands of the Serbian Army in Yugoslavia, another harrowing story is beginning to emerge. As the historian for the National Ex-Prisoners of War Association I have been carrying out research in the Public Record Office and discovered some recently declassified files on the Korean War (originally they were to be closed for seventy-five years, until 2028, but have now been made available). They contain the records of investigations into 1,615 atrocities and war crimes perpetrated against troops serving with the United Nations Command in Korea between 1950 and 1953. Some 10,233 of the victims were American soldiers.

Much of the material in the records is frankly horrific. If there had been a clear victor in the war there is no doubt that war crimes trials would have been held and many North Korean and Chinese soldiers and officers would have been imprisoned or executed as a result. As it is, the perpetrators have gone unpunished, even though the names of some are known. There is no means of extracting them from their homelands today, but it is possible to make known to the general public the crimes they committed.

The scope of this book can be divided into three main parts. The first part covers the first year of the war, at the end of which the two sides had fought themselves to a standstill in roughly the same position they were in when the war began. This is the time period when most of the war crimes, death marches and atrocities took place. The second part of the book deals mainly with the lot of the Allied prisoners of war, by now moved to camps on the Yalu River, the border between China and North Korea. Starvation, sickness and forced indoctrination were three of the things they had to suffer. The third part of the book covers the end of the war and the exchange of prisoners. Then we move on to the mysteries: what happened to the men who did not come home?

Another facet that should be published is the heroism of the prisoners who survived or escaped to freedom. Captain (now Major-General) Farrar-Hockley, for example, escaped seven times before he finally gained his freedom. The fate of those prisoners who were known to be alive at the end of the war but were not returned can also be investigated. One British wing commander was known to be a prisoner in a tungsten mine, together with thirty-five American officers, some three months after the final release of prisoners. One confidential US government document found by the author discusses the disappearance of dozens of American pilots following their interrogation by Soviet intelligence. More than 8,000 US personnel are still 'missing' and unaccounted for. Some are presumed to have been taken to China and the Soviet Union. What happened to them?

Another intelligence document in the author's possession, based on a CIA debriefing of a high-ranking Czech defector, suggests that prisoners of war were used as medical guinea pigs by Soviet, Czech and North Korean doctors. The experiments, performed at 'a Czech-built hospital in North Korea', were conducted to 'develop methods of modifying human behaviour and destroying psychological resistance' and 'to train Czech and Soviet doctors under wartime conditions'. The latter involved such training as amputations carried out on healthy prisoners.

To substantiate these stories we have the account of the B-29 crew that was released by the Chinese two years after the war ended. One of the crew tells of the men they left behind and the instructions by the American government to keep quiet about what they had seen. Did one of the foreign witnesses at the 1992 Senate hearings into the POW/MIA issue really see American body parts in a North Korean War Museum, and were Caucasians seen tending crops in a field in North Korea – prisoners kept back by the communists at the end of the war? What is being done to track down and recover these men and the remains of those killed while prisoners? What are the prospects for the future?

In the summer of 2000 South Korea intends to mark the fiftieth anniversary of the start of the Korean War and veterans from the twenty-two nations which took part will be invited to attend. It would seem, therefore, an appropriate time to release a book on the subject.

Philip D. Chinnery
January 2000

CONTENTS

ONE

A KOREAN DUNKIRK?

SURPRISE ATTACK

Lieutenant Bill Bailey squinted through the windscreen of his aircraft at the four dots fast approaching from the north. Were they the air force F-82s that were supposed to be escorting their supply mission to Suwon? They came nearer and then, to Bailey's surprise, they broke into two pairs, the first pair diving towards the airstrip below and the cargo plane unloading on the ground. The second pair headed directly for Bailey's C-54 aircraft.

Instinctively, Bailey turned the aircraft away and ordered Lieutenant Ahokas, his navigator, to climb up on a stool and look out of the astrodome towards the rear of the plane to try to see what was happening. The two North Korean Yak fighters were right on their tail and as the navigator peered through the glass dome their wings sparkled and a burst of tracer fire flew by his head. Startled, he dived backwards into the plane as the pilot dived towards the ground. For the next thirteen minutes Bailey threw his big plane around the sky, trying to keep one step ahead of the attackers.

Suddenly a bullet exploded in the rear of the cargo compartment with a bright flash and a cloud of smoke. They were carrying 14,000 pounds of 105mm howitzer ammunition and the bullet struck close to the powder canisters stored in the rear of the plane. Bailey increased his speed as the Yaks came round again. Holes appeared in the hydraulic system, the radio operator's station, the fuselage and the wings and much of the engine instrumentation to two of the four engines was knocked out. Eventually, their ammunition exhausted, the Yaks drew level with the plane and stayed there, observing for twenty or thirty seconds. Finally they broke away, towards the north.

Bailey climbed into cloud cover and turned his plane towards Japan and home. Air–Sea Rescue sent a B-17 to escort them to Ashiya Air Base, where ground crew later counted 292 holes in their aircraft. The other C-54 at Suwon airfield did not fare so well. A sitting duck, its crew fled into the nearby rice paddies where the co-pilot received a non-fatal bullet in the backside while his plane caught fire and burned. It

1

was 28 June 1950, and America was at war again.

Three days earlier, at four a.m. on 25 June, North Korean T-34 tanks had rolled south across the invisible 38th Parallel which divided North and South Korea. Equipped and advised by the Soviets, the North Korean advance took the Army of the Republic of Korea (ROK) by surprise and they fell back in disarray.

Although American advisers had been training and equipping the ROK Army, the South Koreans were in no condition to take on the North Koreans. They had no aircraft or tanks, nor any means of destroying the enemy T-34s. As they began to retreat, US Far East Air Force headquarters in Japan despatched transport aircraft to evacuate the Americans in South Korea.

Almost a full day passed before President Truman and his advisers in the United States began to stir themselves into action. By now the invaders were only seventeen miles north of Seoul, the capital of South Korea. The lack of action on the part of the Americans was only to be expected, after all, had they not recently made it clear that they would not fight for Korea? The Russians who had backed the invasion, and the North Koreans themselves, were in for a surprise: despite earlier statements to the contrary, President Truman decided that the United States would contest the invasion.

The United Nations Security Council met the following day. The Soviet Union was not represented at the meeting, having decided to boycott the council, as a member of which they had veto power over action by the international body. It was a great mistake on their part. The Security Council passed a resolution that called on member nations to give military aid to South Korea to repel the North Korean attack. General MacArthur, the World War II hero and now head of the US Occupation Forces in Japan, flew to South Korea to assess the situation for himself and recommended that two American divisions be sent without delay. President Truman agreed, and directed the Pentagon to set the wheels in motion.

On 27 June American fighters shot down three North Korean Yak-7 planes on the way to attack Kimpo airfield near Seoul. Four more were shot down later that day. On the ground, though, things were going from bad to worse. Streams of refugees fled southwards as Seoul was abandoned to the enemy. The bridges spanning the Han River, just south of the city, were blown up on the orders of a panicking minister of defence, killing or injuring 4,000 soldiers and civilians who were crossing them at the time. Much of the ROK Army was stranded on the far bank of the river and had to abandon their transport, supplies and heavy weapons and swim or cross in small boats. By the time the last man had crossed to safety it was estimated that only 54,000 men remained from the 98,000 ROK troops that were under arms on the day of the invasion.

On the morning of 28 June the weather improved and American planes went into action. Flying from bases in Japan, B-26 and B-29 bombers began to bomb roads and railway lines north of Seoul, while F-80 and F-82 fighters strafed troop concentrations and columns on the road. Unfortunately, with the poor ground-to-air communication that existed in those days, South Korean troops were also liable to be strafed by the over-zealous American pilots.

The air attacks alone could not prevent the fall of the South Korean capital, and when the North Koreans entered the city on 28 June they occupied the university hospital, wherein lay 150 wounded South Korean soldiers. Upon the orders of the commanding officer, all the patients were shot or bayoneted in their beds and their bodies buried behind the hospital (Korean War Crimes case number 36/KWC36).

On 30 June President Truman approved the immediate despatch of a regimental combat team to Korea and ordered a naval blockade of North Korean ports. The British had ten ships in the area already, and the Australians two, plus a squadron of fighter planes based in Japan. As the ships began to steam towards Korea, the war had only been in progress for five days.

A couple more days passed while the communist secret police began to arrest or kill any South Korean politicians and other establishment figures still in Seoul and the North Korean Army prepared to cross the Han River. By the night of 3 July the North Korean 6th Division had occupied the vital port of Inchon on the west coast of South Korea. In less than ten days the North Koreans had taken the South Korean capital, destroyed or scattered the majority of the ROK Army and captured the port they needed to ensure rapid resupply of their forces moving south. Their next objective was Suwon, along the main central highway, which had been abandoned in haste by the American Advisory Group. The ROK Army headquarters moved south the following day.

In Japan, General MacArthur put the 24th US Infantry Division on alert. It was not one of his better decisions, for although they were the nearest to Korea of the four divisions stationed in Japan, they had the lowest combat efficiency rating (64 per cent). While the bulk of the division embarked on ships for Pusan, a port on the south-east corner of Korea, a small combat team from the 1st Battalion, 21st Infantry Regiment, was flown in ready to fight. This force was commanded by Lieutenant-Colonel Charles B. Smith, and hot on the heels of 'Task Force Smith' came Major-General William F. Dean, the 24th Division commander. By the time Colonel Smith's men had arrived at Pusan airfield and been driven north in trucks, Suwon had fallen and the enemy were already on the road towards their next objective: Taejon.

Lieutenant-Colonel Smith was ordered by Major-General Dean to advance northwards from Taejon and engage the enemy. 'All we need is some men up there who won't run when they see tanks,' Dean said confidently. The men were cheered by South Korean civilians as they advanced to their allotted positions, about eight miles south of Suwon, where the road ran through a saddle of hills. There the men dug in and Colonel Perry from the 52nd Field Artillery Battalion directed the placement of his six 105mm howitzers to give supporting fire when required.

At 7.30 a.m. on 5 July a North Korean column came into sight, led by no fewer than thirty-three T-34 tanks. As they came into range the howitzers laid down an artillery barrage along the road, but the tanks kept coming. When the leading tanks were 700 yards from the American positions their two recoilless rifles began firing, but still the tanks came on. When they reached the infantry positions a second lieutenant took a bazooka and crawled into a ditch alongside the road. From there he fired twenty-two rockets against the rear of the tanks, where their armour was weakest, but the charges were too weak to penetrate the steel.

As the tanks reached the pass between the hills they were engaged by the howitzers which promptly destroyed two of them. Unfortunately the artillery only had six rounds of anti-tank ammunition, and when these were gone they found that normal high-explosive shells simply ricocheted off the sides of the tanks. Anti-tank mines would have stopped the T-34s but there were none in South Korea at that time.

By nine a.m. the tanks had moved on past the infantry and artillery positions. Behind them now came a six-mile column of trucks and infantry, led by three tanks. When the column was about 1,000 yards away, Lieutenant-Colonel Smith ordered his men to open fire. Their four 60mm mortars began to lob bombs among the trucks and the fifty-calibre machine-guns spewed half-inch bullets towards the disembarking infantry. Instead of tackling the Americans head on, however, the North Koreans began to outflank them, and at 2.30 p.m. Smith ordered a general withdrawal. Amid heavy fighting the infantry and artillerymen started to withdraw, but by the time they reached safety 150 of Smith's 400 men had been lost, together with thirty-two men from the artillery. They had done all they could, but it had barely slowed the enemy advance.

The next objective for the enemy columns was P'yongt'aek on the road south to Pusan. As soon as the 34th US Infantry Regiment arrived at Taejon by train from Pusan on the night of 4 July, General Dean sent their 1st Battalion up to P'yongt'aek and the 3rd Battalion twelve miles east to Ansong, to cover an alternate route the enemy might use. Dean instructed the regimental commander, Colonel J. B. Loveless, to do everything to hold the P'yongt'aek line. It was easier said than done.

Colonel Loveless had only been in command of the 34th for a month and his force of 2,000 men was a third understrength. He had been brought in to replace the previous commander, who had failed to improve the fighting capabilities of the regiment. The rot, unfortunately, went right to the top. General Dean, as commander of the 24th Division, was responsible for its effectiveness, as was General Walton Walker, the commander of the US Eighth Army. The buck stopped at the desk of General MacArthur, whose primary concern at the time, it may be said, was the rehabilitation of Japanese society and the country's economy. He wore two hats at that time, as occupation commander and troop commander, and as a result the troops under his command had become soft and were ill-equipped and poorly trained for the battles ahead.

Lieutenant-Colonel Ayres moved his 1st Battalion/34th Infantry up to P'yongt'aek and surveyed the ground he was ordered to defend. The land north of the town was flat rice paddies, through which ran a road on a ten-foot-high embankment. Two miles north of the town there were hills on either side of the road, ideal strongpoints from which to overlook the advance of the enemy. A Company began to dig in on the west side of the road, while B Company did the same on the east side. C Company remained behind in reserve.

Not only were the companies understrength, with about 140 officers and men each, but their weapons were inadequate as well. Each man had either an M1 rifle or a carbine and eighty to a hundred rounds of ammunition – enough for only ten minutes of firing. Each rifle platoon had one light machine-gun with four boxes of ammunition, and one BAR (Browning automatic rifle) with 200 rounds. The Weapons Platoon had three 60mm mortars and two recoilless rifles, although there was no ammunition for the latter. There were no hand grenades either, essential items for close-quarter fighting.

Another discovery was made by a patrol which came across an enemy tank in a village a couple of miles north of the American positions. They opened fire on a T-34 with their bazookas, but they were not powerful enough to cause any damage to the Russian-built machine. The tank fired back, with its machine-guns, killing one of the men.

That night it rained incessantly and the men's foxholes were soon filled with water. During the early hours of the morning they were told that Task Force Smith had been defeated and shortly afterwards heard the sound of an explosion as the bridge to their rear, which carried the road across a stream and into P'yongt'aek, was destroyed to halt any tanks which might bypass the defenders. It was hardly good for morale, and when dawn broke the men peered through the rain and mist and saw a line of tanks and trucks extending as far as they could see.

As the North Korean infantry fanned out into the paddyfields and began to advance, the first tank shells began to explode on the hills. The men stood neck-deep in water in their foxholes and tried to fire their weapons, but less than half were working properly. With no artillery support and no effective defence against the tanks, the men of A and B Companies began to climb out of their foxholes and withdraw from the hills. As the enemy fire intensified, the retreat became a rout and the frightened men ignored their officers and ran all the way back to P'yongt'aek. When the men of A Company reached the town, one of the platoon sergeants examined his men's weapons to see why they did not work. Twelve out of thirty-one rifles were either broken, dirty or had been incorrectly assembled.

Captain Osburn, the A Company commander, discovered that forty of his 140 men were missing. Some had been killed or became separated during the retreat. A few were shot by the North Koreans as they tried to surrender. Most of their supplies had been lost. Osburn ordered a forced march down the road to the south, warning his men that anyone who fell out would be left behind. The men were not used to marching and as the pace began to take its toll their feet began to suffer. Some took their shoes off and wore them around their necks, others threw them away. By the end of the afternoon they had reached Chonan and found the rest of the 1st Battalion waiting for them.

The next morning, 7 July, found the 34th Infantry Regiment consolidated just south of Chonan. General Dean was furious that his men had abandoned the P'yongt'aek–Ansong defence line, because it was the best natural position north of the Naktong River. He must have been doubly furious to discover that the 3rd Battalion had been pulled back from Ansong to Chonan by General George Barth, the artillery commander of the 25th Division who had been sent over to Korea to assist Dean. The artilleryman had also visited the 1st Battalion the previous day to instruct them to withdraw if they were likely to become surrounded. It was hardly in keeping with General Dean's defence plan.

General Dean tried to recover the initiative and sent the 3rd Battalion back up the road to P'yongt'aek, unaware at that time that the enemy tanks had crossed the stream where the bridge had been blown earlier and that the North Koreans were about to swing around to the south of Chonan. He also ordered the replacement of Colonel Loveless by Colonel Robert R. Martin, who had served with Dean during World War II.

It was essential that Colonel Martin and his newly acquired regiment halt the North Korean advance north of Chonan. If they did not do so, the enemy columns could turn west on the coastal road and flank the American reinforcements moving up the central road from Taejon. One of his first actions was to send Major John J. Dunn forward to report on the situation north of Chonan. Dunn caught up with the 3rd Battalion and found them moving into a defensive position. He then went further up the road and made contact with the advance troops of L Company, who had set off northwards before the 3rd Battalion that morning. They were receiving harassing fire, but Colonel Martin sent orders that they were to stay in position. Then Major Dunn heard that the 3rd Battalion had begun an unauthorised retreat and had to come back to turn them round. Finally, as he drove north again towards the advance company, his jeep was ambushed by an enemy patrol. Dunn and the others in the jeep were wounded and as they lay there they could see the riflemen from the leading company of 3rd Battalion, but they made no effort to rescue them. Then he heard an American officer crying out to the troops: 'Fall back! Fall back!' Two hours later the enemy arrived and captured Dunn. He would spend the rest of the war as a prisoner.

Late afternoon on 7 July found Lieutenant-Colonel David H. Smith and his 3rd Battalion awaiting the enemy just north of Chonan. That night an enemy tank column found its way into the town and their infantry arrived the next morning. In the street fighting that followed Colonel Martin was killed by an enemy tank shell. The 3rd Battalion was encircled and would have been completely destroyed if it were not for a battery of field artillery which arrived in time to give them covering fire as they withdrew. Only 175 men, including Lieutenant-Colonel Smith, made it to safety. The others were killed or taken prisoner.

The two-day sacrifice of the 34th Infantry Regiment at least gave General Dean time to bring the 21st Regiment into position at Chochi'won, fifteen miles south of Chonan. A company of M-24 light tanks and a battery of 155mm artillery pieces came with them.

It was now apparent that everyone, from General MacArthur downwards, had underestimated the North Koreans. Trained, equipped and advised by the Russians, they were more than a match for the Americans at that time. MacArthur revised his estimates and asked for five full-strength American divisions, supported by one airborne regimental combat team and an armoured group with modern tanks. That meant 30,000 men, required immediately.

As is usual practice after a war, the politicians had neglected the US armed forces and allowed them to run down. The men were simply not available in the numbers required, and to supply them meant stripping the army's general reserve back home. The 2nd Division at Fort Lewis, Washington, was the first to be sent to Korea. As the Marines sought to fill the ranks of their 1st Division, they cast their net far and wide, even calling up Marines guarding US embassies abroad.

To try to buy more time, General Dean ordered Colonel Stephens and his 21st Infantry Regiment to defend Chochi'won for four days at least, to allow the retreating ROK forces to cross the Kum River and more American troops to arrive. On the afternoon of 9 July the first enemy tanks appeared, escorted by hundreds of infantry. This time the Americans could call up air support and their artillery had armour-piercing shells. Within an hour five T-34 tanks were burning and the American mortar crews and dug-in infantry were decimating the enemy troops.

That night the North Koreans found a way around the American forward positions and destroyed the mortars essential to the defence. Later, six of the men from the heavy mortar company were found with their hands tied behind their backs, shot through the back of the head. The enemy pressure increased and just after noon the survivors on the forward ridge withdrew under heavy fire. An hour later, Lieutenant-Colonel Carl Jensen, the CO of the 3rd Battalion, 21st Infantry, led his men forward and recaptured the ridge. It was the first successful counter-attack by Americans in the war.

The air force was having some success as well. A flight of jets dropped below the overcast at P'yongt'aek and discovered a long convoy of 200 vehicles from the 3rd North Korean Division waiting for their engineers to repair the bridge blown up earlier by the Americans. The Fifth Air Force rushed every available plane to the scene and they had a field day, bombing and strafing the trucks and tanks stalled below them.

That night the 21st Infantry was pulled back to a position two miles north of Chochi'won. Colonel Jensen's 3rd Battalion moved back as well, but the enemy were hot on their heels. During the night of 10 July the North Koreans reconnoitred their position and launched a surprise attack the next morning. Colonel Jensen was killed when his command post was overrun and the battalion was soon surrounded. Enemy road-blocks had been established between the 3rd Battalion and Colonel Stephens' command post at Chochi'won, so ammunition could not get through and the wounded could not be evacuated. By noon the battalion had ceased to exist. Only a third of the men made it back to Chochi'won and most of these were without rifles, helmets or equipment.

The enemy continued the attack against the 1st Battalion, 21st Infantry at Chochi'won and eventually they carried out a fighting withdrawal to the south, disengaging one company at a time. The remnants of the 3rd Battalion, 34th Infantry helped cover the withdrawal and by the end of the day all surviving American forces had crossed the Kum River.

The war was only a few days old when it became obvious that the treatment of US prisoners of war was going to be different to previous wars. At 11.55 a.m. on 9 July 1950, an American officer of the 24th Infantry Division who had been taken prisoner only forty-eight hours previously, made a 900-word broadcast on the enemy's behalf over the Seoul radio. Purportedly speaking for all American soldiers, the officer said, among other things: 'We did not know at all the cause of the war and the real state of affairs, and were compelled to fight against the people of Korea. It was really most generous of the People's Democratic Republic of Korea to forgive us and give kind consideration for our health, for food, clothing and habitation.' Within a few weeks many statements of this sort were picked up by American listening posts in the Far East. Service authorities were dumbfounded.

THE LONG WALK TO PURGATORY

One of the American soldiers who did not make it back to the Kum River was Ed Slater. He was a member of the 21st Infantry Regiment, sent into action with Task Force Smith near Osan on 5 July. Almost fifty years after the battle he told his amazing story to the author.

'During this battle we were overrun by the North Koreans. We ended up fighting hand to hand. We were trying to protect most of the troops who were withdrawing and trying to cross the river behind us. Many were shot down as they waded across the river and some were captured. I decided to stay on my side of the river, get in the water and go north and circle around behind them. I was familiar with this terrain since I had been stationed near here in 1949.

I crossed the first two hills – or, as the Koreans call them, mountains. There I found a second lieutenant and eight or nine enlisted men, all of whom were complete strangers. I told the lieutenant and a sergeant, who had a bad ankle wound, about a machine-gun nest about a hundred yards away on the other side of the river. He looked through his binoculars and said he did not see it. Then the lieutenant found a civilian and paid him to carry the sergeant on his back.

As we started down to the river bed, all hell broke loose as the machine-gun opened fire on us. I found myself running up the hill in front of the gun with another GI, just a kid. The sergeant, with his ankle wound and foot flopping, was trying to keep up with us both, but he fell behind and I never saw him again.

The kid and I ran over a couple of hills and hid behind some small shrubs. Just then we saw some Koreans pointing in our direction and yelling. The kid got excited and pulled a grenade from his belt. He started crying and said he was going to pull the pin because he wasn't going to be taken alive. I told him to wait until I got out of there first! I crawled over the top of the hill and started running down the other side. A short time later I heard an explosion – he had indeed pulled the pin. For me this was the start of a three-and-a-half-month nightmare.'

For the next few days Ed continued moving south, trying to find food and water. One old Korean civilian took pity on him and gave him some food, but it was too dangerous to allow Ed to stay in his house. A day or so later he was sitting in the shade at the edge of a rice paddy when there was a lot of commotion, screaming and yelling in the nearby village. Two North Korean soldiers ran across the rice paddy and told him to raise his hands. They seemed more scared of Ed than he was of them, but he had to go with them. As they walked along a ridge about twenty feet above a rice paddy, Ed saw a black American soldier, wearing only a pair of shorts and tied to a tree. Bayonet wounds covered his entire body. They had been using him for bayonet practice. Figuring that he would be next, Ed panicked, knocked one of the soldiers down and took off running. When he turned around he saw that the other guard was running away too, in the other direction.

Eleven days on the run, without food and with very little water, takes it out of a man. Finally Ed decided to walk into the nearest village and ask for food. An old couple lived in the first house that he tried, and they invited him in and gave him a large bowl of rice and some water. While he was eating, two young men came in and sat down beside him. When he had finished the meal, Ed thanked his hosts and stood up to leave. Suddenly the two men grabbed his arms and armed North Korean soldiers burst into the room. Ed takes up the story:

'Something hit me across my back and I fell right on my face. They picked me up and told me to eat more rice. I told them I could not eat any more. One held my head back and another crammed rice into my mouth. It evidently amused them because they laughed a lot while doing it. Then I vomited, some of which landed on one of them. They dragged me out into the open and tied my hands behind me. I believed I had seen my last sunrise. I had seen some of our men with their hands tied behind them, shot in the head.

They then took turns hitting and kicking me. It seemed like there was no place they didn't hit! They even stomped on my feet. Suddenly an officer appeared and began asking me, "Where is your radio?" He evidently believed I was a flyer. Every time I shrugged or said something he would hit me across the back with a club. Finally I passed out.

When I woke up I was lying next to a freshly dug grave. Another officer asked the same questions again, over and over: "Where did you leave your radio? Why did MacArthur send you over here? Are the Japanese coming over here? What is your rank?" He finally said he would have his men shoot me if I refused to answer his questions. At this point I was so beat up that I really didn't care. They stood me at one end of the grave and pointed their rifles at me. Something hit me across the back, knocking me into the grave. I fell on my right shoulder and thought I broke it. As I moved, they started shooting around the top of the grave, laughing all the while. At last they lifted me out of the grave by my elbows, then they put a stick under my arms and said, "You go with us."'

Ed Slater was thrown into a large corrugated building together with about twenty civilian prisoners. For three days they were beaten one after the other, and occasionally one of them would be taken out and shot. On the morning of the third day another American prisoner was brought in. He had been worked over pretty well and was very scared. He kept asking Ed what to tell them when they asked questions. He told him to tell them his rank, name and number and that he was a medic. Unfortunately the GI had already told them he was a BAR man.

That afternoon the guards returned and told them to take off all their clothes. Ed was left wearing only his pants. His boots were taken and even his shorts found a new owner. The other GI was left wearing only his shorts. Then they took him outside, beating him at the same time; he was kicking and screaming as he went out. A short while later Ed heard the sound of shots. He began to pray for the other American.

Two dozen American prisoners sit under the watchful eyes of their communist guards in Seoul. A close look at their faces shows the young age of the captives. It was not uncommon to find seventeen-year-old soldiers amongst the American ranks.

Around ten p.m. that night Ed was taken out and forced to march barefoot with two guards to an unknown destination. As the sun came up he entered a large building and found himself among other American prisoners. With his feet aching and bleeding, he sat down against the wall and started crying.

Most of the men had been wounded and captured at Taejon. Their wounds had not been treated and few were in any condition to begin the march northwards the next day. After a while Ed found some rags to wrap round his feet and some rope to use as a belt. He had lost so much weight he had trouble keeping his pants up.

Three days passed before the prisoners were given any food. The guards boiled a large pot of rice until it became sticky, then put some of it into a teacup, scraping it off evenly so that everyone got equal amounts. This they dropped into the prisoners' dirty hands, to eat however they could. There were no mess tins, no knives or forks. You either ate the daily ration of rice with your fingers, or you starved. Ed's nightmare continued.

'The men with the very bad wounds kept dropping out and the guards told us they would bring them up with us later. We never saw them again. To add to our misery we were now covered with body lice. It seemed like they multiplied faster than you could pick them off. Maggots had gotten into the wounds of some of the men. It was difficult to keep them out of wounds. Someone passed the word down the column to tell us to leave the maggots in the wounds, because they would actually keep the wounds clean! You couldn't get them all out anyway.

Sometimes when we did get to take a break we were told to sit down in a large open field or in a large building in a village. For four or five days they made us sit on concrete floors from daylight to dark. We couldn't even lean back on our hands or lean forward or stretch our legs. In this position you felt like your bones would break right through your skin. When it got dark they made us lie down and we had to lie there until daylight. Everyone would lie in a prone position next to each other to keep warm. This meant that when one person turned over, everybody turned over! Early one morning everyone turned to his left. The man next to me failed to turn, so I nudged him a few times, but he had died during the night. His face was about six inches from mine. He had a blank stare and maggots had already started crawling around his eyes. I know I'll see that face in my mind for ever.

One day I went to the toilet and saw one of the men who had a good share of his forearm blown off. He was eating the maggots that had accumulated in his wound. I can't believe I didn't get sick. I guess the shock was so great that I only felt a flash of fear. I couldn't look at him again, so I just walked away.

One of our greatest fears while marching was that our own planes would catch us in the open and mistake us for a column of North Koreans, and this did indeed happen a few times later on in our march. As we marched further north it became colder and colder. As the sun came up we would notice frost around our beards and clothes where it had accumulated as a result of breathing. One day, people in the front of the column suddenly started yelling, "Airplanes! Airplanes!" Sure enough there came Navy Corsairs diving right at our column. We all hit the deck after waving our shirts etc. and yelling to get their attention. It didn't work because they strafed the whole column. We had about four-teen badly wounded men who were riding on an ox cart and every one of them was killed. They killed a lot of the others who had tried to hide in the ditches. Finally they realised their mistake and tipped their wings to acknowledge that they were sorry. I can still see the terror in the faces of those men when I think about it. The only good thing about this day was that they did finally see us and from that point on knew where we were.

By now a lot of us had a severe case of diarrhoea. There were four times during those first few days when men would drop out and squat, if their legs would hold up, to relieve themselves. We would turn around a curve in the road, hear a shot and never see them again.

We were barely able to walk by now and still they wouldn't let us rest. Every time they gave us a drink of water, which was seldom, it seemed to go right through us. The men would let mother nature take her course – right down the backs of their legs. I was no exception. Sometimes the guards would look at me and laugh and point me out to villagers as we marched past. I didn't need any more humiliation. At least I now had a pair of boots that I took from a soldier who died a few days ago.'

By now the air force was trying to keep track of the column of pris-oners. One day, while the prisoners were resting in a large field, a bomber popped over a hill and started to circle at about 500 feet. Suddenly the bomb bay doors opened and a cloud of bundles attached to parachutes blossomed above the prisoners. The bundles were Red Cross parcels and the men cheered and waved anything they could find. However, it was not to be. The North Korean guards began shooting in the air and would not let the men touch the parcels. They had to look on as the guards crammed their pockets full of candy, soap and cookies. Ed and his new buddy Bob discussed what they could do with a para-chute if they managed to get hold of one. They could use it to wash with, perhaps. Neither had washed his face for three months.

Eventually they reached a village and there, waiting for them, was a train. At last, the long-promised train. No more walking. The weakened prisoners crawled into the box cars and lay down. Suddenly there was a burst of firing and Ed was hit in the leg. Apparently the train was going the wrong way and the North Koreans wanted the prisoners to get off again and continue marching. By the next day walking was agony and every step Ed took caused pain to shoot clear up to his arm. The maggots kept the wound clean until another GI helped remove the bullet.

As the prisoners neared Seoul they were put into a schoolhouse. Three Russian officers appeared and questioned some of the men. It was not the first nor the last time that Russians interrogated American prisoners. More will be said about this later in the book. After a few days Ed and the 200 men still alive in his group began marching towards Pyongyang, the North Korean capital.

Hundreds of miles to the south, American staff officers pored over maps of the area. They were planning a rescue mission, but time was running out.

CIVILIAN PRISONERS OF WAR

The unfortunate Major Dunn and the many other American soldiers taken prisoner during these early days were to suffer the most of all the prisoners taken during the war. Starvation, brutality and neglect became their lot, and it was shared for the most part by a small number of American and foreign citizens.

Larry Zellers was a teacher in a missionary school in Kaesong, just south of the 38th Parallel, when the North Korean forces crossed the border on 25 June 1950. He was quickly arrested by the North Korean secret police and taken to Pyongyang, the capital of North Korea, for interrogation. Captured along with Zellers were other missionaries. Fifty-three-year-old Kris Jensen had been a missionary in Korea for half his lifetime. Dr Ernst Kisch was fifty-seven years old and had survived both Buchenwald and Dachau, and had only been in Korea for a few months, working in the Ivy Hospital in Kaesong. Nell Dyer was an American teacher at the Myung Duk School for girls. She first went to Korea to teach in 1927, but left when the Japanese occupied the country. Living in the Philippines when World War II began, she was imprisoned by the Japanese for three-and-a-half years and returned to Kaesong to teach after the war. Bertha Smith, from Marshall, Missouri, was in her early sixties and the best Korean speaker in the group. Her mission was to rebuild the local churches that had been devastated during the Japanese occupation. Helen Rosser, in her mid-fifties, was a public health nurse who first went to Korea in 1924 and worked for many years establishing rural public health centres in Korea.

Within days they were all incarcerated in the headquarters of the National Internal Security Police in Pyongyang. Locked in cells behind steel doors, they were told the rules of the jail. They would rise at six a.m. and retire at ten p.m. During the day they would be given three meals and permission to use the wooden bucket in the corner of the cell three times. For the remaining sixteen hours they had to sit cross-legged and perfectly still in the middle of the room, facing the back wall. There was no back support and prisoners were ordered not to talk, look around or sit with their heads down. If a guard observed someone breaking the rules, punishment was immediate and administered with a slap to the face or a heavy belt to the back. Through the cell window they could hear the gun shots as executions were carried out daily.

Zellers was accused of being an American spy and threatened with death. For days numerous interrogators tried to re-educate him, to purge his old capitalistic thoughts and make him learn to repeat the communist line. Eventually, in the second week of July, their captors decided to move them from the prison, the city was being evacuated because of the American bombing raids. They were to have company on their journey north: Europeans captured in Seoul and other cities. There was the British Salvation Army Commissioner Herbert A. Lord, head of his organisation's work in Seoul and an excellent Korean speaker. The Anglican Bishop of Seoul, Cecil Cooper, and *Monsignor* Quinlan, chief Catholic priest of Ch'unch'on, had also been captured. Neither the Church nor diplomatic immunity meant anything to the North Koreans. The British minister in Seoul, Sir Vyvyan Holt, and his staff of two, Vice-Consul George Blake and Legation Clerk Norman Owen, had been taken prisoner too.

The date and location of Korean War Crimes case number 1512 was not known at the time of writing, but it seems appropriate to mention the incident here. An Irish priest was the victim in this case. He was accosted by an enemy officer while walking down the street with a Korean friend. Their assailant accused them both of being spies for the Americans and took them to his superior officer, who told him to dispose of the prisoners in any way he desired. Accordingly, they were escorted a short distance and then shot in cold blood. The priest died but his friend survived. The body was later recovered and identified, but as the perpetrators were unknown the case was never referred for trial.

The civilian internees, numbering sixty or more, including British, Americans, French, Turkish and Russians, were moved to a school-house in a village some miles from Pyongyang. This period was rather difficult, and a taste of what was to come. The food was bad and living conditions were crowded and unpleasant. The group, however, was not subjected to the full range of North Korean cruelty at this time and on 11 September they were told that because of the serious air raids they were to be taken further north to a more protected place.

The civilians were joined by a large group of captured American GIs, a number of them sick and wounded. They were moved by train to Manpo, a small town on the Yalu River opposite the Chinese border. The train travelled only by night, the internees and civilians spending the day sitting in the hills segregated from one another. On occasion *Monsignor* Quinlan was called upon to bury Catholic GIs who had died of their wounds.

The prisoners remained in Manpo from 11 September to 11 October, the period covering the amphibious landings at Inchon and the recapture of South Korea. Then they were moved to Korang'jin as the United Nations spearhead drove ever nearer, but saw their hopes of an early release dashed as thousands of fully armed Chinese troops marched by them, heading south. On 30 October they were back in Manpo again. The following day they met the North Korean major who would soon be responsible for the deaths of many of their number, civilians and soldiers alike.

DEATH OF A DIVISION

On 10 July 1950 Generals Collins and Vandenburg arrived in Tokyo to discuss the situation in Korea with General MacArthur. Given enough troops, he promised, he could not only drive the North Koreans back across the 38th Parallel, but also destroy their army and occupy the whole of North Korea. Alarm bells should have rung at this point. Would the Soviets and Chinese sit idly by while a unified Republic of Korea was established on their borders? Back in Washington the reserves were called to arms. The movement of 60,000 men was set in motion as the United States began to gear up for war again.

General Walker's advance party established the headquarters of the US Eighth Army at Taegu on 9 July. The next day the 25th Division began to arrive. The all-black 24th Infantry Regiment began to arrive at Pusan on 12 July. By 30 July the UN perimeter would be limited to the south-east corner of the country. It looked very much as though the port of Pusan might become the Korean equivalent of Dunkirk, the French port from which the British Expeditionary Force was evacuated in 1940 with the German Army hard on its heels.

To the east of the country the South Koreans were carrying out a fighting retreat to prevent the North Koreans from flanking the American forces. US Navy aircraft carriers in the Yellow Sea were providing air support and the air force was continuing to establish air bases in the south. By 25 July most of the North Korean Air Force and their airfields were out of action. The ageing equipment of the UN forces was slowly being replaced with newer weapons and a massive airlift began to get men and supplies to Korea.

A KOREAN DUNKIRK?

As the North Korean 3rd and 4th Divisions prepared to cross the Kum River and advance on Taejon, General Dean marshalled his forces to oppose them. Although his 24th Division had 11,000 men on its strength, there were only 5,300 at the sharp end. The 21st Infantry Regiment on the right had 1,100 combat troops and the 19th in reserve had 2,200. The 34th Infantry on the left had received many new replacements and was now up to 2,000. The artillery units contained another 2,000 men. The rest were engineers, service troops and other rear-echelon types. The North Korean 4th Division was at half strength with 6,000 fighting men, but they also had fifty tanks. Their 3rd Division had no tanks, but was at full strength.

General Dean placed the 3rd Battalion of the 34th Infantry at the left of his line and their K Company came under artillery fire on the morning of 13 July. The men cracked under the strain and the whole company pulled back to Taejon, suffering from shell shock. L Company were left out on a limb. There were no working radios available and there was a lack of communication wire for the field telephones. On the morning of 14 July the North Koreans began to cross the Kum River in barges and advanced towards L Company. The company commander ordered his men to withdraw and they hastily moved back to battalion head-quarters. The company commander was relieved of his command on the spot, but it was too late for the 63rd Field Artillery Battalion, three miles south of the river. By 1600 hours the battalion had ceased to exist and their ten howitzers, all their ammunition and eighty vehicles were in the hands of the enemy. The artillerymen who had not been killed or captured fled south. Why wasn't the 63rd Artillery used to destroy the barges carrying the enemy across the river? The answer lay in organisation, planning and leadership, all of which were sadly lacking.

Back at the Kum River, I Company of the 3rd Battalion found itself on its own. Under mortar fire all day long, they held their positions until nightfall then withdrew under orders to Nonsan, where they rejoined the remains of the 34th Infantry.

The 19th Infantry Regiment was involved in heavy fighting on the flank of the 34th Infantry. Eventually they pulled back to discover that the enemy had cut the roads behind them. At one roadblock a traffic jam of a hundred vehicles and around 500 men had built up and the decision was made to destroy the vehicles and make their way out over-land. About a hundred of the men started to assist forty of the wounded soldiers, but the going was rough and many of the wounded could not continue. Chaplain Herman G. Felhoelter and the medical officer, Captain Linton Buttrey, stayed with them. Soon the North Koreans appeared on the scene and the chaplain told Captain Buttrey to run for it, suffering a bullet wound as he did so. The North Koreans then shot the chaplain as he prayed, and killed all the wounded Americans.

One of the private first class soldiers captured on 14 July soon experienced a taste of the treatment awaiting surrendering Americans:

'While on the Kum River between Taejon and Chongju I saw two of the American prisoners shot in the back by the North Koreans. There was no apparent reason why these men were shot. I was placed with about ninety other men prior to being marched to a camp. All the prisoners were tied together in twos. During the march I was beaten with a rifle butt by my captors. This occurred on 18 July between Suwon and Seoul. I was struck repeated blows over my body and was knocked to the ground. This beating lasted about five minutes. A Japanese friend, who had been brought over as a KP, a supplies and munitions porter, was also beaten with rifle butts. Neither of us suffered any permanent injury, but we were both badly bruised.'

On 19 July General Dean and the three regiments of his 24th Division prepared to defend Taejon. The 34th Infantry had taken up positions three miles from the town in a rough arc from the west to the north of the town, with its headquarters at nearby Taejon airfield. The 19th Infantry were in an arc from the south of Taejon to the west. The 21st Infantry were out to the east, tasked with keeping the road open to the south. Once across the river, the North Korean forces would have plenty of different routes with which to approach and outflank Taejon. It was a heck of a place to defend. General Dean must have known what the future had in store for his men. He moved his division headquarters down to Yongdong and moved his forward headquarters in with the 34th Infantry Command Post at the airfield. It was an unusual decision, one that he would later regret, but communications were so bad that he felt he had to be as near the front line as possible.

General Walker arrived in Taejon and told General Dean that he was to hold his position for at least two days to enable the 25th Infantry Division and the 1st Cavalry Division to move up to the front. It was easier said than done.

The enemy had rebuilt the bridge across the Kum River, ten miles north of Taejon, and had moved tanks and artillery across. While the 3rd North Korean Division approached from the north, the 4th North Korean Division attacked from the west, led by T-34 tanks. A gap of one mile separated the 19th and 34th Infantry Regiments and the North Koreans took full advantage of the fact. By midnight on 19 July they had encircled the town and were establishing roadblocks to the south and east. General Dean and his aide spent the night in Taejon and woke at dawn to the sound of small-arms fire. Amazingly, considering his heavy responsibilities, Dean found a pair of bazooka teams and went out tank-hunting.

By the afternoon of 20 July two of Dean's battalions had been surrounded and scattered. The only ray of sunshine was that the few 3.5-inch bazookas that had reached the front soon proved their worth and ten enemy tanks went up in flames. Much of the city suffered the same fate as the fighting increased.

Before long the defence of Taejon collapsed in total confusion. General Dean finally realised that the battle was lost and ordered the withdrawal of those units still under command. The 3rd Battalion of the 34th Infantry began to move south and were met by a platoon of tanks from the newly arrived 1st Cavalry Division which escorted their column to safety. The defenders inside Taejon itself were not so lucky. Towards evening the main convoy tried to leave the town but came under enemy fire. Colonel Wadlington, the regimental executive officer who was leading the column, got lost and found himself in a dead-end school yard. He burned his jeep and headed on foot for the mountains. Fifty other vehicles found themselves in the same predicament and their passengers tried to make it through on foot. Some made it home, but many others were killed or captured.

General Dean's jeep took a wrong turning and soon came under fire. After sheltering for a while in a ditch, Dean and his party made it to the banks of the Taejon River. They hid there until dark and then tried to climb the mountain north of the village of Nangwol. During a pause for rest, Dean decided to go off on his own to look for water for the wounded. He fell down a steep slope and was knocked out. When he came to, he discovered he had a broken shoulder and was disoriented. Up above, the rest of his party waited for two more hours for Dean to reappear, then set off for the American lines. General Dean spent thirty-six long days wandering the countryside before he was betrayed by two civilians and captured. His weight had dropped from 190 to 130 pounds and he was to spend the rest of the war in solitary confinement.

Not only did the 24th Infantry Division lose its general, but 1,150 of the 4,000 combatants became casualties. The majority of these men were missing in action and most would meet their end at the hands of their captors.

WAR CRIMES DIVISION

The stories began to circulate within days of the first American clashes with the North Koreans. They were killing their prisoners without mercy. Korean War Crimes case number 2 (KWC2) described the fate of some soldiers from the 24th Infantry Division captured in a firefight near Chonui on 10 July 1950. Other soldiers said that four Americans were captured and they had to watch helplessly while two of them were murdered. Later all four bodies were recovered, hands tied behind their backs, three shot in the back of the head and the other with his skull crushed by a blunt instrument.

Civilian collaboration with the enemy led to the deaths of two other men, separated from their unit during the enemy offensive. On or about 20 July, two American soldiers were killed by North Korean troops. Their bodies were recovered in November upon information supplied by a South Korean civilian. He confessed that he had seen the Americans hiding in a cave and had reported that fact to the North Korean soldiers, who went to the site and apparently shot them. This statement was corroborated by another civilian who assisted in the burial of the bodies (KWC125).

Later in the month the communists proved that they were no respecters of the Red Cross or the Christian cross. They overran a group of eighteen to twenty wounded Americans being ministered to by the regimental surgeon, who was wearing the Red Cross brassard, and an army chaplain. None of the group was armed. The enemy immediately opened fire on them with Russian rifles and burp-guns. The surgeon, although wounded, managed to survive and escaped. Later, three victims of this atrocity were recovered. The chaplain was awarded the Distinguished Service Cross posthumously (KWC10).

On 14 July, when it became apparent that atrocities were being committed on a large and increasing scale in South Korea, General MacArthur's headquarters delegated responsibility for the 'investigation, accumulation of evidence, preparation for and conduct of trial, and review of cases of atrocities and other crimes committed by the enemy in violation of the laws and customs of war in connection with, or arising during, the Korean War' to the Staff Judge Advocate.

On 27 July a command letter was sent out by General Headquarters, Far East Command to all field commanders, outlining the procedure to be used in the collection of evidence related to war crimes incidents. This directive required that judge advocates or legal officers be used wherever possible in active supervision of the programme. The definitions of war crimes and war criminals were established as follows:

War Crimes The term may be understood as including those acts committed by enemy nationals, or persons acting for them, which constitute violations of the laws and customs of war of general application and acceptance, including acts in contravention of treaties and conventions dealing with the conduct of war, as well as outrageous offences against persons or property, committed in connection with military operations whether with or without orders or the sanction of commanders.

War Criminals The term may be understood as including persons who have committed 'war crimes' as defined above, or those who have aided and abetted, encouraged or conspired in the commission of 'war crimes'.

By October 1950, when the end of the war appeared to be in sight, General Headquarters, Far East Command directed the Commanding General of Eighth Army to establish a War Crimes Division within the Judge Advocates Section. When the war was successfully concluded war crimes trials would be held and the perpetrators brought to justice. Bodies would be exhumed and the cause of death established, photographs would be taken, witnesses would be interviewed and captured enemy personnel interrogated. Civilised retribution would be carried out against those who had killed and maltreated United Nations soldiers and civilians. That was the theory.

The War Crimes Division was established with Colonel James W. Hanley as its head. Twenty-six officers, one warrant officer and thirty-five enlisted men would form three branches: Administration, Investigation, and Apprehension and Trial. Field investigation teams constituted the Case Branch. These teams were given the task of taking the reported atrocity incidents and making an actual check of the sites to determine whether or not the act had been committed. Because most of the case files were opened as a result of a confession of a North Korean or Chinese prisoner, it was essential that every effort be made to discover corroborating evidence to establish the fact that the incident had actually occurred, i.e. the corpus delicti. Whether a prisoner would confess because of 'arm twisting' by the UN prisoner-of-war interrogators or whether the prisoner wished to ingratiate himself with his captors remains open to conjecture. It would become apparent later in the war that the majority of the enemy captured by UN forces preferred not to return home.

Once a case was assigned to an individual officer he would secure a field file of all data pertinent to the case and proceed to the locale of the reported war crime, accompanied by an enlisted driver and an indigenous interpreter. Efforts were made to locate bodies or other physical evidence to confirm that the crimes had actually occurred. Local civilians would also be questioned as part of the investigation.

It was no easy task investigating war crimes while the tide of battle flowed up and down the country. Soon the UN forces would be compressed into the south-eastern corner of the country, then in September they would break out and charge northwards, almost to the Chinese border. Then, in November, Chinese communist forces would swarm across the Yalu River and drive the UN forces south again.

BY THE SKIN OF THEIR TEETH

Although General Dean's 24th Division was routed by the enemy, they achieved their aim and delayed the enemy advance long enough for two more American divisions to arrive in South Korea. The 1st Cavalry Division landed at the port of Pohang and moved out to the north and west, and the 25th Division came in at Pusan. Together with the newly reorganised ROK troops they did their best to slow the advance of the North Koreans, but by 1 August the front had moved so far south that they literally had their backs to the sea. They were squeezed into an area eighty miles wide and fifty miles deep in the south-east corner of the Korean peninsula.

Unfortunately the newly arrived Americans were not much better trained or equipped than the 24th Division and often retreated at the first opportunity. One such unit was the 24th Infantry Regiment, one of whose battalions fled in panic on one occasion, leaving behind most of its machine-guns, bazookas, mortars and dozens of rifles. At the end of July it was taken out of the line. To the army units sailing towards Korea it seemed likely that the defenders would be driven into the sea long before they reached Pusan.

Meanwhile, in Japan General MacArthur was planning an audacious masterstroke to defeat the North Koreans. He decided to land the Marines at Inchon, a port on the west coast not far from the South Korean capital of Seoul, from which they would drive across the peninsula, severing the enemy supply lines. At the same time the forces within the Pusan Perimeter would break out and start to fight their way north. The new arrivals began to trickle in: the 5th Regimental Combat Team, a much understrength 2nd Division and, happily, the 1st Provisional Marine Brigade with their large proportion of World War II combat veterans and their own integrated Marine Air Group for close air support.

The new arrivals within the Pusan Perimeter soon became aware of the type of men they were facing. One story doing the rounds concerned a group of cooks taking food up the line in the 35th Infantry area. They were captured and tortured by troops of the North Korean 7th Division. The one survivor, who escaped by hiding in a haystack, had to endure the screams of one of his comrades who was castrated and had his fingers cut off before being shot. Others had their tongues cut out or their feet cut off before they were murdered.

As the fighting continued around the Pusan Perimeter, the men of the newly arrived 1st Cavalry Division learned the hard way to avoid surrendering to the enemy at all costs.

THE MASSACRE OF THE CAVALRYMEN

On 15 August 1950 the 81mm Mortar Platoon of H Company, 5th Cavalry Regiment, was in position north-east of Waegwan in the vicinity of Hill 303 (DQ4785). At 0330 hours the lieutenant in command of the platoon became aware of unusual activity near his position. He became concerned and concluded that this activity reflected the presence of enemy troops in considerable strength. He was afraid that the enemy might surround his position, so he telephoned G Company and asked for reinforcements. He was informed that a platoon of sixty South Koreans would be sent up to him. One of the survivors of the platoon later described the events that followed (KWC16):

'About daybreak we heard tank motors and Koreans coming in our direction. I thought they were the South Korean replacements because they were coming from the direction of Waegwan, where there was no enemy. The South Korean reinforcements were to be recognised by their platoon leader, Lieutenant Pak. Someone sent out to identify the patrol called out "Lieutenant Pak" but was answered by a blast from an automatic weapon! The lieutenant, still believing them to be friendly, withheld permission to fire. When the advancing patrol was recognised as North Korean it was too late to fire. They were in our foxholes shaking hands and at the same time taking our weapons!'

The North Koreans gathered the platoon together and took them to a nearby orchard. In the orchard their personal property, such as watches, billfolds, dog-tags and boots, was taken from them. Following this the cavalrymen's hands were bound behind their backs with either wire or their own bootlaces. After they had been bound they were led to a road where two large Russian tanks were parked, bearing the numbers 406 and 409. The captives were told they would be taken across the Naktong River that night, then sent to a Taejon prisoner-of-war camp. The North Koreans told them they had about 5,000 American prisoners of war in Taejon.

During the time they were held captive they were moved at night and hidden in ravines during the day. On the night of 15 August two of the Americans succeeded in removing their bonds. This was discovered and the men were beaten to death with entrenching tools. On the afternoon of 17 August the prisoners of war were gathered in a ravine. In the distance they could hear the firing of small arms. Suddenly a group of North Koreans came over a ridge and started firing into the bound prisoners. As suddenly as the firing began it ceased. After about fifteen minutes someone said, 'Are any of you guys alive?' Two men, a private and a corporal, said that they were not hit. After checking their comrades for signs of life and making sure that the enemy had gone, they quietly left the scene of carnage. Later in the day one of the prisoners came upon a friendly patrol and told them of the massacre. The patrol split in two; some went to the scene of the shooting, the others encircled the area and captured two North Koreans, who were later identified as Kim Kwong Taek and Chong Myong Tok. Both men claimed they were mess boys for the North Korean soldiers and that they were not present at the scene of the massacre. However the survivors stated otherwise, identifying Chong Myong Tok as having shot many of the prisoners with a burp-gun.

The two North Koreans were about eighteen years old and had been conscripted from middle school into the North Korean People's Army (NKPA) the previous month. They marched south with others as replacements for the 206th Mechanised Infantry Regiment and first came across the American prisoners when they were chosen with four others to guard the men. Kim Kwong Taek later told his interrogators:

'At the end of two hours a messenger came from the company and told the platoon leader that the company commander wanted us to bring the

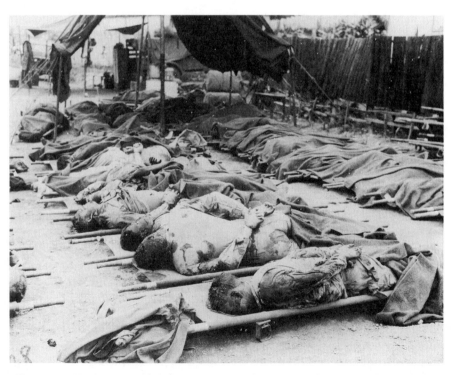

Thirty-four atrocity victims from the 5th Cavalry Regiment, 1st Cavalry Division, killed near Taegu on 15 August 1950. The men were all shot with their hands bound behind their backs.

American POWs up to the company position on the top of Hill 303. At this time there was heavy artillery fire from the enemy and we also heard the sound of tanks. We marched the Americans up the hill to our company position, which was located about 200 metres up the east slope of the hill from the group of seven farm houses. We made the POWs sit down. A few moments later three NKPA soldiers came running to our position. They were very excited and upon questioning stated that the UN forces were closing in and so they wanted us to pack and retreat immediately. Our company commander then told the assembled company, "You must get ready to retreat across the Naktong River. If we take the Americans with us they will delay us, and we cannot go in a large group because of the air raids, so we must kill them!"

Our company, the 4th Company, then consisted of about fifty men, including officers. None of the officers was wearing any epaulettes or insignia of rank. The entire company then marched all the American POWs down the hill to a ravine. Some of the men and all the officers had Russian sub-machine-guns. The rest of us were armed with American M1 rifles and Russian rifles. The Americans with their hands still tied were made to sit in the bottom of the ravine. They did not sit in any particular order or line and some were kneeling and some sitting. The members of the company then climbed on both sides of the ravine. I climbed on the north edge of the ravine. The company commander, who was also on the north edge, gave the order to fire and the entire company of fifty men fired into the American prisoners. I fired exactly five rounds from my rifle, aiming at a different soldier each time. Since everyone was firing at the same time I do not know if I actually killed anyone or not, but each time I did fire I aimed at an American. The firing continued for about fifteen seconds or as long as it took me to fire five rounds with my bolt-action rifle. The execution occurred at approximately 1200 hours, 17 August 1950. All the persons who participated in this execution were members of the 4th Company, 2nd Battalion, 206th Mechanised Infantry Regiment.

Since the fire from the enemy was becoming intense we immediately left the area. No one remained behind to make certain that all the Americans were dead. While trying to get over the hill I was hit in my left leg by an enemy bullet which hit the bone and broke it. I was carried to an aid station at the foot of the hill, along with about twenty other wounded soldiers. About 1400 hours UN forces approached the aid station and all our medics and wounded who could walk ran away. I was left behind with two others, including Chong Myong Tok, and we were captured by the Americans soon after.'

Unbeknown to Kim Kwong Taek there were North Korean tank men present at the execution as well. One of them was Heo Chang Keun who joined the NKPA in November 1949 and at the time of the atrocity was serving with the 3rd Squad, 2nd Platoon, 105th Automatic Gun Company Tank Unit. His unit had arrived in Seoul on 10 July and at the end of the month crossed the Naktong River and took part in the capture of Waegwan. On 11 August they withdrew in the direction of Hill 303. One of their two tanks was put out of action when it drove into a hole caused by a UN artillery shell. The following day the unit received a replacement tank and it was concealed in a trench beside the road at the foot of Hill 303. The two tank crews were still there on 17 August when their unit commander, Lieutenant-Colonel Choi Eul Sook, ordered them to accompany him up the hillside. Tank operator Heo Chang Keun recalled:

'A company commander of the 3rd Division together with fifteen soldiers was guarding about forty-five US prisoners of war, who were standing in a trench with their hands tied. The trench was five metres in length, six metres wide, one metre deep. We were disposed in a line around three sides of the trench and when our commanding officer ordered us to fire the nineteen of us opened fire on the POWs. About ten minutes later, on order of the commanding officer, we stopped firing. He gave us instructions that we have to keep this incident secret.'

Heo Chang Keun was captured by the South Korean Army on 5 October 1950 as his unit retreated northwards. Fortunately for him their treatment of captured enemy prisoners was better than that afforded to the cavalrymen on Hill 303. (It can be seen from the differences in the eyewitness accounts that people recall different things and their memories do not always agree on certain details when they are forced to undergo such traumatic experiences.)

The 8th Cavalry Regiment also suffered their share of atrocities. During the North Korean drive to capture Taegu in early September they sent their 1st and 13th Divisions down the 'Bowling Alley' which was held by the 8th Cavalry. Short of reserves, the regimental commander sent in his combat engineer battalion to act as infantry. One of the officers in D Company was wounded and his men carried him down the mountain and left him in a Korean house until a jeep could pick him up. Unfortunately the North Koreans arrived first, tied up the officer, built a fire under him, then gouged out his eyes and pulled off one of his thumbs before he died. A second officer was tied up, doused with petrol and set alight. Thereafter the Americans had little thought to taking prisoners themselves.

THE NAMWON BUNCH

The story of the Namwon Bunch begins on the night of 31 August 1950. Twenty-five-year-old Terry McDaniel was the supply sergeant for C Company, 23rd Infantry Regiment, 2nd Infantry Division. He had just returned from a supply run to the forward elements of the company at the little town of Masuwan on the Naktong River. The road had been under heavy North Korean artillery fire all day long and he drove as fast as he could to reach the company command post (CP) before they zeroed in on him. He told the author:

'Later that evening, about the time that the heavy shelling began to fall, Captain Bartholdi told me to send the vehicles back to battalion. I asked if he wanted me to go back with them and he told me no, he needed every gun he could get. I thought it was a good try! Soon I heard the word passed to "fix bayonets". Now no time during my seven months in combat in Europe had anyone ever told me to fix bayonets, so this really got my attention.

When we began seeing soldiers withdrawing past the command post Captain Bartholdi told me to stop them and deploy them along the road

Sergeant First Class Terry McDaniel at Fort Knox, Kentucky in December 1950, three months after his rescue with the rest of the Namwon Bunch.

27

that ran along the north side of the CP. We stopped two vehicles, a full track and a half track also, and not long afterwards a jeep approached from the west. It was halted and the occupants were told to identify themselves. They did not say a thing, so the personnel on the tracked vehicles were told to open up on them. Such a display of fireworks: twin forty cannons and quad fifty machine-guns, all spouting death at the same time. I hope they were the enemy.

I looked up at the skyline just south of the CP and saw figures crossing the crest of the mountain in the distance. It reminded me of a chain being pulled across a board, coming up one side of the mountain, being skylined and going down the other side. To quote Jimmy Montoya from B Company, "There were so many of them they looked like a lot of ants running all over." I was sitting down in the valley trying to figure out which side of the mountain I was going to tackle to try to get back to where some friendlies were!

By the early hours of 1 September the company had been reduced to around a third of its original strength and most of those had been wounded. Captain Bartholdi told us that we were on our own and to try to make our way back to the battalion rear. We soon found out that we had unfriendly people completely surrounding us, and even the regiment was seriously threatened.

The company CP was located in a Korean farmer's home, a sort of compound that was enclosed within a rock and mud wall. A number of us went over the back wall and started up a steep slope, heading west. I had Sergeant George Eurich, the commo sergeant, and PFC John Stovall, my supply clerk, with me and just as we hit a little bit of a clearing, up the slope a-ways, I stopped to take a breather. I was never so out of breath as I was then. About the same time as we laid back to catch our breath a burp-gun went off and George, who had been carrying a walkie-talkie in his left hand, let out a yell; he had been stitched across the back of the left hand about three times. We could see movement below, so we got up and took off again, bearing to the left to get in the tree line and out of sight. A few minutes later we stopped and tied a dirty handkerchief around George's wound. I decided to stay on the road side of the hill and Eurich and Stovall went on up and to the right – I don't remember why. Eurich was later captured and rejoined me. Stovall was also captured but at a different location and later rejoined Captain Bartholdi. Both were later executed by the North Koreans at Taejon, along with a number of other C Company men.

As I came downhill I could hear a lot of commotion on the Masuwan–Changnyong road. I noticed a tank and a large number of men, mostly wounded, trying to get aboard to take their chances running a couple of enemy roadblocks to get back to our forces. I had always been squeamish about getting too close to a tank, so I elected to go up to the next hill and continue to make my way west. One of the wounded was Master Sergeant Erwin Ehler and he seemed to be wounded all over. He did make it back to friendly forces and a long stay in a military hospital.

After eluding the North Korean soldiers for something like fifteen or sixteen hours a small group of us were unknowingly herded into a deep gully. There were around six of us, including Master Sergeant Louie Goins, 82nd Anti-Aircraft Artillery, and perhaps Sergeant First Class Al Jamison, C Company, 23rd Infantry, and a lieutenant whom I did not know. A short time before we reached the gully we were crawling at the very top of this hill in a pepper patch, flat on our bellies, hearing the snap of bullets going by, when suddenly I heard Goins give a yelp and move out smartly, still flat on his belly. A bullet had clipped his canteen and it had bent around and tore a hole in the left cheek of his rear end. I didn't let him live that down.

As we started to go out the bottom of the gully I was the point man and I saw a squad of little soldiers coming up the wash. I jumped back into the gully in time to see the lieutenant drawing a bead on the heads at the top of the gully. I yelled at him that there was a bunch of the enemy coming up from the other end and that we had better make up our minds what to do next. There was no question. I threw my carbine behind a big bush and we filed out with our hands above our heads.'

A couple of miles away from the C Company command post, the men of B Company were fighting for their lives. Jimmy Montoya was one of them:

'I finally ran out of ammo and buried my forty-five under a bush. The North Koreans came and dragged me down the hill to the rice paddy. They were beating me and telling me about the "big boom". I must have caused them a lot of damage with my last grenade. They were probably also telling me about all the NKs I had killed with the forty-five, but I didn't understand what they were saying. The only thing I understood was the "big boom" and they would hit me with a rifle butt and I would go down. Then they would stand me up again, yell something about the "big boom" and hit me again. This went on for several minutes and finally they were going to shoot me. Suddenly an NK officer appeared, in a beautiful uniform with about ten stars on his shoulder. Now our Supreme Commander, General MacArthur, only had five stars, so this NK officer must have had more rank than MacArthur!

Now I don't claim to understand the workings of our supreme being, but if there was ever an apparition, that NK officer was one. He was in the rice paddy in the middle of a war wearing full dress uniform and he looked like an angel or Jesus himself. He took time out from his leadership duties to spare me, me who had caused them so much damage with the grenade and my forty-five. God works in mysterious ways.

Korean Atrocity!

The NK officer had a long conversation with his soldiers and finally they stood up and took me as a prisoner of war. I was then joined by Sergeants Gregory, Fernandez, Mackeral and Corporal Simmons. Five survivors out of a group of about 200 Americans. It was sad to see all those brave Americans dead and strewn all over the rice paddy. Nobody to bury them, to put them in body bags, to take their ID tags and to tell the story of their heroism. They would probably become MIAs for ever. But what could we do? We were now POWs at the mercy of the North Koreans. The only consolation we had was that they had died valiantly helping their fellow GIs by taking as many NKs with them as possible. They had put up a terrific fight considering the position they were in, a deadly cross fire, both from the top of the hill and from the rice paddy, by NKs with a humongously large force. I don't know about the NK losses, but they must have been heavy because there were so many targets.

We were marched to the south-west, escorted by about one hundred NKs. We were climbing a very large hill when suddenly one of them hit

Private First Class Jimmy Montoya, another of the Namwon Bunch in Albuquerque, New Mexico in 1951. The 'big boom' of his last hand grenade killed many North Koreans and almost led to his being shot out of hand by his captors.

me on the back of the head with a rifle and knocked my helmet off. The helmet went rolling down the hill and the NKs started laughing. I thought, "Oh well, it could have been worse, my head could have been in it." Shortly thereafter one of the NKs pulled me to the side and motioned to my boots, that he wanted them. I pointed to all the blood, on the right one where my foot wound was bleeding, trying to persuade him that it was no good. But blood or no blood he made me take them off anyway. As soon as I lost my boots I knew I was going to have problems with my foot wound. The boot had been holding my foot tight, like a cast, and this enabled me to walk without too much pain. I started limping and found a piece of wood to use for a crutch. Simmons and Mackeral also had foot wounds and were also having problems walking. Simmons had the worst wound; he couldn't put any weight on his foot at all. The bottom of his foot was completely shattered; you could see the bones sticking out all over. Fernandez and Gregory helped us as much as possible, even though Gregory had a very bad wound on his shoulder. My hip wound didn't bother me, but it was bleeding a lot and I knew that I was going to have problems because of blood loss.

These front-line soldiers did not mistreat us too much. Not like the beatings we got later from South Korean civilians, rear-echelon commandos and some of the sadistic guards. I guess it was because the front-line soldiers felt like we were all in the same boat, infantrymen, and they showed respect for us. The South Koreans were supposed to be on our side, but you couldn't prove it to me. We used to get some of the worst beatings from them. They would use fists, feet, sticks and rocks to beat us with. I guess they were trying to prove to the NKs that they were indeed on their side in order to get better treatment.

We joined up with other POWs and our group grew to over forty. We were marching to the north-west, usually at night as there were too many airplanes that would bomb and strafe us. One time when we had been marching during the day for several miles I was completely exhausted and couldn't continue anymore. I gave up and decided to let the NKs shoot me instead, which they were ready to do. Sergeant Gregory wouldn't let them. He picked me up and carried me, dead weight, on his back for several miles until I finally recovered my strength. This took superhuman strength because he himself was suffering from a wound and injured feet from walking barefooted. He was also exhausted like the rest of us. I don't know how he did it. I will always be grateful to Gregory for this heroic act. I know that I would have been killed if it hadn't been for this great caring person. I owe my life to him.'

Sergeant Gregory took his life in his hands when he helped his fellow GI. It was very dangerous to draw attention to yourself and he could have been killed for interfering.

Terry McDaniel and his fellow prisoners were also heading north at this time and they soon discovered the North Koreans' total lack of feelings or mercy.

'We were carrying a badly wounded young soldier. His left shoulder had been torn apart and as he was transferred from my shoulder to the shoulder of SFC Al Jamison his wound began to spurt – an artery had been severed. Jamison had only gone a few paces when a North Korean officer told Al to put the soldier down. His refusal was cut short when the officer pulled his pistol and demanded, and got his way. A little further down the trail we heard a shot and knew that the kid had been put to death. Life had very little meaning to these adversaries of ours, as we were to find out more personally in the days to follow.

When we arrived at a gathering point, the North Korean soldiers started to confiscate items such as dog-tags, shiny belt buckles, rings, watches, pens, wallets, almost anything except our fatigue trousers and jackets. I had been wearing unlined leather gloves and they were completely covered with blood. While I sat and waited for them to take what they wanted from me, I took off my gloves, wedding ring and school class ring and with my P-38 [GI can-opener] slit the cuff of my trousers and secreted these three items in the cuff. They did not search me there and I eventually brought the items back home with me.

Then we began the long walk that would eventually get us to the town of Namwon. We would wind through the hills and along creeks and rivers in the valleys. Some of the trails were really scenic and kind of reminded me of the hills and valleys around Bernardsville, North Carolina. Most of the days we would hole up under a big tree or in some village, in a 'hooch' or a cell of some sort. One of these homes had the traditional fire built under the floor, which made the place very comfortable because the nights were growing cold. Fatigues don't give a lot of warmth.

We didn't do much daytime walking because of the artillery spotter planes the Americans had flying around, and then also a jet would be seen from time to time. Walking at night was difficult to say the least. Most of the time they would use commo wire to tie us together. This kept us together in the dark and also kept us from trying to escape. Most of our combat boots were taken from us and poor-quality tennis shoes given instead. After they and our socks gave out, a lot of the tender-footed soldiers began to show some bad sores on their feet. I remember SFC Nokel Roach booting a young soldier in the rear end when the kid started to cry about his feet being sore. SFC Roach was from the North Carolina mountains and probably had a lot of experience walking barefoot.

I don't recall too much trouble on the trail. The 'hubba hubba' calls and the occasional bayonet point with an unleashed round from a burp-gun with a seventy-one-round magazine hooked to it kept us on our toes. At one time a call went out from the North Koreans for mechanics. Eventually two young soldiers stepped forward and they went out to repair a vehicle. When they came back they had a lot of potatoes which they shared with others.

Another time when we were on the front porch of this hooch a civilian was giving us a lot of static, something like "Tomorrow you will all die." Sergeant George Eurich, who had spent a lot of time earlier in the Pacific and could speak and understand Japanese pretty well, stepped forward, and with his face in the civilian's face said, "Shoot me now you son-of-a-bitch!" Me, being the type of guy I am, wanting to live two more days, said to George, "George, you trying to get us all killed?" and George let off another string of words about the civilian's ancestors.

A few days after our capture the North Koreans took Captain Bartholdi away and said that they were taking him to Seoul to set up a prison camp. A few days later they came in and asked for our leader, and a lieutenant stepped forward. He also was taken away with almost the same story about setting up a camp. About midway during our capture, when we were in a little town and being held in a large warehouse, the "officials" came again and asked for our leader. MSGT Goins finally stepped forward and they told him to bring a couple more soldiers and go with them. Their mission was to write a letter about how nice the Koreans were and why we shouldn't be there in the first place. They returned to the warehouse and everyone was supposed to sign the letter. About this time the town and especially our building came under attack by some American jets. Most of the prisoners took off for the rice paddy. Whether I was too scared to move, or perhaps thought I was safer in the building, I don't know, but there was a few of us that stayed and some were peppered by rock and metal fragments. I don't recall any more about the letter and we had no more persons taken away from our group.

When we arrived in Namwon and settled into our "interim jail" there was a "gathering of information" of sorts. Some of the questions were: Do you like MacArthur? – No; Do you like Truman? – No; Were you a land owner? – No; What was your political affiliation? With this last question the officials got tired of everyone being Republicans. No one was a Democrat because they were in power in 1950, so we started telling them we were Protestants, Catholics etc. and they bought it.

Our living conditions were tough, at best. Towards the end of September the weather was beginning to cool at night and if we were inside a building everyone would be scurrying around trying to find a big grass mat, either to lie on or use as a cover – a thermal blanket so to speak. At Namwon I was fortunate to share a couple of these, and lying close together and covered with a grass mat at least we didn't freeze.

Food was not something to count on as a regular fare. It could be a rice ball (baseball size) or a barley ball (softball size). Sometimes this ball might contain a small potato or a scrap of meat; as John L. Napier from I Company, 29th Infantry Regiment, characterised it – meowwwww meat! Occasionally there was a bit of "kimche" poured over the ball as we held it in our bare hand. At times we might get a chunk of rock salt, or a dried fish. As we walked along we might pass a pepper patch. If we could snap one of the hot peppers it would sure take your mind off walking and the situation for a while.

When we were on the trail and received our daily rice or barley ball, at times I might not eat the whole ball and I would put the rest of it in the left pocket of my fatigue jacket, to eat later. You can probably mentally visualise what this pocket looked and smelt like after a few days of the local blowfly visits.

Our attention to health and sanitary needs was also irregular. Washing hands and face, when it happened, was usually in some creek as we stopped during our forced marches. Going to the "Benjo" was also a thing, such as going behind a bush, tree or whatever, or out under the big sky. Privacy was not a big thing on our minds.

The biggest failure of this group of prisoners of war was the fact that there was no real attempt to be organised by the senior military men. In fact, possibly just the opposite occurred. There was the beginning of small, exclusive social coteries. And a couple of individuals found out that it was best not to get on the dark side of some groups. It was going to be a timely liberation!'

Jimmy Montoya and his group of POWs had now joined up with the others at Namwon. Their wounds had not been treated once in the month they had been prisoners.

'There was no iodine or any type of disinfectant and no bandages for our wounds. We would wrap our wounds with pieces of rags, but even rags were scarce. Maggots were formed when we got infected. They supposedly kept the infection down. The larger the infection grew the more and larger maggots were formed. My foot wound was infected and several maggots were formed. They were ugly, but they did slow the infection down. Corporal Simmons had the worst infected wound. The whole bottom of his foot had been shattered by a bullet. You could see the bones sticking out all over. His foot was so badly infected that it was swollen to about twice its normal size. The maggots were so numerous and large that they were crawling all over the floor. He was in very severe pain during all the time he was a POW, and yet he never complained. One day, after he had been a POW about twenty-seven days, he was outside the building getting a little sun on his wound. He had the NKs' permission to do this, but the NKs shot him to death and carried him away.

34

A Korean Dunkirk?

One day I had taken my fatigue jacket off to kill some of the many lice that infested us. It was the only thing that I had left; they had taken away everything else that was American; my boots, my wallet, my helmet and even my pants. They replaced my pants with a raggedy pair of torn pants, with torn-off legs. I was squeezing the lice to kill them when an NK saw me and came over. He poked me with his rifle and waved for me to give him my jacket. He gave me a torn-up raggedy shirt instead and there went the last piece of American property I had. Now I would suffer even more from the cold.

On the morning of 28 September we heard a lot of heavy fighting: artillery, mortars and automatic fire, both from the ground and the air. Some of the bullets were hitting the roof of our building. We knew that a big battle was going on. Soon our NK guards came over and took the South Korean POWs, about twelve of them, out of the building with their hands tied behind their backs. Then the guards came back and started tying our hands behind our backs. We knew then that they intended to kill us, because they very seldom moved us in broad daylight, especially when there was so much fighting going on. We started arguing and crowding them. There were about ten guards with weapons and we were over eighty POWs desperate to save our lives. We took some of their

A rare photograph of some of the Namwon Bunch immediately after their rescue on 28 September 1950. Captured in July and August 1950, none have yet had a wash, shave or clean clothes.

35

weapons away from them and convinced them to leave us alone and to just go. They left, but we weren't sure whether or not they were coming back with more help. Sergeant Goins finally went out to the road to check out the situation. He spotted a tank coming up the road, but was not sure whether it was one of ours or an NK tank. Finally it got close enough so that he could see it was an American tank. One of the GIs from the tank yelled at us, asking if there were any Americans in the building. We burst out of that building like a bunch of bats coming out of hell, crying, yelling, screaming and laughing.

We saw the most beautiful big black sergeant on top of the tank, manning the fifty-calibre machine-gun. He came down from the tank and we mobbed him, hugging him, shaking his hands, crying on his shoulder and thanking him. I don't think there was a dry eye in all that group.'

The men were very lucky that day. The South Korean prisoners had indeed all been shot. Apparently an American task force was heading for Namwon with their Liberators tank in the lead. After the black sergeant crossed the river the next vehicle behind him got stuck and the others piled up behind it. He decided to plough on to Namwon and there found a large group of North Koreans who scattered when they saw his tank. Then he heard voices saying 'Don't shoot – we are American GIs' and suddenly found himself surrounded by eighty-six new friends. The sergeant was from an all-black regiment of the 25th Infantry Division. At that time many units were still segregated, but as the war continued the practice was discontinued. Sadly the black sergeant was killed in action about two months later.

Today the Namwon Bunch hold biannual reunions and Terry McDaniel edits their 'Namwon Bunch in Korea' newsletter.

THE INCHON LANDING

At 0500 hours on 15 September 1950 the first fighter bombers began to lift off from the decks of the aircraft carriers in the East China Sea, heading for the port of Inchon. Their target was the island of Wolmi-do and the guns that covered the harbour at Inchon. For five days the navy and air force had been reducing the defences on the island and when the Marines stormed ashore at 0630 hours they found few North Koreans alive to oppose them. After Wolmi-do island had been captured the variations in the tide held up the main landing until the afternoon, but by nightfall 13,000 men were ashore and casualties had been light. MacArthur's gamble had worked.

The North Korean attempt to capture the whole peninsula had finally failed as the Pusan Perimeter held. A considerable amount of effort had

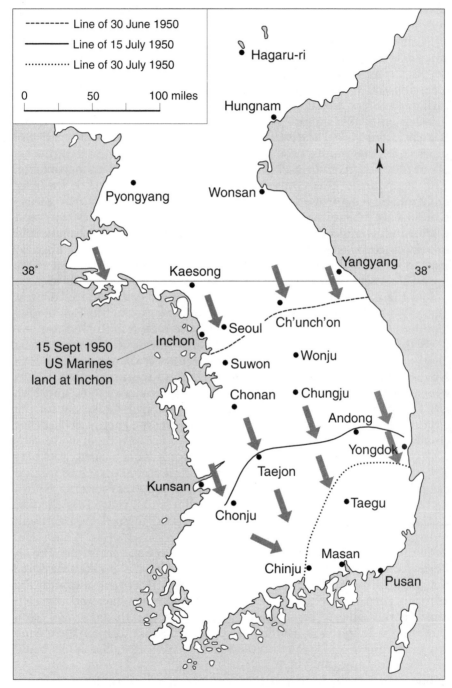

--------	Line of 30 June 1950
————	Line of 15 July 1950
··············	Line of 30 July 1950

0   50   100 miles

Hagaru-ri

Hungnam

N

Pyongyang

Wonsan

38°   38°

Kaesong   Yangyang

15 Sept 1950
US Marines
land at Inchon

Inchon

Seoul   Ch'unch'on

Suwon   Wonju

Chonan   Chungju

Andong

Taejon   Yongdok

Kunsan

Chonju   Taegu

Chinju   Masan

Pusan

The North Korean invasion was finally halted at the Pusan Perimeter.

37

been required to stop them and US casualties exceeded 19,000, including many missing or taken prisoner. However, by September 1950 there were four US Army divisions and a Marine division in action. The first major Allied contingent had arrived in the shape of the 27th British Commonwealth Brigade and the 90,000 ROK troops were now receiving the weapons and training they sorely needed two months earlier. Fighters and bombers of the US Fifth Air Force were being supplemented by carrier-borne aircraft from the US Navy and the British Royal Navy, and warships sailed close inshore to provide fire support to Allied units in coastal areas. It was now time to fight back.

For the Inchon landing MacArthur had almost 70,000 men available. The 1st Marine Division was 25,000 strong and the 7th Infantry Division had been made up to strength with almost 9,000 South Koreans in its ranks. Engineer, artillery and amphibious tank and tractor units would also be required to fulfil MacArthur's initial order to seize Inchon, then Kimpo airfield and finally Seoul itself. The day after the landing General Walker's Eighth Army was to break out of the Pusan Perimeter and push northwards.

The Eighth Army had been reorganised into I Corps and IX Corps. The most reliable units were allocated to I Corps: the 5th Regimental Combat Team, the 1st Cavalry Division, the rebuilt 24th Division, the 27th British Commonwealth Brigade and the South Koreans' best division, the 1st ROK Division. They were to break out of the Pusan area and spearhead the 180-mile drive north to meet up with X Corps which was coming ashore at Inchon. The IX Corps and its 2nd and 25th US Divisions would follow on a week later. On the east side of the country the ROK I and II Corps were to engage the enemy as best they could.

On the positive side of the account, the North Korean Army was now in bad shape. Originally 90,000 strong, it had suffered around 60,000 casualties and many of its new recruits were press-ganged South Koreans who only donned the enemy uniform and moved up the line to battle because they knew what fate awaited them if they refused. Many surrendered at the first opportunity.

At 0900 hours on 16 September the break-out from the Pusan Perimeter began. Unfortunately the eighty-strong B-29 bomber force that was scheduled to carpet-bomb the North Koreans opposing the 38th Infantry Regiment as it crossed the Naktong River was diverted due to bad weather. The advance bogged down and the only significant gain was made by the 1st ROK Division which broke through the enemy line north of Taegu. Two more days would pass before the B-29s could add their weight to the break-out.

The 25th US Division was hampered by the performance of one of its infantry regiments. The 24th was an all-black outfit and they performed so badly during the summer that the divisional commander asked that the unit be disbanded. His request was refused and it was left to the 27th and 35th Regiments to get the division moving. Eventually the enemy began to give ground and a week after the landings at Inchon the North Korean divisions around the Pusan Perimeter were in full retreat.

THE MONTH OF MASSACRES

It is a sad fact that the North Korean People's Army slaughtered most civilians during September 1950. Some 14,602, or 84.6 per cent of the total, were killed during the last four days of the month. Despite the fact that this was around the time of the break-out of UN forces from the Pusan Perimeter and the amphibious landing at Inchon, it became apparent that these murders were as a result of policy dictated by the North Korean leaders.

One atrocity that was still under investigation as the war came to an end may possibly have been the worst of all the atrocities carried out against American prisoners of war. As of June 1953 the only evidence in the file of Korean War Crimes case number 279 was a confession from a North Korean prisoner. After several days of questioning, during which the prisoner gave very detailed information, it was the belief of the interrogators that the facts contained in his confession were well-founded and reliable.

The North Korean stated that as part of his assignment as a truck driver, on 10 September 1950 he was driving from Namchon to Pyongyang and passed a group of twenty-four warehouses surrounded by barbed wire and noticed that many American prisoners were confined therein. Five days later his unit was ordered to prepare for a long trip. He added that about thirty Russian-made trucks were in his battalion, and that they loaded approximately 650 prisoners on them and commenced their journey about midnight. At their first stop they were joined by an additional twenty-four trucks loaded to capacity with US prisoners of war. During the next stop, which was for a meal and rest for the cargo, he noticed that fifty trucks were in the convoy. At the final halt the men were unloaded and led into a mountain valley where they were fed rice and wine, but, upon a blue flare signal, the guards and drivers began firing into the group and continued for about forty minutes, completing the slaughter of the estimated 1,250 prisoners. They then uncovered three large pits which had been excavated earlier, but found them insufficient to hold all the bodies, and so were required to dig another.

Following this macabre execution the trucks returned and later transported all the remaining prisoners from the warehouses to a new camp further north. The confessor was unable to explain why the one convoy load was murdered but the others spared. The interrogators noted in the file: 'To the extent that it has been possible to check, such as locations and units, this confession appears accurate. Every effort should be expended to discover corroborating evidence for this reported atrocity.' (In a conversation with a contact at the Pentagon in May 1999, the author was told that many South Korean soldiers reportedly transited through this holding compound. The possibility exists that the 1,250 poor souls who may have met their end in this atrocity may have been mostly South Korean soldiers together with a smaller number of Americans. Perhaps we will never know the truth.)

At least three war crimes files were opened following a massacre of South Korean citizens at Chonju (KWC case numbers 41, 727, 733). An estimated 600 to 2,000 political prisoners were murdered in a bloodbath of medieval proportions. All the victims had their hands wired behind their backs and most of them bore evidence of having been shot.

The bodies of 300 South Korean political prisoners are removed from caves near Hamhung in October 1950, to await identification. The victims died of suffocation after being forced into the caves by North Korean soldiers who then sealed the entrances.

A number of the victims evidently had been stabbed or bayoneted in the stomach and a few appeared to have had their heads split by an axe or similar implement. Agents from the 25th CIC team counted 315 bodies on the afternoon of 30 September 1950, two days after the families of the victims had begun removing the bodies.

Another mass murder was discovered at Yongchong, where approximately 500 South Korean prisoners, survivors of the 800 who had originally left Seoul on this final march, were led into an apple orchard, lined up in four ranks and shot. Survivors were bludgeoned and all the bodies were piled together, drenched with gasoline and ignited (KWC53). Another group of ninety had been shot and deposited in a coal mine about fifteen miles away, *en route* to Yongchong.

United Nations forces soon discovered that many of the enemy prisoners they were taking were in fact South Koreans who had been conscripted into the North Korean Army against their wishes. Many had been given the choice of changing sides or being killed. On 2 October this procedure was demonstrated at Tong Tang-ni. All the young men of the village were assembled by the North Korean security

The tragic face of this South Korean woman tells the story. She is among others trying to identify the bodies of political prisoners killed by the North Korean Army in Hamhung after being forced into caves which were subsequently sealed.

41

police and given the choice of entering the North Korean Army or being imprisoned. Around forty men refused to volunteer and were jailed. Soon afterwards the prisoners' hands were tied behind their backs and they were divided into two groups. One group was taken to the river bank and shot to death by their five guards. The other group suffered a similar fate after being lined up on the edge of a large pit (KWC56).

THE KILLINGS IN INCHON PRISON JAIL

On 3 July 1950 the North Korean People's Army had occupied the city of Inchon on the west coast of Korea. As was usual practice when they overran a town or city, they arrested many people who were considered to be anti-communist and confined them to cells on the second floor of the Inchon police station jail. On 15 September the UN forces placed the city under naval and air bombardment as a prelude to their seaborne invasion. That night approximately fifty-three Korean civilians were killed and twenty-eight others were wounded when three guards at the Inchon police station attempted to murder all the democratic leaders and United Nations sympathisers incarcerated in the jail (KWC49).

Prior to the mass murder some of the prisoners had been interrogated three or four times and were forced to 'confess' to imaginary crimes after beatings and 'water treatments'. Even though the prisoners would 'confess' to any crime they were accused of, they were victims of the same treatment many times. Some of the prisoners had been arrested for having in their possession leaflets dropped by American planes; others were arrested because they failed to volunteer to join the North Korean Army.

South Korean Kim Chong Won had been in charge of investigations at the Inchon police station until 3 July, when the North Korean Army occupied the city. He later told investigators:

'I was fleeing south when I was captured on 13 July at Sihung, near Suwon, when my companion Pak Kum Soo was killed by the village communists. I was bound and sent to the political department of the Seoul police station. I was interrogated by the use of "water treatment". I was bound in a chair with my head back and water was poured in my mouth; then I was beaten with a leather belt and kicked in the ribs and stomach. After five days I was moved to Nam Dam Library, which was known as Kim Il Sung's personal jail. There I was kept bound and remained for twenty-five days, until I was moved to Kyong-I-Do Reformatory, also Kim Il Sung's private jail. Then I was told I was going to be sent before the People's Court in Inchon. I was imprisoned in the

Inchon police station jail in cell 15 on the second floor along with other political prisoners. There was one soldier, two policemen, members of the Tei Han Youth [anti-communist] Association and former government officials, totalling fifteen in my cell. The first floor contained criminal prisoners. When the UN forces began to bombard the city the criminal prisoners were released.

At 1700 hours four policemen came up and told us to be quiet and that they were going to transfer us to another prison because of the heavy bombing. At about 1900 hours three members of the NKPA security force – Pak Ki Pun, Lee Sun Tol and Kim Dong Sik – armed with carbines, came to the cells and told us to sit in two rows instead of the customary three. Half an hour later the guards returned and began firing into the cells, beginning with cell 16. When they shot into cell 16 I knew they would come to cell 15 and I cried out "Long life to the Korean government!" I told the communist policemen that it was proper for a policeman like myself to die, but the members of the youth organisation should be freed. Then they shot at me, but the bullet missed me and hit the man in front of me. The second shot grazed my left shoulder and I collapsed. They continued to fire into cell 15 for two or three minutes, just as they had done into cell 16. Of the fifteen in the cell, ten died and five survived.

Cell 14 was empty and they went to cell 13, which contained only five women. They killed three of these and the other two survived. They proceeded on through cells numbered 12, 11, 10 and 9 in the same manner. When their ammunition was exhausted, the guards left.'

About twenty minutes after the shooting the five survivors broke out of cell 15 and fled. Before fleeing Kim Chong Won looked into all the cells on the second floor but could not tell exactly how many had been killed in each cell. While leaving the building he found some prison records which one of the jailers had dropped while fleeing. The next day he reported the incident to the United State Marines, but they did not investigate the matter at that time. He then returned to the jail and at that time counted fifty-three bodies in the cells on the second floor. He estimated that more had been killed because, according to the prison records he had found the previous day, 195 prisoners were confined to the jail and relatives of the deceased were then in the process of removing the bodies.

Mr Ha Hei Chu was another lucky survivor. He had left Inchon on 5 July because the communist police were looking for him because of his affiliation with the ROK civilian defence. On 6 September he was forced to return to Inchon in search of food and was apprehended by North Korean security police. He was in cell 9 on the second floor of the jail, together with former ROK policemen, government officials, telegraph operators and members of the Young Men's Association. When shots were fired into his cell he lapsed into unconsciousness for about thirty minutes. When he woke he found thirteen of the occupants of his cell dead and the fourteenth wounded. He left the jail without looking into the other cells and could not state how many were killed in total.

Survivors stated that the following participated in the shooting: Pak Ki Pun, Lee Sun Tol, Kim Dong Sik, Kim Hak Yong, Lim Sang Chan and Master Sergeant Choi Dong Hyun, who was in charge of the jail at the time of the shooting. Kim Dong Sik, one of the jail guards at the time of the atrocity, was later apprehended. Enemy Order of Battle records at the time listed the 6th Battalion, 10th RR Security Brigade and the Headquarters of the 7th Battalion, 10th RR Security Brigade as being located in Inchon from 25 August to 15 September.

One odd postscript to the massacre surfaced the following month on 16 October, when the Bu Byong police reported to the 3rd Logistical Command CIC that they had arrested Lim Sang Chan, a member of the People's Committee, Inchon. Lim had volunteered his services to the North Korean police upon their occupation of the city. His duties with the police had consisted of searching homes and confiscating property. On 15 September, when UN forces invaded Inchon, he apparently massacred approximately seventy people of the ROK Army, police and peaceable rightist citizens who were kept in detention in Inchon. He had then fled to the hills. He was captured, but escaped on the way to the prisoner-of-war camp and hid in the Bu Byong area, where he was found by the local police. When the war crimes investigators contacted the Inchon police in February 1951 to ascertain the whereabouts of Lim Sang Chan they received a negative answer. Perhaps he had already been the victim of summary justice himself.

By the end of September the US forces driving north were capturing up to 2,000 North Korean prisoners every day. Sometimes, for reasons best known to themselves, captured enemy personnel would readily admit to participating in the most heinous crimes. Korean War Crimes case number 102 is a typical example. An obligingly cooperative North Korean prisoner admitted that he was a member of the Education and Cultural Section in the village of Kwangju and that in this capacity, together with two others, on 16 September 1950, he took ten anti-communist prisoners about eight kilometres into the countryside and executed them. He stated that he used a carbine and did not bury the bodies. He offered to point out the site, so, accompanied by a war crimes investigator and Korean detective from Kwangju, he directed them to the spot. Three badly decomposed bodies were found, and the suspect insisted that these were three of the ten victims he had helped to murder.

THE TAEJON MASSACRE

For murderous barbarism, the Taejon massacre will be recorded in the annals of history along with the Rape of Nanking, the Warsaw Ghetto and other similar mass exterminations. Uncounted civilians, estimated variously between 5,000 and 7,500 as well as forty-two American and seventeen ROK Army prisoners, were slaughtered in cold blood for political expediency (KWC28A).

During the summer of 1950, following the capture of the city by the enemy, the North Korean Home Affairs Department was established with the express purpose of apprehending all persons unsympathetic to the communist cause. This 'security' force then proceeded to arrest prominent business and professional men, together with all people in the area who had been employees of the Republic of Korea. Each unfortunate person who was arrested was subsequently brought to the headquarters located in the Catholic mission for inquisition, and those

The bodies of dozens of South Korean citizens killed by retreating North Korean troops near Chinju in October 1950. The perpetrators appear to have fled before filling in the trench to hide the evidence of their crimes.

who survived were then incarcerated in the city prison. This jail consisted of 150 cells, each of which was packed with between forty and seventy of these victims. When it was impossible to squeeze more into these blocks, the overflow was retained within the confines of the mission. The military prisoners were not segregated from the others.

During the imprisonment North Korean soldiers were granted access to the hapless, defenceless individuals for the sport of tormenting them and confiscating any personal possessions that might have been overlooked. Favourite pastimes were the twisting of prisoners' fingers, and kicking and beating them without provocation.

When the recapture of Taejon by United Nations forces appeared imminent in late September 1950, the occupying conquerors determined that prior to withdrawal they would liquidate all the prisoners. Commencing 23 September, several groups of between 100 and 200 prisoners were quietly removed from their cells each night, their hands tied behind their backs with each person bound to the others. They were then transported to previously selected sites, placed in open trenches or ditches dug for the purpose and summarily shot. A check was made to locate survivors, and where found their skulls were crushed. The bodies were then covered lightly with dirt.

By 26 September the security police decided that they must accelerate the rate of murder if they were to accomplish their fiendish task prior to departure. They dug additional trenches in the courtyard of the police station and called in a North Korean Army unit to assist in completing their bloody work. During the early hours of 27 September the American and South Korean prisoners were woken in their cells in the Internal Security Building. Their hands were tied and they were taken down to the courtyard to be executed. They were ordered to get into a shallow trench, or ditch, that ran along the inside of the prison wall. Several wounded American soldiers, unable to walk, were carried out on litters and unceremoniously dumped into the trench. They were then shot or beaten to death and dirt was thrown over the bodies. Some of the victims were covered with dirt before they died.

As time ran out for the murder-gorged aggressors, the remaining South Koreans were dragged from the prison into the already filled trenches and killed. At the same time those who had been retained in the Catholic mission interrogation centre were executed as quickly as possible. When these trenches were filled with bodies, others were slain in the churchyard and basement, and many bodies were thrown down the well until it was completely full. Many bodies were found on a hillside behind Taejon prison and in the Yongoyong River bed. The perpetrators then fled, leaving their latest victims unburied.

Examination of the bodies revealed that many of them had been beaten and mutilated before execution. Of these thousands of unfortunates, there were only six survivors: three civilians, one ROK Army soldier and two Americans. Sergeant First Class Carey H. Weinel survived due to the care of the Koreans who found him. Sadly, the other American, a private, died while being evacuated.

One of the North Korean soldiers brought in to assist with the executions was Song Hong Bom, a twenty-nine-year-old private in 3rd Squad, 2nd Platoon, 2nd Company, 5th Battalion, 9th Regiment, 3rd NKPA Division. He later told war crimes investigators:

'At 0300 hours on 27 September 1950, having prepared to retreat, we were taken to Taejon City Home Affairs Station in a truck under the command of our lieutenant. We were driven into the courtyard of the station through a gate. There were already about twenty-five persons of the Home Affairs Station and trenches were dug in the courtyard in an "L" shape. I could see the people and the trenches well as it was bright moonlight. Here, we and the members of the Home Affairs Station executed forty US POWs who had been confined in the jail under command of the column staff officer of our battalion. First the POWs were taken out in groups of five, tied together with wire, and put into the trenches. Then another group of five US POWs would be taken out. The last group were wounded POWs and they were also thrown into the trench. Then our company commander ordered us to fire and we shot them. I shot two US POWs who were in the trench and killed them. We took out eight groups of POWs in groups of five and we executed forty of them simultaneously. They were all faced to the wall. I did not shoot towards a wall which was on my right side, but I could see a trench and bodies in it on my right side. Immediately after the execution we started to retreat by truck to Chonan. We did not stay to process the bodies. The other people, members of the Home Affairs Station who were in the courtyard when we got there, did not leave from there with us.

I was captured by the Republic of Korea Army on 2 October 1950. On 26 September 1951 I was taken to Taejon police station, which was the place of the execution in which I participated. I was at that time with a South Korean policeman who said he was a survivor of the execution, the lieutenant who took me to Taejon and a captain from War Crimes. I showed them the position where I stood at the time of execution and some photographs were taken at this time. I could recognise my company commander and the column staff officer who commanded the execution if I could see them again.'

Of the helpless prisoners of war shot in the jail, only one survived: Sergeant First Class Carey H. Weinel from C Company, 23rd Infantry Regiment, 2nd Division. He later described his ordeal to army investigators at the 128th Station Hospital at Zama in Japan:

Korean Atrocity!

'I was captured on 30 August 1950. At Chinju our orders were to hold our positions at all costs and that we did until we were overrun by the enemy. I was wounded in my left heel and right hip; then they took me captive before I could gather my senses again. There were approximately nine others taken captive at that time. After taking my dog-tags and throwing them away, then taking my shoes and all personal belongings, they marched us to another place where they had some more prisoners. There were fifteen of us in all. There they held us until a high-ranking officer came and said that he was going to interview us. He had an interpreter with him who wasn't too good at it. He could talk and that was about it. He started asking us all kinds of questions about outfits we were with and whose outfits other outfits were fighting and above all he wanted to find out if any UN troops had come in – Australians or any of them. They said if we told them the truth we'd go to Seoul American prison camp where they told us they had many, many prisoners. Course, we took that half-heartedly and let it go at that. After quite a bit of conflict between the interpreter and ourselves they seemed pretty satisfied with this information and told us in two or three days we would be in Seoul. They took us to our old company command post and kept us there until two days later. They treated us pretty good there; they gave us our own rations and stuff like that. However, by that time our planes were getting pretty warm on our necks. They strafed the building, hitting three of our own men. The rest of that last day they hid us in a ravine close by until dark. After dark we started marching at the town just before you cross the Naktong River – I forget the village's name, but it was right by Chinju. Right close to that they had a field hospital and they took all nine of our wounded men. That is the last I saw of them. They marched us to the river, keeping us there all night until early the next morning when we took a barge across the river and started towards Chinju.

After many days – I don't know how many it was – we arrived at Chinju. We were turned over to the police there and kept for two days. Our planes tore the jail up so they had to move us from there. As luck would have it one man was hit – not bad, but he was hit. From there they marched us to about thirty miles this side of Taejon. I don't know how many days it was. I lost count and track of time. We boarded a train and rode to Taejon where they turned us over to the police.

There was a total of forty-four Americans and twenty-two South Koreans in Taejon police station, although two of the Americans soon died. We got very little food, mostly rice soup and real small rice balls. The station was more or less open to people – you may as well say soldiers – and the North Korean soldiers would come in and harass us. Sometimes they would go as far as beat us up and take other clothing they saw that they wanted. We had very little left at that time. They seemed to get great joy out of letting us know they had the upper hand, that they were kingpins, that they were the boss and anything they could do to show us that they were was right up their alley.

Now on the morning of the twenty-sixth we could hear American artillery from a distance. That day they had what they called a rice festival all day. The American artillery started coming in the night of the twenty-sixth in the village. There was a lot of commotion on that night, all night long. Then during the morning of the twenty-seventh they came and woke up all the South Koreans, tied their hands together and marched them out of the police station. Shortly after their leaving we heard a volley of fire. Then they came up and told all the men that could walk to get up, that we were going to Seoul. They started tying the men's hands together, six and seven in a group. When everyone was tied except the four or five wounded they started taking us out in groups. Shortly after each group left we heard a volley of fire so we figured that they were shooting the men.

I was with the last group of walking men and they got to pushing us pretty close together and I saw the men in the group before me shot and also my group shot. After shooting all the groups they went back and got the wounded and threw them into the ditch and shot them also. Then, believing everybody was dead, they started covering the men up. As luck would have it they didn't put too much over me to smother me. I could breathe through the rocks and dirt. I didn't move. I pretended like I was dead. They shot at my head and hit my hand. That is how my hand got busted up. After they covered us up they left us for dead. I stayed there about two hours before trying to get out, but my binding was too tight. I couldn't get my hands loose. This hand was busted, I couldn't take hold. I finally got myself to a kneeling position and couldn't get any further. I stayed there all that day and up until the next day about eleven o'clock. I couldn't stand the pain any longer so I took a chance of hollering. Finally, South Koreans heard me and after a lot of arguing and persuading and begging and pleading and everything else they really went to work and got us out of there. They took me to one of the houses and hid me until the Americans came that evening. There was another survivor, from New York, who died shortly after he was liberated. We were liberated the evening of the twenty-eighth by the 24th Division.'

At the time Sergeant Weinel and his comrades were being prepared for execution, others were suffering a similar fate outside the jail. The events were described to a war crimes investigator by another captured enemy soldier, this time a Chinese, Moon Byong Ho, who was attached to the North Korean Army.

'I joined the 1st Guard Battalion, rear section, Chinese Red Army on 10 August 1948. I was transferred to the 1st Platoon, 3rd Company, 591st Guard Battalion, North Korean People's Army as the squad leader on 20

May 1950. On or around 1300 hours, 17 July 1950, when we were at the entrance of Suwon City, hiding our truck because of an air raid, we saw one unidentified young man (looked about twenty-five years old) firing at us with a rifle from a distance of about thirty metres. We captured this young man. I shot the young man to death with a Russian rifle by order of Junior Lieutenant Heo Kyong Kook on or around 1800 hours, 17 July 1950. This execution was held at the stone wall which is located about fifty metres from the road of the entrance to Suwon City. This road leads to Seoul. The young man was not blindfolded and his hands were not tied. I fired from about a distance of ten metres into his back. I left the dead body unburied there. I couldn't draw the sketch because the map of the execution site was not available, but I can lead you to the spot of the execution.

I participated in the killing of approximately 360 policemen and political prisoners at the Taejon prison on 25 September 1950. On or around 1800 hours we made forty prisoners go in the hole that was prepared beforehand, which is located at the foot of a hill beside a village which is located about one kilometre south-west of Taejon prison. We made the POWs sit down facing us. The space between the POWs was about one metre. I stood on the right side of the hole. I, together with the officer of Home Affairs Station [name unknown, rank was senior lieutenant], shot the forty prisoners to death by order of the chief of the Taejon prison [name unknown, rank was major]. I killed approximately twenty prisoners with my burp-gun, firing seventy-two rounds. About two hours later we made forty other prisoners go in another hole. We made the prisoners sit down the same way. I, together with the officer of Home Affairs Station, shot the prisoners to death by order of the chief of Taejon prison. I killed approximately twenty prisoners with my burp-gun, firing seventy-two rounds. The prisoners' hand were tied with straw but they were not blindfolded. We buried the dead bodies there.

On or around 1700 hours, 30 September 1950, I killed one un-identified young man who looked about twenty-nine years old, under the bridge which is located about five miles north of Taejon, by order of the junior lieutenant [name unknown]. The reason why he was killed by me was because he didn't show us the road. I shot the young man from a distance of about three metres in his back with a "Model 45 pistol", firing one round. The young man was not blindfolded and his hands were not tied. I left the dead body unburied there. I was captured by the US Army at Taejon on 30 September 1950.'

One man who survived the massacre of the prisoners outside the jail was thirty-year-old Eun Ok Tong, a civilian official in the intelligence section of the 8th ROK Division. Most of the other 4,500 prisoners were either policemen, officers of the Youth Defence Army, chiefs of the South Korean Youth Association or chiefs of the Myong Office and headmen from various villages. Around 1000 hours on 25 September two members of the NKPA Political Security Bureau came to cell 7 and tied up Tong and the other five men in the cell. As they were forced outside to join the other prisoners they overheard a colonel from the Political Security Bureau saying that he had orders to execute all the prisoners before 1400 hours. Tong later told investigators:

'Fifteen hundred prisoners were taken along the road to Nonsan and arrived at a mountain foot behind Toma-Ri located about two-and-a-half miles from the road. They divided the prisoners up and I was taken to a mountain foot with eighteen other prisoners. They made us sit on the ground and began to fire at us with their burp-guns and A-type rifles. They fired at me with their rifles but I did not die, I was only wounded in my face. I rolled over and disguised myself as a dead man until they went back. After they went away I crossed over the mountain and hid myself until the next day. I returned to my home and hid for three days until someone arrived to give me medical treatment.'

Thousands of bodies were later recovered by the liberating United Nations forces who occupied the city. On 30 September 1950 a graves registration team from the 24th Division was given the task of recovering and identifying the bodies of the American soldiers. Apparently there were forty-three men in the prison just before the killing began, but Private Christopher Murphy had been taken away to a hospital, from where he was later liberated. SFC Carey Weinel was the only survivor of the massacre (sadly, he passed away in July 1999); PFC Ralph E. Peters died shortly after the men were found. The other men killed were: PFC James F. Anderson, Capt. Cyril S. Bartholdi*, PFC Earl G. Bumpus*, PFC Doyle R. Brown*, PFC William R. Castleberry*, PFC Frank Cohen, PFC Vernon C. Custer, Pte William A. Dent, PFC George C. Evans, Pte Lester R.Garner, MSGT Robert E. Gentry*, PFC John E. Grow, Pte William A. Hager, Cpl John W. Harmon, Cpl Eugene S. Harris, Pte Lawrence J. Hartlieb, Pte James A. Kearney, Sgt Vernon S. Ledford*, PFC Arnold F. Lobo, PFC Everett L. Mitchell, Sgt Joseph Mlynarski, PFC Willis W. Mobley, PFC Jack O. Newman, PFC Raymond E. Owens, PFC Rufus D. Page, SFC John H. Peterson, Pte Allen M. Robertson, Pte James P. Robertson, PFC John M. Rozenair, Sgt Robert B. Senell, Pte William G. Sewell, Pte Tony J. Sherard, Sgt Howard R. Shuck*, Pte Raymond A. Snyder, PFC Robert J. Stein, PFC John R. Jr Stovall*, Sgt Armour D. Strother, SFC Herbert Tarnopol, PFC Gilmor W. Wilson* and Cpl Ralph E. Winthrop. (All asterisked names were members of C Company, 23rd

Infantry Regiment, captured 1 September 1950 at Migu-ri. See 'The Namwon Bunch' story.)

NO MERCY

Because of the number of atrocities which took place during the Korean War it is impossible to detail and discuss them all in one volume. However, some of the other incidents which took place in the fateful month of September should be mentioned.

On 26 September, 269 captured Republic of Korea soldiers plus one reported American were marched to the base of a mountain about eight miles north-west of Hamyang, after being told that they were to be evacuated to the north. At this point they were divided into groups of ten, bound together, led off into the hills and summarily shot. Several suspects were found among captured enemy prisoners and they confessed after being identified by the six victims who managed to survive (KWC92).

Another incident which took place on the same day, 26 September, involved the first report of a war crime involving British soldiers. After his capture, a North Korean prisoner, Kim Do Beum, Prisoner of War number 28702, stated that on this day a master sergeant of the Supply Platoon, 3rd Battalion, 29th Regiment, 10th North Korean People's Army Division executed one wounded British prisoner at a mine twenty-five kilometres north of Koryong (DQ3554). (KWC667) According to Kim, the sergeant killed the prisoner on orders of the 3rd Battalion commanding officer. Kim saw the body later in the day (Public Record Office file number WO208/4005).

In the absence of further information the author can only speculate that the unfortunate soldier may have been a member of the 1st Battalion, Argyll and Sutherland Highlanders, part of the 27th British Commonwealth Brigade. The brigade comprised the Argylls, a battalion from the Middlesex Regiment and later a battalion from the Royal Australian Regiment. The Argylls went into action on 23 September, crossing the Naktong River and advancing along the road to Songju. Ordered to capture Point 282 a couple of miles north of the river, they were holding their own until the US artillery support was withdrawn and a flight of USAF Mustangs bombed their hill instead of the nearby Point 390. Around ninety of the Highlanders were killed or wounded and a handful were listed as missing. The enemy unit facing them was the 10th Mechanised Division.

Kongju received its demonstration of red ruthlessness the very next day (27 September) when the thirty-five male and one female 'political' prisoners confined in the city jail were eliminated. In the late afternoon these people were told that they were to be given a lecture by an officer of the North Korean People's Army and were led into the open and seated in a semi-circle. As soon as they were settled as comfortably as possible, the officer ordered the guards to open fire and the slaughter commenced. Fortunately there were two survivors and most of the bodies were recovered from the place of execution. Two prisoners of war, in separate confessions, admitted participation in this crime and each implicated the other.

At approximately 0100 hours on the same day the jail and the Registrar of the Courts Building at Suchon were burned by the North Korean Occupation Forces just prior to their withdrawal (KWC32). The prisoners, consisting of Korean land-owners, policemen and government officials, being held in the buildings perished in the blaze. The local populace alleged that there were 280 victims. On 3 October 1950 thirty-two charred bodies were counted at the scene by Colonel Burton F. Ellis of the Judge Advocate General's office, Headquarters 2nd Infantry Division. He reported:

'I visited the site of the Registrar of the Courts Building at Suchon, Korea. There I observed that the building had been recently burned to the ground. Adjacent thereto was the remains of a small brick building of approximately eighteen by twenty-four feet, outside dimensions, which appeared to have been a jail. This building had recently had the roof burned off and the inside was completely burned out. Inside this jail building I observed the burned remains of three human bodies. Outside and in the immediate vicinity of the jail, all within the compound of the Registrar of the Courts Building, I counted an additional twenty-nine human bodies, making a total of thirty-two that were charred and burned. Those bodies appeared to be of male Koreans who had been dead for four or five days.'

Yun Kap Tuck, chief of security at the Suchon police station, said that he saw the fire but could not go near it. He said that North Korean troops were surrounding the building and he could hear the prisoners yelling 'Republic of Korea, Victory'. He went on to say:

'On 28 September 1950 at 0800 hours the door of the jail was opened and at 0830 I went to the jail. The families were taking the bodies away and I estimate about thirty were being removed. The guards at the jail were Chung Uck and Kim. The others I do not know but they belonged to the North Korean security police. I do not know where they are. The Communist Party is responsible for the burning of the prisoners at the jail. During the communist occupation, Lee Ku Myong was the province governor living in Suchon. He was thirty-five years old and a North Korean. He organised the communist underground here.'

Rim Wan Sun, a member of the city police at Suchon, was taken to the jail with about forty other prisoners at about 2100 hours on 24 September. He later stated:

'At 0100 hours, 27 September, a large number of additional prisoners were crowded into the jail. There were approximately 150 already in the jail at that time. The guard asked for those who were relatives of communists and I said I was and they released me. I then went to my home about 100 metres north of the jail. When I reached my home I noticed that the jail and the Registrar of the Courts Building was on fire. I never returned to the jail until today and then I saw many charred bodies that showed they had been in the fire. I do not know the names of any of my fellow prisoners.'

The day after the Courts Building was burned, 28 September, 282 South Korean political prisoners were confined in the Mokpo People's Prison when United Nations forces were approaching the city. Realising that defeat was imminent, their North Korean jailers held an emergency conference and decided to follow the usual pattern of executing these

The horrors of war. The charred bodies of South Korean land owners and government officials burned to death by North Koreans in the Suchon City Jail.

people for the crime of being 'reactionaries'. The victims were taken from the jail and had their hands handcuffed or tied behind them. They were then loaded on to four trucks and taken to different murder sites. Although most of these unfortunate people were shot to death, a few managed to escape when one of the trucks broke down. When the liberating forces overran the city they took many prisoners, six of whom confessed to participation in the mass killing (KWC117).

Also on 28 September, at Naju, a junior lieutenant in the North Korean Political Security Police Unit took six political prisoners from the jail, and as usual, without trial, shot and bayoneted them (KWC189). This lieutenant confessed to the atrocity, but maintained that he had acted under orders of his superior. The hands of the victims were tied behind them, they were shot and the bayonet was used for the *coup de grâce* where deemed necessary. Despite this treatment five of the prisoners survived, although one died shortly afterwards. The others identified the confessor as the perpetrator.

Two

NORTH TO THE YALU

THE DEATH MARCH TO PYONGYANG

As the US Marines fought their way from Inchon to Seoul, arrangements were being made by the North Koreans to march all American prisoners of war out of the city and up to the North Korean capital at Pyongyang. The events of this episode were recorded as Korean War Crimes case number 75.

Many American prisoners of war lost their lives on the Seoul to Pyongyang 'Death March'. The ordeal began about 26 September 1950 with 376 men and ended at Pyongyang on or about 10 October with an estimated 296 survivors. The prisoners had been captured at various places. Many were taken in the Taejon and Hadong areas. Approximately eighty of the prisoners had made at least a part of the journey from Taejon to Seoul on 15 or 16 August. These prisoners had walked about fifty miles north from Taejon where they were put on flat cars and taken to the outskirts of Seoul, arriving there on 20 August. The men were taken off the train and forced to parade throughout the city. Later they were taken to a school house where other American prisoners were held.

The men remained at Seoul, and set off for Pyongyang on 26 September. An estimated twenty-eight of the more seriously wounded prisoners were kept at Seoul. These prisoners were told that they would be taken by train to Pyongyang later; however, the wounded were forced to march or were carried on ox-carts behind the main group. The column of wounded men actually caught up with the main body on the second day.

During the march the men never received sufficient food or medical attention. Requests for additional food and medical supplies were frequently made by the ranking American officer, a major, but they were never fulfilled. Some of the men received first aid when initially captured, but that was the extent of the medical care they received. Each day men died from lack of medical attention. Some of the wounded managed to ride on an ox-cart, but with no medical care their wounds became infected and maggot-laden. The senior officer

56

constantly pleaded with the captors for medicine, water and more food. For his efforts this officer received only additional abuse and beatings. At one time, when an opportunity to escape afforded itself, he refused to accompany those leaving, stating that he felt his duty required him to remain and do what he could to alleviate the suffering of the men.

During the ordeal of the march many of the sick and wounded were unable to maintain the pace. At this time the communists demonstrated a policy that runs like a connecting thread through all the reported atrocity cases: the summary execution of any prisoner whose physical condition would burden their operations. These bodies were always left unburied along the roadside.

Beatings from the guards were commonplace throughout the march. Not only was no medical care provided, but the only food given to the men was one or two rice balls per day. The unfortunate survivors had to find water for themselves, drinking from roadside ditches and adjoining rice paddies. As a result most of them suffered from attacks of diarrhoea and dysentery. Once an American plane flew over the hapless column and dropped supplies for them, but the North Koreans immediately and methodically collected these items, appropriating them for their own use.

Combat boots and personal items had been taken away from all the prisoners. Most of the men were given tennis shoes, Korean rubber

Forced to remove their boots, dozens of American prisoners of war are assembled in a building in Seoul to hear US aggression denounced by their communist captors.

shoes or rice-straw sandals, but they would last only a few days due to the rough roads. Twenty-five of the men had no footwear at all.

During the journey thirty-three men escaped. In each case where the escapee was recovered by UN forces he was found to be suffering from malnutrition and dysentery. The recovered prisoners stated that they were fed very little. Occasionally they were given soup and some days they received no food or water at all. Due to the mistreatment and lack of food some of the prisoners lost as much as fifty pounds before their arrival in Pyongyang.

One of the escapees was First Lieutenant A. G. Makarounis. The twenty-seven-year-old officer from Lowell, Massachusetts, was a member of I Company, 29th Infantry Regiment. He was captured after being shot in the back as he lay in a rice paddy at Hadong on 27 July.

'On that same day, or shortly thereafter, I joined another, larger group of prisoners of war. There were approximately fifty of us who had been wounded and around one hundred who had not. At the time of my capture the only medical attention I received was a first-aid bandage that was applied to my back by another United States soldier. The North Koreans removed all the personal equipment I had, which was my wallet, watch, pen and pencil set and my fatigues. They left me with my trousers and boots. It was a full day and a half before we received some rice in a pail. The average food we got for the length of time I was a prisoner of war was usually a rice ball and corn-meal ball mixed together, which was mostly the size of a good fist. We had that on average twice a day and sometimes three times a day. Every now and then we would receive a bowl of soup to about three prisoners. At Seoul and Pyongyang we would receive bread rations and soup rather than rice. Between the time I was captured until liberation my weight went down from 190 to 137 pounds.

I escaped on the fifth day after my capture, but I was recaptured again. We were all expected to march, even the wounded men, and at least two dozen of our group were barefooted. The majority of the men had these tennis shoes or sneakers or these loafer rubber shoes that the Koreans wore. The combat boots were removed from the men continuously during my time as a prisoner of war. The North Korean soldiers and police officials would come and at the point of the bayonet would remove the combat boots from the men's feet.

After touring what felt like all of South Korea, our first march started from Taejon north towards Seoul. I don't recall the date. We were under the jurisdiction of civilian guards for this part of the journey. At that time we were supposed to march twenty-two miles to reach a railroad station, and the wounded men and the other prisoners who left Taejon assumed that they would march at the most twenty-two miles, but I estimated that we marched at least forty-five to fifty miles before we caught our first flat-top railroad car. Then it was a question of getting on a railroad car or marching into Seoul.

While we were quartered at Kanggyong they put us first in a civilian dungeon. While we were there a civilian would come in, kick us and hit the ones that were wounded around the wounds and would also take a rifle, cock it and point it at us. He was about twenty years old and had been wounded in the neck and shoulder. He never hesitated to point out that a plane had given him this wound.

When we reached Seoul they put us on a forced march throughout the entire city, which must have been at least ten miles without a break and at a fast rate of speed. We arrived at a schoolhouse at Seoul where the other prisoners were quartered. Many of the men, including myself, suffered black-out spells from sheer exhaustion.

American prisoners are forced to carry communist propaganda banners through Seoul. Some of the men at the front of the column have already been relieved of their boots and jackets.

Korean Atrocity!

The North Korean interpreter on the march to Pyongyang was a Mr Kim. It was reported that prior to the war he was a newspaper reporter in Seoul. At one schoolhouse where we were quartered after a night's march, Mr Kim, who was always cursing at the prisoners of war, came in with a bamboo stick in his hand and started to hit everybody within his reach, because the prisoners apparently had not complied with the order he had put out. These beatings did not inflict any wounds on anybody, but it did hurt the men inasmuch as they were tired and sick from their wounds.

Our next march started on or about 20 September, from Seoul to Pyongyang. We marched all the way into Pyongyang. The march ended on about 10 October, and during this march the American soldiers who were not capable of catching up with the group and were not carried by the other soldiers in the group usually dropped to the rear of the column. The North Korean second lieutenant in charge of the column would continuously beat the prisoners who fell to the rear of the column, who could not physically make the forced march. On one occasion he personally beat Lieutenant —, an American officer. He had fallen out and he beat him with a riding crop, I think, that he had in his hand until a Japanese-American soldier who was trying to help Lieutenant — burst into tears and was able to get him on an ox-cart. Lieutenant — later died on the march.

There was another prisoner of war who continually kept falling back to the rear of the column. Some of the men fell back with him and tried to assist him, but they could not carry him as they were too weak, and as we were going along the road a North Korean guard took this soldier and started to throw him into a ditch. The soldier made a feeble attempt to get up and about ten minutes later a group sergeant came up and said that this second lieutenant whom I have mentioned had shot and killed him with a carbine alongside the road. I believe his name was —. He was short, weighed about 130 pounds and I believe his home state was on the East Coast.

We started the march from Seoul with approximately 376 American prisoners of war and when we arrived at Pyongyang there were approximately 296 left. The others had died of malnutrition, had been killed on the road by the Korean guards or were strafed by accident by American planes. Well, we arrived in Pyongyang on 10 October and we stayed there until 14 October. At that time the group moved out, but some of us, including myself, escaped again. The group moved out on foot, but I understand that it was split up into two groups and that they caught trains out.

We remained at the school building for six days and six nights. We were helped by three Korean school teachers. They fed us food and water. When we were liberated the same three civilians came in, took us out of the cellar and took us down one of the main streets of Pyongyang, and we saw the South Korean troops of the ROK Division and then the newspaper correspondents who were our first American contacts.'

As the sick and weary American prisoners approached Pyongyang, another massacre of South Korean civilians was taking place not very far away. Later allocated the Korean War Crimes case number 141, it was known as the Changhyon Massacre.

Three North Korean prisoners of war confessed to the killing of approximately 1,800 South Korean civilian prisoners on 8 October 1950. The victims were residents of Seoul and Kaesong who were alleged to have been friendly with the UN forces. The victims were force-marched to Pyongyang with their hands bound, little food and scanty clothing. After reaching Pyongyang they were confined in the Military Academy building. Later they were divided into smaller groups and taken out and shot. The bodies were buried by nearby villagers. Two American officers investigating the atrocity made sworn statements concerning their observations of the mass graves. They stated

Discovered by advancing UN forces, the bodies of South Korean civilians beaten to death in a mine shaft at Kum Bong San by North Korean forces after being taken from the prison at Chinnampo.

that the stench of death was everywhere, the ground was sunken and that upon digging they turned up a human skull. There was also a grave marker which stated in Korean: 'To our comrades from South Korea'.

By 28 September 1950 Seoul was again in the hands of the United Nations forces. As General Walker's Eighth Army fought their way north and linked up with the Marines, discussions were taking place in Japan and Washington on the next phase of the war. There were many good arguments for halting at the 38th Parallel, but General MacArthur was determined to pursue and destroy the North Korean Army and reunite Korea by force. Unfortunately he did not give enough thought to the possible reaction of the Chinese, and his soldiers would pay the price for his lack of foresight. Despite warnings from diplomatic sources that China would enter the war if American troops moved into North Korea, President Truman and his advisers reluctantly agreed to give MacArthur the benefit of the doubt. It was a fateful decision.

The South Korean Army were in no doubt about their future plans. Advance patrols from the ROK 3rd Division crossed the 38th Parallel on 30 September. As they moved up the east side of the peninsula General MacArthur decreed that X Corps would cease combat operations in the Seoul–Inchon area and carry out an amphibious landing at the east coast port of Wonsan. It was largely a wasted exercise. By the time the Marines came ashore at Wonsan they found ROK troops already waiting for them. American patrols began to cross the 38th Parallel on 7 October, and on the ninth the 1st Cavalry Division crossed over in force.

On 15 October President Truman met General MacArthur for the first time. It was on Wake Island in the Pacific and a confident MacArthur sought to allay the President's fears about continuing the war north of the 38th Parallel. MacArthur stated his belief that formal resistance would end by 23 November (Thanksgiving) and that he hoped to withdraw the Eighth Army to Japan by Christmas. The X Corps would be reconstituted and comprise the 2nd and 3rd US Divisions and UN detachments. Elections would be held shortly afterwards. Regarding the possibility of the Chinese or Soviets interfering as the UN forces destroyed the balance of the North Korean Army, MacArthur gave his opinion thus: 'We are no longer fearful of their intervention. The Chinese have 300,000 men in Manchuria. Of these, probably not more than 100 to 125,000 are distributed along the Yalu River. Only 50 to 60,000 could be gotten across the Yalu River. They have no air force. Now that we have bases for our air force in Korea, if the Chinese tried to get down to Pyongyang there would be the greatest slaughter.' He also told the President that he planned to use South Korean troops as a buffer between the UN forces and the Chinese and

Soviet borders; the other troops would remain south of a line twenty miles north of Pyongyang to Hamhung.

General MacArthur returned to Japan and the President to Hawaii, then San Francisco, where he made a speech referring to 'a man who is a very great soldier – General Douglas MacArthur'. No doubt he would have used different words had he been aware that the first Chinese troops had crossed the Yalu River on 14 October, the day before he met MacArthur on Wake Island.

THE HOUSE ON THE HILL

On 13 October 1950 it was the 1st Cavalry Division's turn to fall foul of the North Korean policy of executing their prisoners if recapture was imminent. The details of this atrocity are to be found in Korean War Crime case number 67. One potential victim lived to fight another day. He was Captain John H. Brewer, a supply officer with the 7th Cavalry Regiment.

'At about 0930 hours on 13 October my driver and I left the battalion CP and started back to pick up the battalion trains which were located near Paeckchon. The battalion CP was located near Kumchon. While proceeding along the road about two miles south of the CP we were fired on from a hill direct to our front. There was a two-and-a-half-ton truck in front of me with a fifty-calibre machine-gun mounted, so I directed the men to open fire with it. The driver opened up with the fifty and two enemy waved white flags and we directed them down to the truck and put them in the back. We proceeded another hundred yards down the road and were fired on by several more machine guns, burp-guns and rifles. The driver of the truck jumped in the back and started firing the fifty-calibre. I moved up behind the truck in my jeep, dismounted and moved up to observe the fire. I saw that they were firing at the fifty-calibre from two directions. So I ordered the driver to leave the fifty, which he did. We continued firing with our carbines and M1s until the enemy pushed forward and pushed us back up the road around the nose of another hill. Here we met two tanks and a platoon of infantry, which I understand had been sent by S-3. They took over, deployed and commenced firing and drove the enemy back over the hill. The mess sergeant from headquarters, CP, 2nd Battalion, who was on the truck, was hit in the arm. The rest of us were not hit. I sent the truck with the two prisoners and the mess sergeant that was hit back to the battalion CP.

My driver and I proceeded down the road to pick up the battalion train. I don't know how far down the road we went before we hit the other roadblock, but it was about two to three miles above the 38th Parallel. Around the bend in the road which was a hill we came under direct fire of machine-guns, burp-guns and rifles. I started to pass and go on down the road and was attempting to run the blockade, but everyone in the ditch started hollering, "Captain, you will never make it – they are all down the road and all around us." I told the driver to pull over and hit the ditch. After getting in the ditch, finding approximately ten to eleven people there, we started to organise to defend ourselves as best we could. The firing continued to get heavier with occasional hand grenades, and in a matter of a few minutes they closed in on us from both ends of the ditch and over the top with hand grenades.

We were taken prisoner and marched off the road and up the hill to one of their dugouts, and there we were searched and everything taken off us: our watches, billfolds, fountain pens, rings, everything. Then we were marched up to the house and seated in the yard for a short time while one of the non-coms went to the house and then returned. We were marched into the house and seated on the floor in the room where there were a lot of tables – it looked like it had been used as a dining room or mess hall.

The guards tried to make conversation with the soldiers, and one tall officer who said he was a captain spoke English. He asked why the US

A posed propaganda picture released by Peking, China, showing Chinese soldiers capturing a jeep full of American soldiers.

forces crossed the parallel and went into North Korea. He also asked us if there were any Japanese or Chinese fighting with us. He asked every one of us his age, how long he had been over there, if he was married and if he wanted to return to his homeland. A terrific firefight was going on outside and we could hear a fifty-calibre and either some of our artillery or our tanks firing into the hills near where we were seated. We were sweating it out in fear that they would hit the house with our artillery. This firing seemed to irritate the guards and other enemy in the room and they would scream out to get our hands higher. Then they asked us why our planes came over and bombed them and talked among themselves with apparent irritation. Then they asked some of the men what they did. They wanted to know what the insignia was on my collar and I told them "Tank". So they thought I was a tank driver. Before I was captured I took my bars off and stuck them in the ground. I don't believe they knew my rank, except they did have my billfold with ID card that could have been easily checked.

Approximately half past five or six o'clock there was a lot of confusion and running in and out of the building as the firefight was continuing outside. One of the officers came back and said something to the guards. They immediately began putting on their gear and equipment, preparing to leave. One of them motioned to us and said something to the officers outside. Then they loaded their rifles and all of them opened fire on us. As they opened fire I fell flat on the floor and laid there during the firing. I felt one bullet go across my right leg, cutting a groove; something hit my left leg which I assumed was fragments from a grenade. Then a number of rounds went right over my head into the concrete wall, knocking concrete into my face. Then the firing stopped and someone came round with a rifle and jammed the butt of it into my back and across my legs, during which time I did not move at all. Evidently they left the room.

I continually heard voices just outside the building and running around and talking up until around eleven o'clock. Then all the firing ceased outside and I didn't hear any sounds in the house or outside. I still continued to lie in the same position, not moving for fear that an outpost or someone from outside the building might be looking in the window to notice movement and return to finish us. Then, about 0200 hours in the morning, I heard some of the boys moving their legs and I knew that they had not all been killed. At this time they began to whisper and I worked my way slowly back to them and whispered to them to be quiet and not move, for fear that they would return. We laid in the same positions and I determined that there were approximately three that were not killed. Listening for any movement of the other group lying on the floor, I determined that the rest of them must be dead.

At approximately 0500 hours I moved my head and surveyed the room to determine if there was anyone in or about the room. Not seeing anyone or hearing any movement, I got up cautiously and went to the windows and looked around the building. I listened for any signs of the enemy. Not hearing anything, I got the rest of the group – four besides myself – and told them that we must get out of the building and get away. I told them that we would go out the back window, across the road, that I would lead the way and get down and find a vehicle and send them some medical aid. I jumped out the window. They followed, and we took off over the hill and passed a trench not too far from the building where two enemy soldiers lay asleep with their rifles against a tree. We moved on across the hill and made our way on down the road. One of the men and I went on down the road till we made contact with a captain out of the 24th Division who sent transportation to pick up the boys that were wounded. I found a 77th Field Artillery jeep in the ditch, got it out and went back to the battalion train, took two of the boys on down to the aid station, then returned to my organisation that night, with the train.

I would know one of the North Korean officers again if I saw him. He did not have the dark colour or slant to the eyes of most NKs. He was the one that spoke English and asked most of the questions, and he was quite a bit taller than the rest of the NK soldiers [a Russian perhaps?].'

A more detailed account of the incident was given by Corporal Frederick C. Herrmann of the Service Company, 7th Cavalry Regiment. He recalled:

'On 13 October 1950 when my guard, Private First Class —, and I were returning from a town twenty miles north of Kumchon, which is approximately twenty miles north of Seoul, after having delivered a truckload of gasoline to the front, we reached a point in the road about ten miles from Kumchon, and heard shooting. Then we saw several vehicles in the road in front of us. The one directly in front of us was Captain Brewer's jeep. Ahead of that was a two-and-a-half-ton truck and in front of that was another jeep. I stopped my truck because of the shooting. Private First Class — and I grabbed our rifles and jumped from the truck into the ditch beside the road, in which were Captain Brewer, Private First Class —, Sergeant First Class Bryant and the supply sergeant from — Company, who were all members of the 7th Cavalry Regiment. Six other men were in the ditch but I do not know their names, but since they were with Captain Brewer I believe they were from the 7th Cavalry as well. We shot at the North Koreans but we saw that we were surrounded, so we surrendered.

About ten or fifteen North Koreans captured us; there were about 150 of them in the surrounding area. The North Korean soldiers who actually took us prisoner were dressed in the light khaki uniform of the North Korean security forces. After these North Korean soldiers had captured us they made us take off our helmets and they marched us down the road about 200 yards in front of the first jeep. At this point we turned east and climbed a hill.

At this time there was a United States L-5 airplane circling overhead. I believe the pilot saw the ambush because he kept circling in the area above us. We got about halfway up the hill when they stopped us and these North Koreans took all our personal property and our identification. Then we continued to march up the side of the mountain trail. When we had travelled about seventy-five yards we arrived at a house. This house was rectangular and it was constructed out of mud and wood. It was one storey high. We never entered the house but we sat against its outside wall for about twenty-five minutes. Then we were marched to the top of the mountain where there was another house. This house was also one-storey, and it was either painted or white-washed white. It was made of wood, with a sloping roof which extended over the side of the house. Around three sides of the house was a flush boarded wood fence – that is, there was no fence on the south side of the house. This fence was about ten feet high. There was only one gate in the fence, on the north side of the house, approximately fifty feet east of the north-east corner of the house. On each side of the gate there were two poles about the size of telephone poles, and these two poles formed the jamb for the gate. The fence was not painted, but it was dark and dirty from being exposed to the weather for a long period of time.

We entered a room in the house which was approximately fourteen feet by twelve feet, and it was about eight feet high. The floor was hard dirt. After we entered the room they motioned for us to sit down, and we sat down in a line which formed a "U".

The supply sergeant and one other had been wounded in the leg at the time of our ambush and we tried by the use of sign language to make our little North Korean guard understand that we wanted to take our shirts off and bind their wounds. He did not understand what we were talking about. The guard was about five feet tall and was pretty husky and I believe he weighed about 160 pounds. He was one of the ugliest people I had ever seen. He had a scar on his right cheek, about a quarter of an inch from his nose. It was perpendicular and shaped like a half moon and it was about an inch long. His hair was cut very short. He carried a carbine in his hand and had the habit of thrusting it out in front of him, as we had been taught to do during bayonet practice.

Then a North Korean soldier came in who had one star on his shoulder with a single stripe running through it. I believe he was a junior lieutenant. He was about five feet ten inches tall and weighed about 140 pounds. His only distinctive feature was that the top eyelid of his left eye was slightly closed. He did not stay very long, but a short time later he returned. The second time he came we asked him about bandaging the legs of our two wounded men, but he could not understand us very well since he only spoke broken English, and bad broken English at that. We made him understand what we wanted, and he allowed us to bandage the wounds with our shirts. He started questioning us about the number of Japanese and Nationalist Chinese troops fighting in Korea. We laughed and told him that somebody had been kidding him because there were no Japanese or Chinese troops fighting in Korea. He asked us why we started the war in Korea. When we told him that we did not start it, he had us stand up and move to the east side of the room where there was a bulletin board on the wall. On the bulletin board were some newspaper clippings: one was an American jeep and trailer with American GIs lying dead; the next was a picture of a firing squad showing some dead men tied to poles, and he told us that it was a picture of South Koreans shooting North Koreans.

After looking at the pictures we all sat down on the floor in the same position. Upon our request he got us a one-pound coffee can filled with water for us to drink. He then asked us if we were hungry, and if we could eat rice. We said that we could, but we never received any rice, nor were we fed at all. We received permission to go to the latrine though, which was outside the house. The ugly little guard went with us, and he made us walk by the side of the house under the cover of the sloping roof so that the L-5 airplane that was circling overhead could not see us.

During the time when we were going to the latrine, the lieutenant left the room. He came back in a little while and started talking to us about the troops of the United Nations in Korea. During this conversation a North Korean soldier came into the room and motioned for the lieutenant to leave the room, which he did. Through the open door I could see they were looking down the road with binoculars. Then this lieutenant called another lieutenant, who had two stars, and they went outside. There was shouting and all the North Koreans left us except our guard. Later we heard shooting, which lasted about an hour.

In the evening, just before complete darkness, the lieutenant with two stars, the lieutenant who spoke broken English and another lieutenant with one star, who was about five feet seven inches tall and weighed about 140 pounds, came in and some excited conversation passed between the officers and the ugly guard. The ugly little guard pulled back the bolt on his carbine, and someone said, "This is it." Just about this time I heard a shot and Grimmig fell forward. I could see blood coming from his head. When he fell towards me I yelled, "Look out," and I turned completely around to the right and dived face down in the dirt under the table. The only part of my body sticking out from under the table were my arms and legs. The only North Korean soldiers I definitely know were in the room at this time were the ugly little guard and the three lieutenants.

I don't remember how many shots they fired, but there were a lot of them. I lay under the table holding my breath. I saw Clare fall and his head came down on my shoulder. The next thing I remember is that I felt something kick me, but I did not move. Then I felt something on the back of my neck which seemed to me to be the butt of a rifle, which somebody was using to see if I was alive. But I did not move. Then I heard a shot and my leg felt as if it were completely knocked off. I was shot in the left leg just above the knee. As I lay there, not daring to move, I heard the North Korean soldiers yelling and running around.

After a while it was quiet. Then I heard some tanks driving on the road outside. Although they might have been ours, I did not know, so I did not make any noise. About midnight I heard the clock on the wall strike the time, and I heard somebody moving in the trash pile which was at the north corner of the room. Because I did not know who it was, I remained still and silent. Several times a voice asked, "Is anyone alive?" But I did not answer and nobody else did either. Finally the voice said, "God damn it, I'm a GI; is anyone alive?" Then I told him that I was. I asked if anyone else was alive and Bryant said that he was. Another GI, whose name I did not know, answered that he was too. We received no other response from anybody else in the room.

Because we didn't know whether the North Korean soldiers were still outside or not, we decided to stay in the house all night. The next morning Captain Brewer stood up and this was the first time that we knew he was alive. According to the striking of the clock on the wall it was about six o'clock on the morning of 14 October 1950. We decided that we would leave the building by going out of the windows on the south side. Before we left we inspected the rest of the members of our group and discovered that all of them were dead. I inspected the bodies of the supply sergeant and Grimmig to determine that they were dead. Both had been shot in the head. Out of the twelve of us, the only ones who were alive after the shooting were Captain Brewer, Bryant, two of the men whose names I do not know, and myself. I had been shot in the leg and Bryant had been shot in the ankle.

Captain Brewer and one of the GIs went out the window first, and they were supposed to help us out, but once they got outside we never saw them again. Finally we got out of the house and crawled three miles to the south, where we found a road, and beside the road we crawled into a hollow bush. I believe this was the same spot where the 77th Field Artillery had been ambushed earlier. While we were sitting in the bush Captain Barnes and Lieutenant Erickson found us. They were attempting to start some of the vehicles that were left on the road as a result of the ambush. At this time a US Army truck column came down the road and we were rescued and returned to our forces.'

While the Marines of X Corps sat in their ships in Wonsan harbour, the race for the North Korean capital of Pyongyang was under way. Three ROK divisions were driving northwards, together with the US 1st Cavalry Division, the 24th Division and the 27th British Commonwealth Brigade. On 19 October units of the 5th Cavalry entered Pyongyang, just minutes ahead of the ROK 1st Division.

On 24 October General MacArthur conveniently forgot his previous assurances to his President and removed all restrictions on the forward movement of non-Korean forces. He ordered his commanders to move forward with all possible speed, using all their forces. The Joint Chiefs of Staff questioned this decision, but did not order MacArthur to rescind his instructions. The war was nearly over, wasn't it?

On 26 October advance units of the 6th Division of the ROK III Corps reached the Yalu River. Over the radio came the first reports that they had killed a small number of Chinese troops. At the same time the ROK 1st Division captured Chinese prisoners at Sudong. The next day, 27 October, the Chinese first-phase offensive was launched.

THE SUNCHON TUNNEL MASSACRE

When Lieutenant Makarounis escaped from the column of prisoners as they departed from Pyongyang, he had unwittingly saved his own life. Little did he know at the time, but he would never see the majority of the others again. Ed Slater takes up the story:

'Two days after our arrival at Pyongyang they herded us outside and told us we were going to march to a train. Nobody wanted to go. Quite a few said, "To hell with it, we won't go." Some did refuse and then there was some shooting outside. I don't know if anyone was killed or not. That building was not only dark but cold as well. I scooted along the hall and managed to get to the bannister and pull myself up. Then a guard told me to get out as I got to my knees. There was a lot of flashing lights and shooting going on inside now. I managed to get up to hold on to the bannister. Then a guard pulled me down and hit me with his rifle butt four or five times. He told me to get up and when I told him that I couldn't he kicked me in the back and I rolled down the stairs. I landed at the bottom barely conscious, tried to get to my feet, but finally just laid there. I cursed the guards two or three times as loud as I could and told them to go ahead and shoot me because I was not going to go any further. Fortunately someone grabbed me and, with the guards still poking at me with their rifles, got me to my feet. Now the column was being formed again and we took off into the cold, dark night.

I really believed that we all thought the same thoughts: they will either shoot us or let us freeze to death! October in Korea can get very cold, especially at night. Several of us had stuffed newspapers and old rags inside our shirts to help keep us warm. Every so often a guard would make us take them out and throw them away. Rice rations were getting smaller and smaller and we were being fed with less frequency. We became weaker and weaker.

Once again they told us there was a train waiting for us. Finally there was a train and we were loaded into the four boxcars. We were packed in so tight you couldn't fall if you wanted to. Some of the men panicked at the close quarters. They started screaming and clawing at each other in an effort to get out. What with the odour from wounds, the smell of human waste, yelling and screaming, I thought I would lose my mind. Later, after what seemed to be an eternity, the train stopped inside a tunnel. We were told they didn't want to travel in daylight because of our fighter-bombers. We were to wait until dark to start moving again. In the meantime they said they would take the men, one car at a time, and feed us. We began thinking we might be better off now. At least we weren't walking and a train would get us to a permanent camp quicker. How wrong could we be?

The last car was unloaded and the men were told to go to the mouth of the tunnel where they would be fed. They were told to sit down in groups and then, without warning, they were machine-gunned. In the scramble a few men actually got away, but for the most part they were all murdered. Later, when I got back to the USA, I saw pictures of what appeared to be that very massacre. At the time it was hard to realise, but we knew what was happening and we wondered if we would be next.

The next morning our train started moving slowly, very slowly. The train left the tunnel and we were locked in our boxcars. We had two little windows at each end of the car, about two feet by two feet. Those that could see out said our guards were running back into the tunnel. Then they screamed that planes were coming. "They are ours! They are ours!" they yelled. Then they were silent and a rocket tore into the train. I still don't know if the prisoners tore the door off the car or if the rockets blew it off, but in any case it came off. Soon people started jumping off the train. The guards had set up machine-guns and the prisoners the planes didn't hit were shot by the guards. The planes made another pass, strafing the train. Another rocket hit in the middle of our group and exploded just as I reached the door. The planes made one more pass and this time didn't fire a shot. Perhaps they recognised us as prisoners? This was an even worse scene than the massacre of the school yard.

We were herded back on to the train. They loaded everyone that was left, even though several had some body parts missing. The guards shot some of the worst wounded where they lay. Then the train was moved back inside the tunnel. A lot of good men died there that day. That night, after dark, the train was on its way again at last.

What we feared would happen, happened. We were told to leave the train and start walking again. We were told, "You no walk, we shoot." Some of the men were reluctant to leave the cars, so the guards started throwing them out. Then we saw flashes of gunfire which lit up the area inside the cars. We could hear screaming as some men were being bayoneted by the guards. All I could do was scoot along the wall and head for the door.

When I got to the door I just fell out and rolled down a fifteen-foot embankment. The guards were throwing bodies from the train which were landing on me. Some guards were dragging more bodies to the growing pile. They shot fifteen or twenty who were still standing and added them to the pile. Then they poured diesel fuel over us all. The man on top of me had been shot and his blood was dripping on me. I smeared it all over my face. I heard him moan and told him to lie still and be quiet. I had no idea that he would turn out to be my buddy, Bob. He quietened down and didn't move. Then something hit my head a tremendous blow and I passed out.

It was daybreak when I regained my senses. I had a very painful headache. My arms were pinned under a pile of bodies and it took me quite a while to work free. I got my left arm free and reached up to my head and felt a bayonet stuck into my head. I managed to pull it out. Bob's body was still warm, so I thought he must be alive. Rigor mortis had set in for most of those in the pile. As a result I could hardly move, nor move Bob. The boxcars were burning and the warmth felt good. I could only think what would happen if those guards came back and found me alive. I finally got free and told Bob I was leaving. He pleaded with me not to leave him. I told him I would come back to get him. I really didn't want to leave him, but I was afraid the guards would return.

I remembered seeing a train station a few miles back, so I headed down the tracks in that direction. When I got there it was empty. The floor was warm from the fire they had built the night before. I was flat exhausted and lay down, and quickly fell asleep.

That afternoon I woke up to the sound of army trucks and the noise that troops make. I really needed to look for water, but I knew I had to get out of there. So I figured it was back to the hills again. I stumbled across a bird bath full of green, brackish water. I drank my fill, then slid down a steep bank on my butt. When I reached the bottom I found a small boy standing there. He said, in pretty good English, for me to follow him and he would get me some food and water. He said GIs had taught him English. By this time I was just about at the end of my rope. I told him I couldn't get up, let alone follow him. He helped me and said we didn't have far to go. We went to a house where he told an old lady to get me some food and drink. I sat there on the warm floor half asleep. She brought me a bowl of broth like soup. It really gave me a lift.

Now I began worrying about the North Korean guards coming back and catching me. I wondered if I could eat and quickly get out of there. The young boy left, saying he would be back with help. I was still eating when I heard someone talking just outside the door. The door slid open and there stood the biggest master sergeant I had ever seen. It's hard to believe a big old master sergeant could look like an angel, but this one did! He held out his hand and said, "Let me take you home," I cried all the way to the next village.

He took me to see General Allen, who was the head of a task force who had been trying to liberate us. The general asked if any of the prisoners I had been with were still alive. I told him that I thought there was at least one that could be alive. He asked if I would go with him in a jeep and show him where I had been. We got into the jeep and went back to where I had last seen Bob. Bob was still there and still alive. I told Bob, "Buddy, we are going home!" General Allen said, "No, not yet. Not until we clean you up a bit and feed you."

I had never liked tomato soup, but that was what they first served us. It tasted great, though it burned the hell out of the cuts in my mouth – but it was still good! When we drove away in the ambulance towards our lines neither Bob nor I bothered to look back.' [KWC76]

Ed Slater now spends three days a week at his local VA hospital and is a national service officer for the American Ex-Prisoners of War Association.

AT THE MERCY OF THE TIGER

The Tiger Survivors are a unique group of prisoners of war. They were captured between 5 and 25 July 1950 and were later joined by a few others captured at the Chosin Reservoir in November. They were combined with seventy-nine national civilians, as mentioned earlier in this book, and all suffered from maltreatment, starvation and neglect throughout the summer of 1950. In the beginning the group numbered 850, including civilians, but by the time they gained their freedom in 1953 there were only 265 still clinging on to life. As of April 1999 their numbers had dwindled to 145. One of them was Shorty Estabrook, now living in California.

'I joined B Company, 19th Infantry Regiment, 24th Infantry Division when it was on occupation duty in southern Japan in June 1948. Our division was closest to Korea and that is why we went in first. We were not trained properly and ammo was in short supply. We still used the old World War II bazooka and didn't have anything to knock out the Russian tanks. The first wave of North Koreans to hit us were combat-proven men from the China campaign and they were well trained and equipped. We were greatly outnumbered and they went through us like a dose of salts. The 24th managed to hold the commies back via a series of delaying actions. If this had not been done they would have taken South Korea. As soon as we got the 1st Cavalry in with the firepower they had, the war turned.

My little part of the war was on the Kum River about fifteen miles north of Taejon. I was a corporal at the time and was sent from my company to provide security at battalion headquarters. I didn't like that because I didn't know anyone. I had that sinking feeling in my gut.

The North Koreans overran our positions on 15 July 1950 and we started moving south along the road. Suddenly, where the road cut back with a sort of meadow on either side, we came under fire from a road-block. They had enough firepower to blow jeeps off the road. This means that they had been there for some time and we didn't know it. A makeshift squad was organised, me too, and up the hill we went. I was the only one to come back alive.

At this point I wanted to rejoin my company and headed towards the

Tiger Survivor Shorty Estabrook and his wife Marti today. Corporal Estabrook was captured on 15 July 1950 when his company of the 19th Infantry Regiment was overrun north of Taejon.

river which was about 500 yards away. Others were ahead of me. They entered the river and turned south when all of a sudden two of our jets appeared and cut them into pieces. I went straight up a mountain and crawled through several North Korean tank positions and the next day I came to a peaceful valley, with birds singing etc. Unbelievable. A beautiful day.

I hiked all day heading south, hoping to rejoin any friendly unit. Towards dusk I came upon the crest of a small hill and below were several South Korean soldiers, standing around smoking. I yelled and ran towards them. They started shooting and I couldn't understand why. Then I found out they were North Koreans in South Korean uniforms. They got me right there and then.

It was now October and the Chinese were streaming in from Manchuria by the thousands. We were housed in a town called Manpo-jin, right on the Yalu River. The Chinese commandeered our buildings and we had to move from town to town. We were in very bad shape and wearing the summer fatigues of the US Army. Many of us had our shoes taken away as well. We were dying at an increasing rate from exposure, malnutrition and wounds received at capture.

On Halloween a new commandant arrived. His record had preceded him and he was a very bad man. He had already killed a great number of people at a tunnel south of Pyongyang. We would later call him the Tiger. On 31 October we were living like animals in a cornfield just south of Manpo. The Tiger started us marching back through Manpo and we slept beside the road that night. It had already snowed in North Korea and it was turning very cold.

The Tiger death march started on 1 November and we had gone just a few yards when the Tiger, who was leading the group of thirteen sections, looked back and saw several American POWs sitting beside the road. One of the guards had given permission for them to stay, saying they would go to the People's Hospital. When the Tiger asked what was going on, the guard denied he had said that. The Tiger had given the order that no one would fall out of the march.

The Tiger had seven American officers come forward and he was going to shoot them all as an example. Commissioner Lord of the Salvation Army was being used as an interpreter. He begged the Tiger to spare their lives. The Tiger backed down and decided to shoot the officer in charge of the section the majority of the men were from. That was Section Seven, and Lieutenant Cordus Thornton from Texas was their officer [L Company, 34th Infantry]. Like a man he went to the mound and went to his knees, and the Tiger shot him through the head. POWs were so close that blood and brains splattered on them. This was, perhaps, the first witnessed atrocity of the Korean War. We now knew that this mad man meant business.

On the march we had to carry the sick and dying and the dead until we were told to leave them beside the road. We were already weak from malnutrition and became weaker by the hour. Commissioner Lord begged again and the Tiger said, "March till they die." The march ended on 9 November and eighty-nine bodies were left behind, discarded beside the road like garbage. Some of the civilian group were among those who lost their lives.'

The civilians varied in age from small children to numerous aged missionaries headed by Father Wilmor, an eighty-two-year-old Belgian priest who had served the Korean people for fifty-eight years. Among the many women in the group was sixty-seven-year-old Sister Mary Clare, and Miss Smith of the Kaesong missionary group, well over sixty. Some of them were not only old but sick as well. Father Hunt of the Anglican mission was partially crippled with gout; Bishop Byrne was elderly and far from robust; Bishop Cooper was seventy and had been subjected to prison cell confinement. All had endured weeks of poor food and exposure, being forced to sleep without protection in open fields as winter approached.

Almost a hundred people died on the march, and when the survivors eventually reached their destination a further eighteen civilians died of the effects of the march. Father Hunt, over sixty, no longer had any flesh on his feet at the end of the marching; he walked on bone. Some days after reaching the camp he died. So did Sister Mary Clare, and eighty-two-year-old Father Wilmor and several of his elderly Belgian and French Catholic colleagues. Following the nine-day march to the prison camp at Chungyang almost 250 prisoners died from sickness, starvation and exhaustion.

Shorty Estabrook continues the story:

'Now we were in Chungyang and we stayed for a few days. People began to die at a very fast rate. On 17 November we moved about a mile to a place called Hanjang-ni. Two hundred and twenty-one people, including some of the civilian group, died in that awful place. There was no medical attention at all. A simple thing like a boil could mean you would die.

In the spring of 1951 we moved again to an old Japanese Army camp at Andong. It was in this place that Royal Marine Jerry Ahern, the only British soldier with us, died in my arms on 7 May 1951. Jerry had been machine-gunned in battle and both his legs and feet were riddled with bullet holes. We knew he wouldn't make it short of us getting liberated. Perhaps one of the reasons he did last as long as he did was that they took him into Manchuria and that group had to sleep outside in the freezing cold. That, I think, prevented him from bleeding to death. We had a battalion surgeon with us and he could have saved Jerry if he had some sulpha and a medical kit. Without any medical attention Jerry was doomed. He died like a man, far away from his beloved England. He was among friends and we loved him like a brother. He suffered great pain. I can still see the look in his eyes as he passed. He was fighting even then and I bet they had one hell of a time getting him into the pearly gates. For years I carried Jerry's green beret. I met a little man from England who came over to attend one of our ex-POW conventions and gave him that beret, telling him to give it to Jerry's unit 41 Commando. He was supposed to write to me and tell me about the beret, but he never did. I am sorry now that I gave up that beret. I don't know if it ever got to Jerry's unit.

In October 1951 our group was sent to be turned over to the Chinese POW system. The officers were sent to the officers' camp and the civilians were kept by the North Koreans but moved to another town. The non-commissioned officers were also sent to another place, but they were returned and lived just below our place at Changsong Camp number three. Ten more were to die at Changsong.

The Chinese started to feed us and we started to gain some weight and get our health back. The reason they were feeding us was because they wanted to brainwash us. We would jokingly say, "You feed, we listen." The Chinese had no luck with our group because of everything we had already seen. It was common to disrupt classes by asking a question they couldn't answer. This would make the instructor appear stupid. Of course we had to sit through the whole thing. They handed out a form letter for us to fill out. It asked what parties your parents belonged to, and we would write, "Smoking, sex and beer." We simply didn't cooperate and the Chinese didn't try very hard. They knew we were a lost cause

I am proud that I was put in a reactionary squad with six other guys. We were not required to attend any more classes and that suited us just fine. I like to joke and make people laugh and I did so at every opportunity. That was a disruptive thing and that was why I was sent to that reactionary squad.'

One of the other Tiger survivors who lived to tell his story was Lupe G. Rodriguez, a nineteen-year-old medic with the 34th Infantry Regiment, 24th Infantry Division. At 3.30 p.m. on 21 July 1950 he was captured and his three years of misery began.

On 9 October 1950 Rodriguez and his fellow prisoners staggered into the town of Kosan, North Korea, more dead than alive. Shortly after arriving in Kosan Rodriguez made friends with J. C. Fain from headquarters, 1st Battalion, 34th Infantry, and James R. Dowling from Medical Company, 21st Infantry. The three friends immediately began plotting their escape. They had no maps, compasses or food; they only knew that they were going to escape.

On 13 October they crawled from the outhouse to a cornfield, immediately collected some corn to take with them and headed for the nearby mountains. Looking back at the camp, everything was quiet. The three men talked about going back, but decided it would be too risky. Scared, thirsty, cold and hungry, they went to sleep around midnight.

The next day was crisp and beautiful. Frost was on the ground and the three escapees woke to more hunger, thirst and cold. But they soon found some wild figs and turnips and enjoyed breakfast. Heading south, they found a small stream of water and quenched their thirst. Following the stream west, skirting a small village, they came upon a canoe and started paddling downstream. Suddenly the canoe tipped over and they fell into the bitterly cold water. They struggled to the bank and immediately ran into a Korean male who ran away, yelling at the top of his voice. On and on they walked, with no sign of pursuit. Their food was soon gone, though, and they spent another freezing night under the stars.

The following day they continued their journey, hungry, thirsty and cold. In the late afternoon they came upon a mud shack and walked right in, startling a Korean family. One of the two children, a little boy, ran off yelling. The meal that the Koreans had started was quickly finished by the escapees.

Suddenly they heard the sound of men's voices. They assumed they were North Korean soldiers and they were correct. They quickly hid in a haystack and the soldiers went right by them. 'Good luck, once again,' Rodriguez thought. But the soldiers soon returned and their luck changed for the worse. One of the North Korean soldiers saw or heard something and they all started firing their weapons into the haystack. Diving to the rear of the haystack, Rodriguez could hear Dowling and Fain scream in pain as the bullets tore into them. Playing dead, Rodriguez was dragged from the haystack and his feet were placed in a fire. Deciding this was no way to go, he jumped out of the fire, scaring the North Korean soldiers.

Rodriguez prayed that his death would be quick and painless. The North Koreans tied his hands behind him and led him to where Fain and Dowling lay lifeless on the ground. Then the two were shot again at close range. A firing squad was formed to finish off Rodriguez; commands were yelled and bullets were slammed into gun chambers. But good luck came to rescue the brave American once again. This time it was a North Korean officer who stopped the firing squad.

The North Koreans untied his hands, applied handcuffs and led him away to a small headquarters, hitting and kicking him all the way. At the headquarters he was forced to kneel by a desk where many Koreans paraded by, kicking and spitting on him. Dried blood was still on his head where a bullet had grazed his skull. Another stroke of luck. Then a very large dog was brought in. Fortunately the dog just looked at the hapless American and did not attack. Because of the dog's size, Rodriguez thought he must be very special. Most dogs in North Korea become 'stew of the day' long before they live to grow that big.

On 16 October Rodriguez was returned to the group of American prisoners of war in Kosan. He was ordered to kneel down and hold a heavy rock above his head. Another large rock was placed over the calves of his legs. If he rested the rock on his head he was kicked or beaten. Then the North Koreans poured kerosene all over him, but never lit the match. Another lucky break. This took place in the presence of the other POWs to make an impression on them. A North Korean officer ordered him to tell the others that to escape was certain death and the next time no one would be spared.

On 1 November 1950 the death march began. Rodriguez survived that ordeal too. The winter of 1950 was spent in a death camp called Hanjang-ni where 221 people died. He survived that as well and went on to live through a further thirty-eight months in captivity.

Lupe Rodriguez now lives in San Antonio, Texas, and is proud to be called a Tiger survivor. He earned the title, but his nightmares often take him back to Kosan where he still sees the faces of his friends, Fain and Dowling, lying by a haystack of death.

THREE

THE CHINESE WILL NOT ENTER THE WAR

BUGGING OUT

By the end of September 1950 the invaders had been driven out of South Korea. All of the territory south of the 38th Parallel was in the hands of Lieutenant-General Walton Walker's Eighth Army and Major-General Edward Almond's X Corps. In October General MacArthur decided to send his forces across the parallel with the intention of defeating the North Koreans and reunifying the country. By the end of the month it appeared that they had almost achieved their objective, but the sudden appearance of Chinese formations south of the Yalu River took the UN forces by surprise and two South Korean divisions and a regiment of the 1st Cavalry Division were badly mauled. This was the start of the first phase of the Chinese campaign, and it lasted from 25 October to 8 November. The UN forces on the west side of the Korean peninsula fell back to south of the Chongchon River, about fifty miles south of the Manchurian border. On 6 November, however, the Chinese broke contact and withdrew.

General MacArthur ordered the advance to continue. The Eighth Army began to move on 24 November and the X Corps in the east were due to follow three days later. Suddenly massive Chinese attacks sent the UN forces reeling backwards again. The second phase of the Chinese campaign had begun and would last until 25 December. During that time the American forces suffered one defeat after another. X Corps, including the 1st Marine Division, performed better than its fellows to the west and actually defeated the enemy 9th Army Group. But in the Eighth Army area of operations no attempt was made to fight a unified defensive battle and for the next month a race developed to the south, with the Chinese hot on the heels of the American and ROK forces. 'Bugging out' became a catchphrase with the American troops.

Probably the worst mistake made by General MacArthur was his determination to allow American troops to pursue the North Korean Army up to the border with China. The Joint Chiefs of Staff were already concerned when he ordered the UN forces to cross the 38th Parallel and carry the war into North Korea. Did MacArthur really give enough thought to the reactions of the Chinese as he urged his troops on towards the Yalu River? Were his intelligence experts doing enough to monitor the intentions of the Chinese? Apparently not. The Chinese had been massing an army of half a million men in the mountain valleys just across the border, waiting for the order to march into battle.

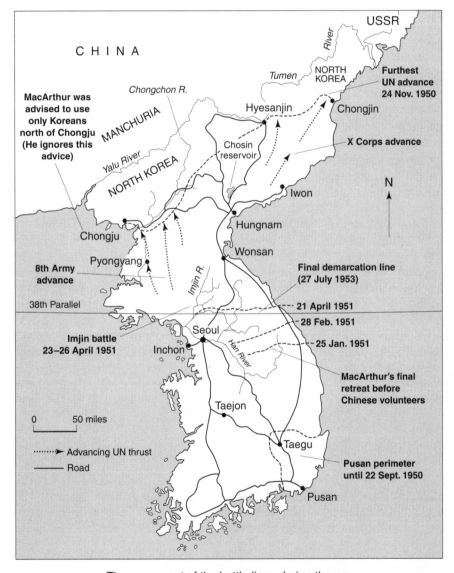

The movement of the battle lines during the war

81

The US Air Force also criticised MacArthur's decision to continue the advance to the Chinese border:

'Failing to appreciate the fact that Far East Air Force air attacks against the North Korean rear had enabled the relatively weak United Nations ground forces to advance to the 38th Parallel, General MacArthur made a fateful decision in October 1950 to press forward to the Yalu. As United Nations supply lines grew longer and longer, those of the communists would get shorter and shorter. Because of the United Nations ground advance and the politico-military restriction preventing air attacks north of the Yalu, United Nations air forces would have less and less opportunity for interdictory attacks against the rear of the communist armies. Because General MacArthur's strategy did not allow sufficient opportunity for air attack, it met defeat in North Korea when inferior numbers of United Nations ground troops were surprised by the sudden appearance of fresh Chinese communist forces.*'

As the United Nations forces were pushed back by the Chinese the enemy rear again became vulnerable to air attack, and FEAF later estimated that they inflicted nearly 40,000 casualties on the Chinese, delaying the southward movement of the Chinese 4th Army and allowing the UN Eighth Army time to prepare its defences.

If the politicians in Washington had given their approval to MacArthur's requests and the intelligence-gathering and communication processes in UN Command had been up to the job, nuclear weapons could have been employed with some success and would probably have changed the outcome of the war. An Army Research study estimated that if one forty-kiloton air-burst weapon had exploded over the dense enemy concentration at Taechon on the night of 24/25 November 1950 it would have destroyed 15,000 out of the 22,000 troops. If six such bombs had been exploded in the air over the communist assembly areas in the Pyongyang–Chorwon–Kumhwa triangle between 27 and 29 December 1950 they might have killed half of the 95,000 men in the area.

THE LAST STAND OF THE 8TH CAVALRY

The ROK II Corps, which was positioned on the right flank of the US I Corps, faced the full fury of the Chinese onslaught and crumbled as its scattered regiments were ambushed or cut off by elements of the 40th and 38th Chinese armies. As its flank was being laid open by the retreat

---

* *The United States Air Force in Korea, 1950–1953*, Robert Frank Futrell, page 701.

of the South Koreans, I Corps came under attack as well. The ROK 1st Division fell back through the US 1st Cavalry Division, as the cavalrymen fought to stop the enemy hordes. The 8th Cavalry Regiment was under attack from three directions, but they held out until 6 November when they carried out a fighting retreat through the enemy roadblocks. They lost nineteen officers and six hundred of their men during the fighting.

One of the cavalrymen about to face the full fury of the Chinese Army was Harry Gennaro. He told the author:

'On 5 August 1950 I arrived at Pusan on a Japanese fishing boat. I was assigned to the 1st Cavalry Division, which was engaging the North Koreans near Taegu. I was assigned to E Company, 2nd Battalion, 8th Regiment. We spent days on end taking a hill and giving it up the next day. We fought in an area called the Bowling Alley and No Name Ridge. Our squad consisted of four Americans and three South Koreans. I witnessed atrocities where the retreating North Korean Army had executed prisoners by tying their hands behind their backs before shooting them. I saw soldiers wounded in battle where they held their intestines in with their hands.

We began to push ahead, rather than taking and giving back hills. In the battle around the Walled City and on the push to the 38th Parallel I was wounded by a mortar round that exploded within six feet of me. I was hit with shell fragments in my left leg, left arm and in the neck. I was evacuated to the rear aid station and the next thing I remember was being on a helicopter headed to the hospital. I woke up in a hospital in Fukuoka, Japan. The shrapnel in my neck and leg was removed, but the shrapnel in the left arm was too deep and they decided it would be better for it to work out on its own. I recovered quickly and news came in that the Inchon landing was highly successful. The communists were routed and only mop-up operations and gathering of prisoners remained.

I returned to duty on 11 October and rejoined my outfit near Pyongyang, the subsequent capital of North Korea. There were a lot of new faces. Soon we began saluting and turning in ammo and talking about being home for Christmas. Things looked good. Then news was circulating that thousands of communist Chinese were massing on the Manchurian border. On 25 October we were rearmed, boarded on to trucks and moved north to Unsan. This was north of the Chongchon River and Kunu-ri and about twenty-five miles south of the Yalu River. It seemed like an Indian summer. We received winter clothes, mail and a hot meal. The ROK Army was near the Yalu River and G Company was up and in front of E Company. The tranquility did not last long.

The Chinese launched their attack around 27 October and G Company was attacked on the thirtieth. As wounded came by our position, they said

Chinese were pouring in like water running through a tin horn. We could hear and see the sky lighting up from the battle. Eventually it stopped. We waited. The night was quiet and still. I was in a machine-gun position overlooking a cornfield. My orders were to rejoin my squad if there was an attack. The night was deadly quiet, no stars or movement of any kind. Soon there came muffled noises from the cornfield. All hell broke loose. There were bugles blaring and the sky was lit up like the fourth of July. It was like kicking up an ant hill where ants began swarming. There seemed to be thousands of hollering, attacking Chinese. Within a short while we were engulfed and surrounded.

Wounded and fallen soldiers were everywhere. We fell back three times to the road. Two tanks were leading the retreat. They were drawing a tremendous amount of gunfire from the enemy. I saw several GIs shot off the thirty-calibre machine-gun on the top of the tank. I was on the right side of the rear tank. It felt as if I were in a sandstorm the way the shells were hitting off the tanks. I fell into the ditch. There were several others there too. We climbed the bank of the ditch and regrouped. There were twenty to twenty-five gathered. We planned to make our way over to the third battalion that was on our left flank.

We spent the next night on top of a mountain ridge. We could hear gunfire from their position. We waited until dusk. We had to make a dash across an open field that was in the firing line of the Chinese. We made a charge waving yellow bandanas and shouting loudly. We joined up with L Company, 3rd Battalion. They thought we were rescuing them and we thought we had made it to safety. This was a bad situation. The companies had formed a crescent-shaped perimeter. However, their ammo was exhausted. Ammo was passed to the foxholes from a knocked-out thirty-calibre machine-gun. We stripped the rounds from the band and reloaded them into the empty M1 clips.

My foxhole buddy was also eighteen years old and was from Ohio. Between hand grenades and reloading clips we repelled six charges. My M1 would only fire twice and had to be manually ejected to remove the second spent shell. On the seventh charge I was wounded. A Chinese six feet in front of my foxhole opened fire at point-blank range. The shells burst through the piled-up dirt and tore through my helmet, ripping it from my head. The blast knocked me down to the ground. My face was covered with blood from the head wound. I could hardly catch my breath and almost went into shock. Fortunately the Chinese did not attack again as dawn was drawing near and they did not usually attack during the day. The navy sent two jets over us to keep the Chinese at a distance. The jets came in so low and close that spent fifty-calibre clips from their guns fell into our foxholes.

The situation was hopeless. Completely out of ammo and with no chance of any reinforcement, the order was given: try to get out the best way you can. As dusk was setting in, bleeding from the head wound, I began making my way to the rear of our perimeter. Two South Korean soldiers asked to join me. The three of us made our way to the Chongchon River near Kunu-ri. We swam the river. Between the head wound and the water filling the pockets of my field jacket and pants, I was being pulled down under the water. If it was not for the two Koreans pulling me from the river, I might have drowned. We made it to the road and within minutes a squad of Chinese spotted us. We were captured.

We were searched and my wallet, dog-tags, watch and other personal effects were taken. The two Koreans were beaten and taken off in another direction. I was beaten about the head and back. I was put into the ranks of the Chinese Army. It was raining and we must have marched fifteen miles. The only break they took was from a steady trot to a walk. We came under fire from what I believed to be a British brigade. The Chinese did not return fire and retreated.

I was constantly hit with a rifle butt and pushed to force me to stay in step and not lag behind. I felt as if I was having a nightmare and would

American prisoners under Chinese guard cross the Han River over a temporary bridge on their way north. The profusion of bandanas suggest that many of the men are from the 1st Cavalry Division.

85

soon wake up and discover it had been a dream. It did not happen and the situation grew worse. I was pulled out and turned over to three Chinese guards who appeared to be heading me north towards the Yalu. The guards forced me into peasant storage corn cribs at night. On the first morning the guards marched me up into the hills. I was told to drop my clothes via hand signs and ordered to kneel. The guard threw a round into the rifle chamber. I prayed as I thought the end was at hand. A shot exploded just behind my head. I thought I was dead, but I was still breathing and the guards were doubling over with laughter. On the third morning of what was becoming their routine I refused to show any outward sign of fright and it spoiled their fun, so it stopped. However, it did not earn me any points with the guards, as their attitude of slapping and pushing continued.

After six or seven days I was shoved into a dark hut. Someone asked what outfit I was with. At that moment I realised I was not the only one captured. Were were lined into a column and marched to Pyoktong, carrying our wounded.'

THE BRAVE PRIEST

Emil Joseph Kapaun was a captain in the US Army, but instead of the crossed rifles of the infantry he wore the cross of the Corps of Chaplains and was addressed by his men as Father. A priest of the Catholic Church, he now lies in an unmarked grave near the Yalu River. But he is not forgotten by the men who knew him. As chaplain to the 8th Cavalry Regiment of the 1st Cavalry Division he was already a legend long before he was taken prisoner by the Chinese.

When his unit was fighting along the Naktong River his jeep was blown up by enemy fire and his driver was wounded. He commandeered a ramshackle bicycle and, pockets stuffed with apples and peaches he had scrounged from Korean orchards, he would ride down the rocky tracks and across the paddyfields until he came to the forward outposts. He would then drop into the nearest foxhole beside a nervous rifleman, offer him a peach, crack a joke or two, say a prayer with him and then move on to the next hole. He was never far from the fighting, often setting up an altar on a litter stretched across two ammunition boxes and, with mortar fire coming closer and the enemy gathering for an attack, hearing confessions, celebrating Mass and administering Holy Communion to the men about to go into battle.

When the battles raged, his place was at the battalion aid station where he would cheer and comfort the wounded. He would joke with the lightly wounded and, over the dying, whatever their faith, he would say the last prayers of the Church. He had no fear of dying himself and at

Kumchon, early in the war, when word came back that a wounded man lay exposed in full view of the enemy, he and an officer went out and brought him back through fire that was so intense his pipe was shot out of his mouth.

The day of reckoning came on 2 November 1950 at Unsan. For thirty-six hours the 8th Cavalry, fighting a perimeter defence, beat off a fanatical Chinese attack. The enemy finally broke through early in the morning and hand-to-hand fighting went on around the command post and aid station for most of the day. At dusk the order was given for every man who could still walk to try to break through the enemy lines. Father Kapaun refused to go. His place, he said, was with the wounded, and together with Captain Clarence L. Anderson, the regimental surgeon, he tended the wounded until the Chinese arrived. Most of the survivors were captured as they tried to break out and they were all soon on their way north, towards the enemy prison camps on the Yalu River.

Stories from Hell

During the last two months of 1950, the atrocities continued. The Chinese would eventually realise the value of keeping their prisoners alive and would bend over backwards to convince the world of their 'lenient policy'. In the meantime it became obvious that they were just as adept at mistreating and killing their prisoners as the North Koreans, a fact to which Sergeant Nazervo Santini testified:

'On the night of 1 November 1950 I was captured near Wonsan, Korea. It was very cold at this time and I was clothed lightly. One of my Chinese captors took my sweater from me, causing me to suffer from the extreme cold. At the same time we were forced to lie down on a bank and a Chinese attempted to stab another prisoner, but he evaded the attempt and was unharmed. On the same night a Chinese soldier hit Private — in the back with a heavy metal piece off a machine-gun. This caused him much pain and made it difficult for him to walk.

During late 1950 and early 1951, while at a temporary camp near Pyoktong, we were fed very poorly. The meals consisted of a small bowl, two times a day, of barley, millet, corn or occasionally rice. However, I observed a ration dump at the camp which appeared to have a large stock of rations available.

From January until March 1951 we were given lectures by the Chinese on open, bare ground or in unheated theatres. Most of the PWs were clad only in fatigues, and as a result many became sick from colds, pneumonia or influenza. The Chinese would give these PWs shots, and many of them died a few hours after they received the shot. During this period approximately twelve PWs died daily as a result of pneumonia, malnutrition, lack of medical treatment and possibly the previously mentioned shots.

In January or February 1951 the PWs of Compound 105, Camp 5, because of lack of toilet paper, used some Chinese propaganda literature for toilet paper. The Chinese heard of this and forced the entire compound of about sixty-four PWs, including the sick, to stand on the ice of the nearby Yalu River for approximately two or three hours. These PWs were clad in the clothes they were captured in, mostly fatigues, and suffered extremely from the bitter cold.

In February or March 1953 Private First Class — and Private First Class — were confined in a cell for about twelve days without adequate clothing. As a result both PWs suffered from severe frostbite of the feet.'

Five days after Sergeant Santini's capture, on 6 November, men from the I and R (Intelligence and Reconnaissance) Platoon of the 27th Infantry Regiment, comprising two officers, eleven enlisted men and three ROK Army soldiers, were ambushed and captured by North Koreans in the vicinity of Togan-ni (KWC143). The prisoners were stripped naked – even their shoes and dog-tags were removed – and marched for about five miles to the headquarters of a communist unit for interrogation. One of the officers was singled out for questioning and subjected to particularly brutal beatings for having warned the men to withhold all information other than that required by the rules of warfare. Having been promised a warm meal, the prisoners were then led to the vicinity of Yultong-ni. Their captors held a conference and, laughing among themselves, started shooting their victims in cold blood. There was one survivor of this atrocity, who managed to return to friendly lines and tell his story. In addition the bodies were recovered later at the scene and all of them identified. The following day a captured North Korean confessed to participation in the crime, completing the chain of evidence.

Sergeant Bobbie P. Stringer was captured on 5 November. 'On 8 November, myself together with approximately 200 American POWs were marching to Camp 5. During the march I saw an unidentified American POW, who had fallen by the wayside, beaten to death by a Chinese guard. The POW's head was completely crushed by the guard's rifle butt and I feel sure he was dead.'

A lieutenant survivor of a patrol ambushed that same day, 8 November, stated in an affidavit: 'I saw my men who were wounded in action taken by the Chinese and hung up by their hands and then their clothes were set on fire, and the men that were dead and unconscious, they would push sticks in their eyes, and bayonet. They took most of the dead men's clothes off.' This was later corroborated by a medical officer who examined the condition of the recovered bodies (KWC113).

The next month, December, a South Korean patrol discovered the bodies of five American airmen near Muju. It was apparent from the condition of the remains that the victims had been subjected to fiendish torture, the flesh being perforated with multiple punctures apparently inflicted by sharpened sticks or bamboo spears. An investigation of the incident disclosed that the men were members of a truck convoy that had been ambushed by North Korean guerrillas (KWC164).

Also that month, on the twenty-first, thirty American prisoners were shot and bayoneted to death about four miles north of Ku-jang-dong (KWC63). They were being moved north by train when it was strafed and disabled by United Nations planes. Their North Korean captors decided to murder all those who were wounded before continuing the evacuation northwards. Shortly after that a friendly patrol moved into the area and discovered the bodies, seven of which had been covered with oil and set alight. While searching the area three survivors were discovered, one hiding under a straw mat with half his face shot away and the bone of his left leg exposed. The other two had sought refuge in a nearby Korean home and were seriously wounded, as well as being weak from malnutrition. They all agreed that the person who gave the massacre order was a South Korean traitor.

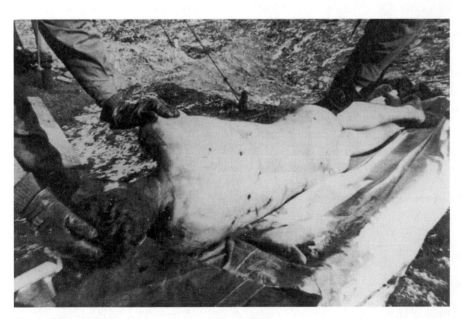

The body of this American serviceman exhibits multiple puncture perforations suggesting torture by bamboo spears. Five US airmen were killed in this manner in December 1950 in what was later known as Korean War Crime case number 164; the Bamboo Spear Case.

THE BEAN CAMP

Harry Gennaro, captured while fighting with the 8th Cavalry at the end
of October, survived the trek north with the other American prisoners.
On 15 November they arrived at Pyoktong on the Yalu River.

'We were ushered into houses evacuated by Koreans. Several of us were
taken to a command post and interviewed by a bad English-speaking
North Korean. I now wished I could have answered his questions differently. They were: Question. Why are you here? Answer. I'm here to halt
communist aggression. Question. Who is the Premier of China? Answer.
Chiang Kai-shek. At that point I was pushed and returned to the hut. I
later learned that twenty-two soldiers were taken south near our lines
and released. I knew one of the released: Donald Campbell from
Pecatonica, Illinois. He informed my parents that I was a prisoner of war.
On the same day our air force came over and dropped bombs on us. I
do not believe anyone was hit.

On 19 November the Chinese decided to move us to a valley that some
called the Bean Camp. Conditions worsened each day. Dysentery, diarrhoea and lack of food and medical attention was taking a heavy toll.
People were beginning to die at a rapid pace. Winter weather was hitting
twenty degrees below. Clothing was being stripped from the dead though
still covered with the dead man's waste. Corn that we stole from a field
and roasted over hot coals sustained us.

A fellow POW, W. W. Smith, and I made plans to escape. We gathered, with other POWs' help, a supply of roasted corn. At nightfall we
slipped past the guard and made our way up the steep mountain slope.
Korea was a God-forsaken place. We travelled the top of the mountain
ridge until morning. About mid-afternoon we decided to chance
advancing towards our positions. We noticed that the artillery sounds
were getting very distant and the flashes that were lighting up the skies
at night were fading. Without warning we were discovered by the Korean
guard and promptly recaptured. We were beaten the entire way as they
marched us back to the Bean Camp.

Upon our return I was interrogated by an English-speaking Korean. He
asked me if I knew martial law. The only Marshall I knew, I replied, was
a World War II general. This really upset him. He pulled his pistol and
stuck it to my temple. I thought he was going to shoot me. My heart sank.
He snarled, "If you are caught outside the compound after six p.m. you
will be shot." I understood perfectly.

After a time it became hard to determine time or dates as one day faded
into the next. We again were force-marched back to Pyoktong. There
were a lot less of us returning than went.'

The Red Cross Makes a Good Target

Sidney Esensten was the battalion surgeon for the 2nd Battalion, 27th Infantry Regiment, 25th US Infantry Division. At the end of November the division was positioned just north of the Chongchon River. At the centre of the line Task Force Dolvin had been formed to spearhead the division's attack north towards the Yalu. It was a strong force of tanks, artillery and infantry and Dr Esensten's battalion joined the force around midnight on 25 November. On the night of 26/27 November the Chinese launched a massive counter-attack and decimated the task force. The medical company detachment and some of the trains of the 2nd Battalion were ambushed south of the battalion perimeter and destroyed. Dr Esensten was there when they were overrun.

'The Chinese began an attack on 27 November about midnight and I got captured around two a.m. at a place called Unsan, which is north of Pyongyang. We got captured simply because, in the Korean War, medical people were the military's target. The enemy enjoyed shooting at our Red Cross helmets because they were good targets and they knew that if our troops did not have medical support their morale would drop. So aid stations, regimental stations, anybody who had a red cross on their helmet was a prime target.

They attacked at two a.m. as we were setting up an aid station to take care of the wounded. Because medical people didn't carry guns we didn't have anything with which to fight back. Therefore my whole aid station was destroyed. Out of twenty-seven medical staff only five were alive after the attack. My jeep driver was shot in the thigh, the bullet hitting his femur but not breaking it, so he had difficulty walking. The Americans discovered that the Chinese were behind them, attacking us, so they counter-attacked and the Chinese immediately took off into the hills with us as their prisoners.

The wounded man could not walk. He outweighed me by about forty pounds, but I carried him on my back, up and down the mountains for two nights after we were captured. Korea is a strange land. The only flat land is the area between Seoul and Pyongyang; otherwise, the rest of the land is valleys and 5,000–10,000-foot mountains. I carried him up and down the mountains. I emphasise this point to show you what stress can do to an individual.

Finally, two nights later, the Chinese put him in a truck to take him to one of their hospitals. [The jeep driver survived his wounds but died later of malnutrition in the POW camp.] The next night I couldn't even carry myself up the hill. In fact I passed out because we were at about 10,000 feet and I was hyperventilating. I couldn't go on because I couldn't breathe. A Chinese guard came by and he was going to stab me or throw me off the cliff, because that was their usual habit. If you couldn't keep up, they shot you, stabbed you or got rid of you somehow. The only thing that saved my life was a sergeant who picked me up and carried me up the hill until we had a rest period. My stress was over.

After we were captured, everybody had to march north. The distance from where I got captured to the area where we were going to stay was probably about 150 miles as the crow flies. We had 150 people in our group, and fortunately no one died. It depended on who was leading them. I pride myself in that I was the senior officer and kept everybody alive. Other groups didn't fare so well, depending upon whether they were captured by the North Koreans or Chinese. The Koreans were very malicious. They had no problems shooting people, throwing them off the cliffs or getting rid of the ones with dysentery. The worst group of all was the 600 men who were captured in April 1951. They started north with 600 men and they arrived at Pyoktong with 200 alive. They were all sick and within one week only 100 of them were left.

During the march we got fed irregularly, many times going for forty-eight hours without food. They did not provide us with water, so the men drank water out of the contaminated rice paddies. The Koreans fertilised the rice paddies and cornfields with human faeces. Men drank water from these paddies and fields and got diarrhoea.'

THE FROZEN HELL OF THE CHOSIN RESERVOIR

Battlefield environments are always hostile, but the bitter cold of the winter in Korea in 1950–51 made it unbearably so, particularly for the men fighting in the mountains near the North Korea–China border. At times the temperature dropped to twenty degrees below zero, with a windchill factor of twice that number as the north winds swept in at forty miles an hour. Snow squalls hindered both visibility and the mobility of the troops. Many were afraid to fall asleep in case they froze to death. Carbines and Browning automatic rifles had to be fired every half-hour or so to keep them from freezing. Some medics reported that they were unable to use life-saving plasma because it would not go into the solution at such low temperatures and the tubes would clog up. When the shooting started the medics popped morphine syrettes into their mouths to thaw them out, so that they could inject the drug into the seriously wounded men. Very often blood froze on wounds before it could coagulate.

Water canteens froze too. Perspiration in boots and on beards turned to ice; damp socks meant frozen feet and possibly frostbite, a major cause of non-combat casualties. One soldier reported that at Koto-ri several GIs set a boxcar alight and crawled inside until the flames drove them out. The Chinese suffered as well in the hard winter. Many wore only canvas shoes and 90 per cent of them reportedly suffered some degree of frostbite during the winter of 1950. Arctic clothing finally arrived for the UN troops, as did special non-freeze lubricants for the engines, but there were still many lessons to be learned about fighting in the depths of a Chinese winter.

Following the landing of X Corps on the east coast of North Korea, two of its divisions, the 7th US Army Division and the 1st Marine Division, were pushing northwards towards the Chosin Reservoir. They were isolated on the eastern side of the peninsula, with eighty miles and the central spine of the North Korean mountains between their left flank and the rest of the Eighth Army. General Almond, the corps commander, was trying hard to motivate the Marines commander, General O. P. Smith, to push on faster, but the Marine would have none of it. Suspicious of Almond's lust for glory and well aware that Chinese were waiting in the mountains ahead of them, Smith wanted his division

Men of the 3rd Battlion, Royal Australian Regiment bring one of their casualties down a snowy hillside. In the extreme temperatures blood plasma and morphine would freeze.

moving closed up and fully supplied with ammunition and ready to fight. Time would prove that Smith was right and Almond and MacArthur were wrong in trying to hurry the men north to the Yalu, for ahead of the two divisions, moving undetected along the trails and valleys in the mountains, were ten divisions of Chinese infantry.

Almost eighty miles long, the road from Hungnam to the Chosin Reservoir heads north-west and then divides in a Y-shape when it reaches the base of the reservoir. The 7th Division took the right arm of the Y and advanced along the eastern side of the frozen reservoir; the Marines took the left. By 25 November two of the Marines' three regiments, the 5th and 7th, had reached Yudam-ni at the western extremity of the reservoir. The 1st Marine Regiment was deployed along the main supply route between Hagaru and Koto-ri, while the 3rd US Division covered the coastal area to the rear of X Corps.

By 27 November the 7th Division was the most advanced American formation in Korea, almost on the banks of the Yalu River. Unfortunately, in their haste to comply with MacArthur's orders they had outrun their artillery and tank support and many of the men had not yet received the belated issue of winter clothing. That morning, as the two Marine regiments at Yudam-ni began to move forward for an eventual link-up with the Eighth Army, the Chinese struck. Violent assaults were launched along the thirty-mile length of the main supply route by three Chinese divisions – 30,000 men. In the face of such an onslaught the Marines pulled back and were soon concentrated in three isolated perimeters: at Yudam-ni at the west of the reservoir, at Hagaru on the base of the reservoir and at Koto-ri, ten miles further south.

The US 7th Division was virtually wiped out by the 10,000 men of the Chinese division which attacked it on the east side of the reservoir. Without heavy weapons to support them the companies were broken up into platoons and then squads, and finally it was every man for himself as the survivors fled across the frozen reservoir towards the Marine outposts. Of the 2,500 men of the division who faced the initial Chinese assault only 1,000 made it back to safety, and of these fewer than 400 were fit enough to join the Marines in their defence of Hagaru. Many of the wounded had to be left behind to die. Survivors told of one convoy of trucks carrying wounded that was stopped at a Chinese roadblock. The Chinese ordered all those who could walk to dismount and they had to watch in horror as North Korean soldiers set fire to the vehicles, with the wounded still inside them. The walking wounded were then marched away to the north, to live or die on another death march to the prison camps on the Yalu River.

While all hell was breaking loose around the Chosin Reservoir,

British Marines were moving north to join their American cousins. Three months earlier 41 Independent Commando, Royal Marines, had begun to arrive in Japan. This small unit of 300 men, under the command of Lieutenant-Colonel D. B. Drysdale, was employed in coastal raiding operations until the UN advance northwards put them out of business. On 16 November they boarded a US transport ship heading for Hungnam, where they were to join up with the 1st US Marine Division.

On 28 November the Royal Marines reached Koto-ri and were ordered to join a task force leaving the next day to reopen the road to Hagaru and reinforce the garrison there. Task Force Drysdale, totalling 900 men including US Marines, Royal Marines and US infantry plus a small number of tanks, set off on the ten-mile journey at 0930 hours on 29 November in a bitter north-east wind. Less than halfway along the route the column met heavy enemy resistance in a valley later named Hell Fire Valley by those who fought there. The American tank company commander, who was not under Drysdale's command,

British Royal Marine Commandos placing charges on an enemy rail line south of Songjin. The Commandos were later sent north to join the US 1st Marine Division at the Chosin Reservoir.

insisted that all his tanks should be at the front of the column. While a second tank company protected the rear, the centre of the column was unprotected by armour, and when a truck was set on fire, blocking the road, the centre of the column ground to a halt. In the meantime Lieutenant-Colonel Drysdale and the front of the convoy continued on to their destination, reaching Hagaru ten hours later. Now out of radio contact with Lieutenant-Colonel Drysdale, the centre of the convoy was stalled and became surrounded as the rear of the column and its protecting tanks turned around and returned to Koto-ri. The 300 men in the centre of the convoy were left on their own.

There was nowhere to hide. The only cover for those men on the road was their vehicles or the ditches at the side of the road. As night fell and mortar bombs exploded along the line of trucks and machine-gun bullets raked the banks of the ditches, the Chinese crept closer and closer. US Marine Major John McLaughlin made his way along the line of men in the early hours of the morning. He said that the Chinese had captured a man and sent him back with word that if they did not surrender in fifteen minutes they would be wiped out. He said that if the majority of the men wanted to fight, they would fight. If the majority wanted to give up, he would tell the Chinese they would surrender, but only if they would give safe conduct to the wounded back to friendly lines. At that time ammunition was running low and most of the men were either wounded or beginning to freeze to death. The temperature had fallen to twenty degrees below zero.

There was really no choice in the matter. McLaughlin went away and shortly afterwards the enemy fire slackened and the Chinese surrounding the convoy stood up, some now only feet away from the defenders. They disarmed the surviving Americans and British and began to loot the trucks. Initially the wounded were put on some trucks, but then they were told to dismount. The Chinese reneged on their promise to permit the evacuation of the wounded. Those badly injured were left to die, the others, around 140 men, were marched away to captivity. The Royal Marines' casualties for the day were approximately seventy, killed, wounded or missing.

For the next nineteen days the captives were marched north through rugged terrain to a town named Kanggye, an interrogation centre. Many men died on the march due to wounds, frozen feet, exposure and illness. Others were shot by the guards. Medical care was non-existent and the meagre food rations were inadequate. Men soon began to succumb to dysentery.

The guards were provided by whichever sector they were marching through at the time. The North Korean guards were worse than the Chinese, beating or shooting men who could no longer walk or refused to continue. Those with frostbitten feet suffered terribly as the flesh broke down into sores and scabs formed on the sores during the rest periods. When they began to walk again the scabs would tear loose, causing the prisoners to cry out in agony. Eventually, for some, gangrene would set in and the prisoner would die.

The men were marched by night and hidden from American planes during the day. They marched along high ice-covered mountain trails where the bitter wind cut through their clothing and trudged knee-deep in snow in the valleys. There was no water available to them; they had to eat snow instead. It was the same story as the other death marches: you either found the reserves inside you to keep going – perhaps a Good Samaritan would assist you during the worst times – or you gave up and joined the spectre of death, who marched at all times alongside the tortured souls.

On 1 December 1950 the men of the 5th and 7th Marines broke out of Yudam-ni and began their epic fourteen-mile fighting retreat to Hagaru. During the daytime they could count on Marine air support, but in the hours of darkness they had to fight the hordes of Chinese on their own. General O. P. Smith was urged by General Almond to leave everything behind and pull back south as fast as his men could march and ride. Smith, however, was determined to conduct 'an orderly and honourable withdrawal' and that meant bringing all his vehicles and guns as well. It was the most credible performance of any American unit during that winter. As the Marines fought their way south, they also brought their wounded with them, and their dead, stacked like logs in the back of the trucks.

By the evening of 4 December the long Marine column had entered the perimeter at Hagaru. Two days later the 1st Marine Division began the eleven-mile journey back down to Koto-ri, suffering over 100 killed and 500 wounded along the way. As they passed the burned-out vehicles of Task Force Drysdale in Hell Fire Valley, they collected the frozen dead and amazingly found one wounded man in a hut by the road, still alive.

The retreat continued past Koto-ri and on 10 December the first Marines began to arrive at the east coast port of Hamhung, where a vast armada awaited them. By Christmas Day almost 100,000 men, Marines, US Army and ROKs, had been evacuated back to Pusan, but the battle had been lost. The Marines alone suffered over 4,000 battle casualties and nearly twice that in non-battle casualties, mostly frostbite victims. The Chinese suffered terribly themselves, with possibly 35,000 men succumbing to the fighting or the cold itself. The difference was that the Chinese could replace their casualties a lot more easily than the Americans.

The Destruction of the 2nd Division

In order to prevent the encirclement of its units, the Eighth Army ordered its divisions to withdraw from the Chongchon River front. On 30 November the one major unit still in contact with the Chinese in the Chongchon Valley area was the 2nd US Infantry Division. General Laurence Keiser, the division commander, planned to break contact with the enemy that night and withdraw south from the vicinity of Kunu-ri to Sunchon, about twenty miles further south.

Keiser's new command post was established on the Kunu-ri–Sunchon road early on the morning of 29 November. Before long some members of the Turkish Brigade arrived to report that the Chinese had established a roadblock several miles south of the CP and had ambushed some of their trucks. It was disturbing news, but the Chinese usually made a practice of trying to encircle American units and cut their withdrawal routes, so it was not entirely unexpected. A military police patrol was sent to investigate and made contact with the enemy a mere three or four miles south of the CP. The 2nd Reconnaissance Company was sent to open the road and found that the Chinese had not established a roadblock, physically blocking the road, but rather a fireblock: they were in firing positions on both sides of the road. A second company was despatched to join the first with instructions to get the route open so the division could begin to withdraw the next day.

Around noon a platoon of tanks ran down the road and through the fireblock to make contact with the British Middlesex Battalion, which had been ordered to attack northwards to support the withdrawal of the 2nd Division. They realised that a whole battalion of the enemy was around the fireblock, but there is no record that this message was received by the 2nd Division CP. Chinese reinforcements were arriving hourly and at this time 2nd Division HQ did not realise the serious predicament they were in.

By the evening the size of the fireblock had grown and expanded northwards to within two miles of the division CP. To the division's front the 23rd Regimental Combat Team and the 9th, 23rd and 38th Infantry Regiments fought to keep the enemy back. That night the division CP came under enemy fire for an hour and General Keiser became increasingly concerned about the Chinese fireblock. He ordered the 9th Infantry to attack the next morning and moved the 2nd Combat Engineer Battalion to occupy the ridge which dominated the division CP area.

The tanks supporting the 2nd Division hardly covered themselves with glory on 30 November. During a Chinese attack on B Company of the 23rd Infantry early that morning US tanks opened fire towards the enemy, but their fire on the crest of Hill 201 fell among their own men and twenty were killed with seventy wounded, and a further twenty were lost as missing in action as they fled to escape the friendly fire. Later in the morning the ROK 3rd Regiment was sent to help the 9th Infantry open the road to the south. As the ROK infantry stormed one of the ridges above the road friendly tank fire fell short and killed a number of them. When they resumed the attack the same thing happened again, and this time the ROKs simply turned around and walked down the hill, some throwing away their weapons in disgust.

Four more tanks ran the gauntlet through the fireblock, now six miles in depth, and reached the defensive position where the Middlesex Battalion had remained overnight. Instead of attacking northwards to assist the withdrawal of the 2nd Division, it had pulled back. IX Corps should have been aware of the tactical situation and acted accordingly, perhaps sending further reinforcements if the Middlesex Battalion was encountering heavy opposition. As it was, the 2nd Division was left on its own and time was running out.

Around 1000 hours on 30 November General Keiser gave the order for his division to start to force its way through the six-mile-long fire-block and through the heavily defended pass at the end. The 38th Infantry Regiment led the way, mounted on tanks from the 38th Tank Company. When they found the way ahead blocked by burning trucks or swept with heavy enemy machine-gun fire, the infantry would dismount and take cover in the ditches at the side of the road until the way ahead was cleared. Then they would remount and continue aboard the tanks. Six miles down the road the lead tanks entered the half-mile-long pass, a cut with steep fifty-foot-high slopes from which the Chinese poured mortar and machine-gun fire down at the oncoming tanks. Many of the infantry on the tanks were killed or wounded, but the rest got through safely. Such was the extent of the panic that spread later in the day that many following tanks would not wait for the dismounted infantry to regain their positions on the tanks, but would roar on down the road without them. E Company of 2nd Battalion, 38th Infantry, is one example. At the first stop the forty-two men riding on the tanks had to dismount to return fire. The tanks started to move off without the men and only two managed to climb on the lead tank; the rest were left to their own devices and only seventeen of them made it down to Sunchon.

The two battalions of the 38th Infantry and the 2nd Battalion of the 9th Infantry had a comparatively easier ride to safety than later units as the road was not yet too littered with abandoned or destroyed vehicles or wounded men needing help. As the day progressed, all that was to change. The Chinese soon realised that the pass was one of their best roadblock positions and sent more men and weapons to the area.

It became clear after the event that both General Keiser and IX Corps headquarters were under the impression that the road was open at the time the 38th Infantry began their ride through the fireblock. If they had been aware of the problems facing the division as it prepared to run the six-mile gauntlet they would no doubt have mounted a division attack along the route.

Around noon on 30 November the 2nd Division Headquarters Group pulled out of the CP and started down the road through the fireblock. They had only gone about a mile when the first bullets started to fly around the jeeps and command vehicles, overhead, planes swooped down to drop napalm on the Chinese occupying the ridges above the road. During the many halts Keiser would leave his jeep to fire at the Chinese with his favourite Springfield rifle. The jeep was hit half a dozen times and Keiser's bodyguard was killed while manning the machine-gun on the jeep. The road was now littered with almost every type of equipment that the army had in Korea. In the ditches the wounded lay, while those on their feet tried to hitch a lift on any passing vehicle. As darkness fell the group was held up at the pass by enemy mortar fire until an F-80 jet cleared the way for them. General Keiser and his head-quarters people passed through Sunchon and stopped ten miles south of the town. With the coming of darkness and the cessation of air support the Chinese infantry climbed down the ridges to the roadside, to wait for the rest of the division to make its way down the road.

During the afternoon General Walker, the Eighth Army commander, had flown over the withdrawal route in a liaison plane and must have been aware of the problems the division was facing in the fireblock. Why, then, did he not order the IX Corps or army reserves into action, or indeed send the Middlesex Battalion towards the pass? The fate of the whole division was now hanging in the balance.

The rearguard for the division was the 23rd Regimental Combat Team (RCT), commanded by Colonel Freeman. They had been facing ferocious opposition for days, trying to defend the road junction to Anju and Sunchon, south-west of Kunu-ri. Freeman was between the proverbial rock and hard place. He knew that, as the division rearguard, his unit would incur heavy casualties trying to force a way through the fireblock. On the other hand, at that time the road was open to Anju and there was a chance of escaping that way, before the Chinese cut it off as well. It did not take a tactical genius to figure out that by doing so it would lessen the chances of the other units yet to run the fireblock. Around the time that General Keiser and his group fought their way clear of the pass, Colonel Freeman ordered the 23rd RCT to pull out and drive hell for leather down the road to Anju. The approval for the 23rd RCT to ignore its previous order was apparently given by the division commander, General Bradley, based upon Colonel Freeman's presentation of his current circumstances. The die was cast.

The next unit to follow the division command group down the road to Sunchon was the 17th Field Artillery Battalion and its eight-inch howitzers. They stopped to gather up a number of ROK and Turkish stragglers on the way and fought their way through as darkness fell, losing around thirty vehicles and one howitzer which fell into a ravine, together with eight ROK soldiers who were riding on it. Compared to the other artillery units that were to follow, the 17th was very lucky indeed. When the 1st Battalion of the 38th Infantry followed the 17th Artillery, they noted around two dozen burning vehicles and over a hundred more damaged or abandoned along the road. Whenever their vehicles stopped, wounded men would crawl towards them from the roadside, hoping for rescue.

The 2nd Military Police Company and the Provost Marshal's staff were next in line behind the 1st Battalion of the 38th. Their three dozen vehicles came under machine-gun fire at one point and the men sought cover in the roadside ditches. Suddenly half a dozen friendly 155mm howitzer shells landed on the convoy, destroying half a dozen vehicles and wounding over a score of men.

When the 23rd RCT pulled out and headed down the Anju road around four p.m., at least half the division had yet to run the gauntlet along the road to Sunchon. With the rearguard no longer in place, only two or three miles separated the Chinese from the remaining units of the division, the 38th and 105th Artillery and the 2nd Engineer Battalion. One other artillery unit, the 15th Field Artillery Battalion, fired off all its remaining ammunition, destroyed its 105mm howitzers and pulled out with the 23rd RCT. A platoon of infantry covering their withdrawal was never seen again.

The 37th Artillery had already run the gauntlet, following the 17th Artillery with its eight-inch howitzers, but losing ten of its eighteen howitzers on the way. Next to follow was the 503rd Artillery Battalion with its heavy 155mm howitzers, then the 38th Artillery Battalion. One mile down the road B Battery of the 503rd was overrun by Chinese infantry who swarmed over the road, killing and looting. The rest of the battalion were assisted by some of the AAA vehicles mounting quad fifty-calibre machine-guns or dual 40mm weapons. These fearsome guns made short work of the machine-gunners holding up the convoy, but once beyond the pass they found the road under heavy fire and many of the men moved away into the hills to try to walk out. The 82nd AAA Battalion lost almost 300 officers and men during the withdrawal, mostly from its headquarters battery after two ammunition trucks blew up and blocked the road. The Chinese then swarmed down to the road and overran the convoy.

The 38th Field Artillery Battalion found its way ahead blocked by the tail of the 503rd and decided to destroy their guns and vehicles and make their way out on foot. The last unit of the division to move down the road was the 2nd Engineer Battalion. All day long they had held two hills at the side of the road while the artillery tried to run the fireblock. As night fell they were under attack from all sides and were practically wiped out. From its authorised strength of 977 men, only 266 could be counted when the remains of the division reassembled days later.

The final figure for the number of men killed, wounded or missing for the 2nd Division at Kunu-ri was 4,037. Some units, such as the 2nd Engineer Battalion, were almost wiped out. Others, like the Turkish Brigade, lost 90 per cent of their vehicles and reported 68 men killed, 238 wounded and 630 missing in action. Of the five artillery battalions with the division, three (the 15th, 38th and 503rd) each lost all eighteen of their guns, while the 37th made it out with eight of their eighteen howitzers. The 17th was the first of the artillery battalions to go through the fireblock and they made it out with eleven of their twelve pieces. It is sad, but true, to point out that many of the howitzers that were not destroyed by their crews were soon in action again, this time fired by Chinese gunners against UN targets. The 82nd Anti-Aircraft Artillery Battalion lost twenty-three M-19 dual Bofors automatic 40mm gun vehicles and twenty-six M-16 quad fifty-calibre machine-gun vehicles. On 7 December Major-General Robert McClure took over as commander of the much-reduced division.

So what happened to the 4,037 men of the division who did not make it through the fireblock to friendly lines? Some of them lived to tell the tale, like Sergeant Robert Lee Wyatt.

'On 30 November 1950, near Kunu-ri, North Korea, while a member of B Battery, 503rd Field Artillery Battalion, we were stopped by a roadblock and attacked from both sides of the road by Chinese. The Chinese later moved in, killing wounded prisoners and spraying ambulances loaded with wounded with gun fire. Approximately one week later the captured Americans started to march north, picking up more prisoners along the way. The march lasted about three weeks and finally ended at a mining camp called Death Valley. Approximately 400 prisoners died during the march, from lack of food and clothing. During my two-week stay at Death Valley approximately 500 men died there from malnutrition, dysentery and lice. On about 14 January 1951 I was transferred to Camp 5 near Pyokdeng, along with about 1,200 other men. Men died every day along the route of the march and were left lying in the snow. I personally saw one man from 2nd Company tied by his wrists to a tree and beaten with a strap. A man named — was beaten with a rifle butt; a man named — was beaten to death by the Chinese for trying to escape in approximately February 1951; Private First Class — was beaten by the camp headquarters staff, as was —; — was strung up by his arms and beaten with a rubber hose until he was unconscious. Men were forced to stand in the snow suffering from trench feet and pneumonia to listen to political speeches, and many died. Medical treatment consisted of aspirin and opium pills. Shots were given to the men to make their resistance low. No records were kept of the prisoners' deaths until prisoner-of-war lists were requested, and there are approximately 1,700 to 2,000 unmarked graves at Camp 5. Any man imprisoned for an infraction of the rules was beaten while in jail; if imprisoned for over four days he usually emerged with frozen feet.'

Sergeant John R. Worley was also captured on 30 November.

'The Chinese walked the prisoners of war in circles at night and then for a twenty-five-mile hike to the rear. This happened every night until we reached the hospital area on Christmas night. At the hospital area I saw over 200 men die. They had no food and were lice-infested. I also saw men die on the march from exhaustion and hunger. Sometimes we would not eat for two or three days. I left the hospital area on approximately 7 February. We started walking towards Puckdong. Some men were put on ox-carts and the rest on foot. There were about 150 men in the group I was in. When we got to Puckdong there was no food in the

Taken from a communist pamphlet 'Communism and Prisoners of War' this picture shows a column of UN prisoners or war making their way northwards.

camp. Men were dying by the hundreds. While in camp at Puckdong about 1,700 men died, American, Turkish and other prisoners of war. The majority of the men who died were Americans. I watched two Chinese nurses giving shots to men. They did not know how to give shots. Some men died immediately after receiving shots. None of them lived for more than twenty-four hours after receiving the shots. I showed the nurse how to give shots and took one myself. It did not harm me.

The Chinese instructor named "King" – I don't believe it was his correct name – was forcing men to go to lectures. He threatened men who did not want to go. He would pull men out and force them to go. An airman escaped, and after he was caught he would not answer their questions. He was beaten to death by several Chinese with sticks, belts and clubs. Another man was tied and beaten by several Chinese. Men from the squad had to bring him in. This happened around the last day of March or the first of April 1951. Men were still dying but at a slower pace. We were fed when we would attend lectures. Food was so bad and there was so little that men were eating grass and bark off the trees. This went on until Christmas 1951. We had an influenza epidemic from January until February 1952. There was very little medicine.'

DEATH VALLEY AND THE MASSACRE OF THE LITTER PATIENTS

US Army doctor Gene Lam survived captivity and wrote about his experiences after he returned home. He described the fate of the men of the 2nd Infantry Division and attached units who were captured in the fireblock area south of Kunu-ri between 25 November and 1 December 1950. The majority of the men captured had been in constant contact with the enemy, were cut off from the rear, their ammunition supplies were exhausted and they had been fed sporadically. Most of them did not have the winter issue of clothing and a morale-shattering factor to the men was the knowledge that the regimental and divisional commanders had left and taken their staffs and remaining armour with them.

Gene Lam arrived in Korea in August 1950 and was attached as a medical officer to the 2nd Infantry Division.

'In the beginning we had adequate supplies and the casualties varied, depending on the type of action engaged in, as we started off in the Naktong Perimeter, Pusan defence, and continued north through Pyongyang and Kunu-ri. From 25 November until we were captured we had a tremendous number of casualties. There were three battalions in the area at the time and from our battalion we had a little over 300 men left, plus the attached service units – a total of between 500 and 600 men

– when we ran into the roadblock, and a majority of these were captured.

We were about thirty-five miles north of Kunu-ri when we first encountered heavy enemy fire. We pulled back to eleven miles south of Kunu-ri when we were caught in the roadblock. They had come in from behind us to set it up. Originally the report was that a company of communists had set up the block, but after I was captured I saw thousands of Chinese. We heard reports that there were anywhere from one to three divisions taking part in the action. Our last casualties had been evacuated on the afternoon of 29 November and when the regiment started pulling back our medical company had 119 litter patients in ambulances, trucks and jeeps, all casualties of the day's fighting on 30 November.

Around midnight the column of trucks stopped and when it became evident that the convoy couldn't get through the officer in charge ordered us to leave the vehicles and try to escape on foot. The wounded were to be left behind on the orders of the senior officer in charge of the regiment at that time. It should be noted that at four o'clock on the afternoon of 30 November Major Coers, the regimental surgeon, had asked for permission from division headquarters via radio to take the wounded out by way of a different route. This route at that time had not been cut by the enemy and evacuation was possible. Permission, however, was denied and the wounded were taken with the rest of the regimental vehicles into the roadblock.

When the order was given to take to the hills and attempt to walk out it was about one a.m. and the weather was well below freezing. We took off, but six of us were captured together. In the meantime the Chinese slipped down and mercilessly slaughtered the wounded as they lay on their litters. One man survived to be repatriated in 1953; the remaining 118 men were killed. I didn't see them actually shooting the litter patients, but I heard the machine-gun fire and then when they marched us back past the convoy I saw the bodies. There's no doubt about what they did.'

Captain Lam later said that few men got out alive from the roadblock area. He only knew of about five other officers and eight or ten enlisted men who did. He was then marched to a graphite mine where the six were held captive along with about 300 others who had been captured. Detained there for a week, he saw the Chinese troops as they were marched in and out of the mine from time to time. He counted over 2,000 Chinese soldiers at one particular time. They had good weapons and shoes, unlike most Chinese soldiers who wore tennis shoes.

Apart from observing the enemy, Captain Lam also observed the attitude and condition of the American prisoners during their time in captivity.

'Nearly all the men in the first few days of captivity were in a semi-state of shock. They were bewildered, confused, afraid of what the enemy would do with them, and felt deserted. Most of the men had a period of amnesia for four to five days and can only give sketchy accounts of their location and activities. Most of them were strafed by our air force in its attempt to destroy our abandoned vehicles. They seemed to slump into a state of lethargy and had no concern for their personal safety. The most notable thing during this period was the extremely low morale of the men. The subject of conversation was their personal safety, shame of their unit organisations and loss of faith in their commanders, who they felt had left them the day before their capture.

Within twenty-four hours of their capture the men also started to talk about food. They seemed to have fantasies and dreams about food. Fantastic menus were devised, which they were going to have when they were rescued or released. The usual soldiers' conversation about women, automobiles and pay would not be discussed until 1952 when conditions improved.

Within several days the small groups of men were assembled and started towards the rear. These marches were made at night and were from fifteen to thirty-five miles at a time. The weather was extremely cold, perhaps fifteen degrees below zero or more. The men had in-adequate clothing and were fed only approximately 300 grams of whole kernel corn per day. When we stopped we were jammed in unheated buildings, twenty or thirty men in an eight-by-eight room. There were a number of wounded men who were carried grudgingly and numerous cases of frostbite of the hands and feet started to appear.

It was noticed that many men fell out of the column due to illness or injury, and when they did a Chinese guard also dropped out. At times we would hear a shot and the guard would reappear alone. The night marching continued until the morning of 26 December when we arrived at the camp called "Death Valley". The most seriously wounded men had been taken from us about a week prior to our arrival and were never seen again.'

Dr William Shadish also took part in the march and he later recalled his first Christmas Day in enemy hands.

'For eighteen days we had marched; now, as it grew dark on Christmas Eve, our march was nearing its end. One more hill to climb and the other side of the hill to go down, and we would be there. But it was twelve miles up the hill and on the steep grade and rocky road we couldn't do better than a mile and a half an hour, so we had more than seven steady hours uphill. We hadn't forgotten it was Christmas and every now and then somebody would start a carol in a thin voice, but one of the communist guards would stop him. They don't like religion.

106

Anyhow, there wasn't any breath for singing. It took all our strength to keep marching uphill. We hadn't been prisoners very long and our clothes were still in good shape, but it gets awfully cold over there. I've seen it go down to thirty below. If anybody dropped out of line they just left him there to die.

At about midnight on Christmas Eve they marched us off the road and into a big unheated shed. There wasn't any floor, nothing but the frozen earth to sleep on, but everybody was too tired to care. The next morning we marched again. After two or three hours we turned the top of the hill and after that we made better time. Christmas night we reached the camp. I'd say we were more dead than alive if it weren't for those who really were dead somewhere along the way. We were cold and tired and hungry; they hadn't fed us for twenty-four hours. There was no singing that night and our prayers were silent prayers.'

[The prisoners had carried a supply of rice which they hopefully thought the guards would feed them as a holiday meal; instead the guards ate it themselves.]

Despite the horrors they had seen, the four US doctors smile for captive AP photographer Frank Noel in Camp 2 on the Yalu River in 1952. Left to right Captain Gene Lam, Captain Sidney Esensten, Captain Andy (Clarence) Anderson, Captain Bill Shadish, all doctors, together with Captain Chet Osborne.

This particular camp had formerly served as a mining camp. Its buildings were poor, there was no heat and a number of the huts did not even have doors. About twenty-five to thirty men were placed in rooms about ten feet square, and luckily so, as it was the only way they had of keeping warm. Pneumonia had been a minor problem on the march, but in the camp, where the men led a more or less sedentary existence, pneumonia became the major cause of death.

Most of the men were suffering from one illness or another. They had been given little food or water and they ate snow or drank from streams or puddles. The diet of corn, with perhaps a few half-raw turnips thrown in, started many cases of diarrhoea and those who were not yet affected soon developed diarrhoea after they were fed partially cooked soy beans one day. Eight hours of boiling was required to properly cook the beans, but the lack of wood meant they were usually undercooked. Six to eight bowel movements per day was commonplace, but those with severe diarrhoea could be afflicted up to thirty times per day, with associated fever, dehydration and subsequent death. Personal hygiene was non-existent; there was no opportunity to wash and no eating utensils were provided. Men had to eat out of hats, hands or pockets torn from their tunics.

All the men held at Death Valley had dysentery at some time during their stay there. Doctor Lam later described the effects of this awful illness:

'The usual case developed diarrhoea, ten to fifteen stools per day; loose, light-coloured stools with no blood. This progressed over two or three days, increasing in frequency of stools to twenty-five to forty per day. About the third or fourth day the stools became mainly mucoid and were streaked with dark unclotted blood. After a few days many of the men had stools consisting mainly of blood. The patients became extremely dehydrated, weak and toxic. In the majority of cases the men lost their appetites and refused to eat. This, of course, hastened their deaths. Of those who continued to eat, many recovered. Death in the average case occurred about the fourth or fifth day of severe dehydration and toxicity. The average case after onset lay down and refused to move around. This contributed to the rapidity of death. In those cases which remained ambulant, death was postponed or averted in some cases. Our main attempt at treatment was ambulation and hydration. We attempted to keep boiled water for these patients, but it was not possible to have an adequate amount. Doctor Shadish contracted dysentery and became very toxic within a short while. I obtained ten half-gram tablets of sulfaguanidine from the Chinese and successfully treated him.'

On several occasions the two doctors were taken to camp headquarters and fed together with the Chinese officers. Perhaps they recognised the advantages of having two fully qualified, albeit American, doctors in the camp and wanted to maintain their health. They ate rice, beans and vegetables with each meal. They also frequently had pork or chicken, and occasionally eggs. The Chinese troops also ate rice and vegetables, in spite of the propaganda they put out that the Chinese ate the same as the prisoners. The doctors were allowed to take any leftover food with them and distribute it to the men in the hospital.

The camp in Death Valley was divided into two main parts, an upper and lower camp. The lower camp contained about 900 American and Turkish prisoners, while the upper, smaller part had about 300 to 400 American and South Korean prisoners. Above the upper camp was another camp containing an estimated 800 South Korean prisoners. About fifty South Koreans were held with the Americans and used mainly for burying the dead. The barracks of the lower camp consisted of seven long mud-walled buildings divided into six rooms about eight feet by eight feet square. The number of men in each room varied between twenty-four and thirty-five. The upper camp had a similar arrangement except the buildings were scattered throughout the area.

About a week after Doctors Lam and Shadish arrived, they persuaded the Chinese to let them set up a hospital to care for the sick. Three rooms were patched up for the hospital, two for the sick and wounded and one for the medical personnel of the 9th Infantry Medical Company, which helped to run the hospital. These men cannot be praised enough for the job they did in Death Valley, and later in the other camps. Without them many more would have died and many of them selflessly gave their lives helping other prisoners. A fourth room was used as a morgue, and it was never empty. Doctor Lam later described the living conditions at the camp:

'Facilities for sanitation were practically non-existent. There were three small pit latrines around the camp, but they were soon filled and frozen. The men then relieved themselves whenever and wherever the urge moved them. As a result, in a few weeks the area was littered with frozen faeces and urine. Without the extremely cold weather a very serious problem would have presented itself. We attempted unsuccessfully to keep the area clean but could not do this due to lack of cooperation. The water supply came from the nearby river, but as it ran on a lower level from the latrines it was contaminated at all times. The men were instructed to boil the water for drinking, but many did not heed this advice and suffered diarrhoea and dysentery.

No clothing was issued, so when a man died his clothing was stripped from him and given to others without proper clothing. Even so, at no time did the men have adequate clothing to protect themselves against the cold.

They were "kind" enough to give us one pound of DDT for 1,100 men. We had approximately a hundred sulfa tablets and the other doctor and myself actually stole other tablets so we could treat our sick. They made the mistake of showing me where they kept them. Unfortunately, very few men who went into the hospital came out of it. All it was was a place to die.

The main group of 800 to 900 men were moved to Camp 5 late in January 1951. The Chinese had Captain Shadish and myself go through the camp and select those men who could not make the march at that time. They told us that those who were too sick or wounded would get better food to make them strong and we would take them to Camp 5 in about a month. We selected about 250 men. Of these about fifteen to twenty were medical corpsmen from the 9th Infantry who were to help us with the sick. It should be noted here that about a week later the food was cut by about a quarter instead of the promised increase. Of the men left behind, 109 lived to leave Death Valley on 13 March 1951. Of those who left before us, over half died after reaching Camp 5. On our march to Camp 5, between 13 and 19 March, eight men died and were left along the road. The distance was about ninety miles. The sick were transported on sleds and ox-carts most of the way, but there were some who should not have walked, but were forced to walk the entire distance. Some of these men were suffering from acute hepatitis.'

Doctor Gene Lam kept a record of 256 deaths. The Chinese knew he was keeping a record but didn't bother about it for nearly a year. By that time they had made three copies and had them hidden, one in a bar of soap. Together with Lieutenant Howard Eichelsdorfer, Lam took one of the one-dollar military script bills and tediously split it into two pieces. Using fine print they recorded the names of the more than 300 men who they knew had died. Then they pasted it back together and were able to keep it when they were freed. After his release Lam ensured that the next of kin of all the dead were notified.

THE CAMP

During the early months of the war the North Koreans made little attempt to establish prisoner-of-war camps for the many South Koreans and Americans who fell into their clutches. Holding centres were established at which prisoners of war would be collected, but there was little thought given to feeding, housing or caring for them. Survivors often reported being marched all over South Korea, wandering aimlessly while the sick and the weak fell by the wayside or were put out of their misery by their cold-hearted guards.

When the Chinese entered the war at the end of 1950 they began to organise proper prison camps up near the Yalu River, and all through that terrible winter of 1950 weary columns of prisoners trudged through the snow, hoping that the promised camps were just over the next mountain. For many it was to be a rude shock. The first permanent prisoner-of-war camp to which American and later British prisoners of war were evacuated – as some of the preceding testimonies have already stated – was Camp 5, located near the city of Pyoktong in North Korea on the Yalu River. It was several hundred miles from the front line, with an endless series of mountain ranges separating it from the combat zone.

The climate at Camp 5 was extremely cold in winter and moderately

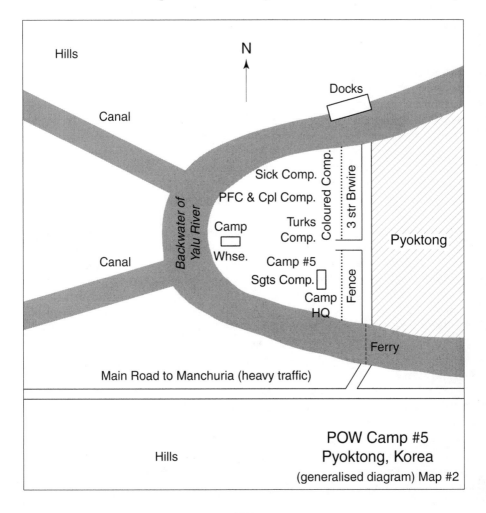

POW Camp #5
Pyoktong, Korea
(generalised diagram) Map #2

warm in summer. This camp, like all other communist camps in North Korea, was actually a Korean village whose inhabitants had been evicted in order to make room for the prisoners. There were no electrical fences, spotlights or guard dogs at any of the compounds, although barbed wire was sometimes used to enclose prisoners. The main means of securing the camps were walking guards or static guard posts. For the most part the guards were Chinese, as were the camp staff and commandant.

Camp 5 was the largest prisoner-of-war camp and was the enemy's model installation. In addition to serving as the communist 'showcase', Camp 5 was also the headquarters for the Prison Command in North Korea. The Chinese general who served as commanding officer for the camp also served as commanding general for the communist Prison Command.

The camps were not like the World War II camps, run in an efficient manner by the Germans with regular visits from the Protecting Power and the Red Cross. The Red Cross was not allowed into North Korea and the Geneva Convention meant nothing to the North Koreans or the Chinese. During that first terrible winter the prisoners largely went without medical treatment; the food was poor and inadequate, and the housing and sanitation conditions abysmal. Thousands of prisoners would die before the spring of 1951 when conditions began slowly to improve. Harry Gennaro recalled his arrival at 'The Camp':

'We were herded into small dirt shack houses made from mud. The rooms were small: eight feet by eight feet or eight by ten, with sixteen prisoners to a room. We slept in a sitting position with our legs to the centre of the room. Our diet consisted of half a bowl of millet, canary food seed, each morning and evening. Prisoners of war were dying off in great numbers. Some POWs were taking the millet ration from the dying. I woke one morning to find that each POW on my right and on my left, named Sparks from Washington State, had died during the night. Each morning we went on burial detail. The dead were laid out on grass sacks with two sticks forming a litter bearer. Two POWs and two reliefs were made up to haul the dead to a burial place across the frozen Yalu. Graves were shallow as tools were not available to dig deeper into the frozen ground. At the beginning the Chinese marched us, carrying our dead, through town. The Korean civilians would hurl rocks and stones and curse us. To this day I have not forgiven or forgotten.

Due to lack of medical attention 1,500 POWs died during the first winter of captivity. Some died from combat wounds, some from malnutrition because they did not handle the rations, some from sickness contracted in camp and some because they just did not want to live in that situation. The entire camp was infested with hog-like lice. These lice would actually suck all the blood from your body if left unchecked. We would take turns in front of the door squashing the lice that covered the inside seams of our clothing. Some POWs who were not able to remove lice daily were thrown out of the hut.

It was at that time that the shell casing shrapnel worked its way out of my skull. This was from the gun shot in the head from the perimeter attack.

The situation did not improve throughout the winter. Details were formed to collect fallen wood from the hills (we were not allowed to cut a tree down) for building fires in the huts. A fire would be started in a chimney open at one end of the hut and the heat travelled through a trench covered with mud-covered stones on the floor. This provided the heat for the hut. When the stones got hot they would stay hot most of the night. The problem was you would scorch your clothes early and freeze again by morning. Even with all the deaths the camp was grossly overcrowded.

Nearing the end of winter, around March, I contracted a severe case of double pneumonia. I felt as if I was in another world. My hands felt as if I was rubbing silk together. Somehow I was taken up on the hill to the hospital compound. Very few returned from there. They gave us warm soy-bean milk and boiled water to drink. One of the most horrifying sights I experienced was when I saw Dunlap. He had been with E Company on the front line and would go for thirds on SOS breakfast. He was a large individual. He stood over six feet and weighed near 240 pounds. I did not recognise the skeleton I now saw. He had no control of his running bowels and had to be washed down by throwing buckets of water over him. He was infested with maggot-like worms. When he coughed he would catch them in his hands. He also passed them and you could see up his rectum due to the skeletal appearance. He died. Praise the Lord. Many died there. I was happy to be able to leave that place and return to the 3rd Platoon.

My feet were beginning to get feeling back from the frostbite. My teeth were loose. I could not stand the air to hit them as I suffered from pyorrhoea. My gums were actually rotting away. I would go to the river and rub the rot away with a wet cloth. I could press my finger into the arm or calf of my leg and the indenture would remain. I had night blindness and had gone down in weight from 165 to 105 pounds.'

Corporal Dorland F. Guinter also recalled the deaths and suffering of those days:

'I was taken prisoner on 1 December 1950 at a place located near Kunu-ri. I was a member of C Company, 2nd Engineers Combat Battalion, 2nd Division, attached to the 38th Regiment. I was first taken to a camp which was called "Death Valley". From this camp a group of 500 prisoners was marched for about four-and-a-half days at night. We

113

arrived at Camp 5 on 19 December 1950. Approximately seven days later seven copies of a magazine called *People's China* were distributed to the group in our room, Squad 36, Compound 105. Later the books were collected by our corporal, who then returned the books to the Chinese. Of the seven books, two were returned. The remaining books were either thrown away or retained for latrine paper.

About thirty minutes later two Chinese, one named "Limb" [phonetic] and an unknown Korean, came to the room and told us to fall in outside. We were then taken to the river bank about fifty yards away. The group consisted of approximately thirty-five men. At this time the temperature was below zero and a strong, cold wind was blowing. None of the prisoners was well clothed. We were made to stand with our hands in the air. If anyone moved or lowered his arms he was struck with a limb from a tree. We remained exposed for approximately four-and-a-half hours. As a result of this exposure many of the prisoners had frozen limbs. After we returned to our room no medical aid was given. As a result approximately half the men in this group died.

When a prisoner was so weak that he could not move the Chinese came and gave the man an injection. About three to ten minutes after this injection was given the man died. During this period I asked for medical aid and was refused. I was threatened with the punishment of being thrown into the "bomb hole". I was told to return to my compound and not to return asking for more aid. About two weeks later I became sick and had to be carried about. During the first portion of this period I received no medical aid. Soon thereafter an American medical doctor was brought in from the officers' compound to treat the prisoners. He was responsible for treating me and my being alive today. He had very limited facilities to work with and could not receive the proper supplies from the Chinese to treat those who needed medical aid.'

Sergeant James C. Williams also survived Death Valley and the march to Camp 5.

'On 1 December 1950 I was taken prisoner and was taken to an area called Sunshine. From time of capture we went three days without food and drink. When we were fed after three days, they gave us red peppercorns. When we spat we spat pure blood after eating this food. During the march they put us in holes while resting. They took us to Huffman Mining Camp, called Death Valley, and we arrived on 26 December 1950. During that time I saw — from 9th Infantry Headquarters Company, whose feet were frozen. He was beaten by the Chinese and Korean guards because he couldn't walk and keep up with the rest of the prisoners. I saw many more beaten by rifle butts and kicked and called capitalists and slaughterers.

After arriving at Death Valley we found the buildings were not fit for hogs; the boards of the buildings were separated. We received no medical care. The Koreans gave shots to sick men and these same men died in the evening. Sergeant — died from one of these shots given by a Korean doctor. I believe that these shots were some type of poison. They put us in rooms about six by eight. About eighteen men to one room. No doors or windows. I saw men trying to keep warm in rooms with only an M-7 overcoat between two men. These men still died. While we were in camp we still did not receive medical care; wounds were never treated. At Death Valley they fed us old cracked corn and soy beans out of fifty-gallon oil drums. They had wood but would not let us use it to keep warm. There was no place to acquire heat in the buildings. We had to cook our food, which consisted of old millet by this time, with green wood from trees. The smoke choked and blinded us. On 1 January 1951 they gave us rocky rice, rice with rocks in it, and about five pounds of ham for a hundred men.

They took us to Camp 5 – arrived 25 January 1951. We travelled over a hundred miles in four days and nights, with just a little rest – sick men too. Some of the men died on the way. — was one; also — of the 503rd Field Artillery Battalion, and —, who was on a sled. While on the way to Camp 5 the communists took some of the men's shoes and made them walk barefooted.

We received 600 grams of food per day. I saw Koreans beat men at Camp 5. One was a man named —, who later died because of sickness. They made — stand out in the cold in an exposed condition. The communists use dope for their medicine. I saw men stood out in snow and ice for two or three hours for not saying "South Korea started the war with North Korea". I was punished this way myself. I saw men forced to write derogatory letters about the United States by being beaten. I saw a man in Camp 5 with hands tied behind his back, beaten to death with sticks and clubs. In November 1951 we were forced to have our picture taken for propaganda purposes. We were supposed to be new troops that were captured. They made us work in mines, and we were used as labourers for the Chinese. They forced us to go to propaganda schools. I saw the communists beat — of B Battery, 503rd Field Artillery, for not paying attention in classes. I saw the communists make one man stand in sub-zero degrees holding a pole above his head until he dropped from exhaustion.'

Arriving at a prisoner-of-war camp in one piece was an achievement. Another prisoner described his journey to one of the newly opened Chinese prison camps.

'On 2 December 1950, while a Chinese prisoner of war and on the way to a prisoner camp, our group, which was riding in a jeep, passed an American two-and-a-half-ton truck with an estimated twelve American

Camp 1 Chongsong
Camp 2 (Branch 1) Pin Chon-ni. Officers' camp.
Camp 2 (Branch 2) Ogye-dong. Penal camp.
Camp 2 (Branch 3) Chang-ni. Officers and aircrew.
Camp 3 (Branch 1) Changsong. Enlisted men/other ranks
Camp 3 (Branch 2) Songsa-dong. Established August 1952 for new prisoners.
Camp 4 Kuup-tong. Sergeants.
Camp 5 Pyoktong. Enlisted men/other ranks after October 1951.
Camp 9 Kangdong. Known as The Caves, consisting of tunnels in the hillside.
Camp 10 Kanggye. Indoctrination centre established in October 1950 for UNC troops
          captured in north-east Korea
Camp 12 Near Pyongyang. Established in May 1951 for six months; prisoners then
          transferred to Pyoktong.
Pak's Palace, also known as Pak's Death House.
The Bean Camp, Suan.

The main prisoner of war camps in North Korea

wounded in the back. There were several Chinese soldiers around it. Just after we passed I heard the motor being gunned and looked back to see the truck go over the cliff and heard the wounded scream. About 10 or 11 December, while we were temporarily in a Korean village, I saw two men pulled out of a Korean house by North Korean soldiers and beaten for about three minutes with fists and rifle butts until they were stopped by an old Korean male civilian. On 14 December I saw three American prisoners and one Turkish prisoner shot and killed by Chinese guards, at different intervals, because they were too sick to keep up.'

Main POW Camps in North Korea Housing British Troops
All in North Korea and all administered by the Chinese unless otherwise noted (Ministry of Defence)

CAMP 1: Chongsong. Approximately fifty miles north-east of Sinuiju. Established March 1951. Held the majority of the British prisoners, around 600 in June 1953, plus more than 1,000 American prisoners. Held only other ranks (enlisted men) after October 1951.

CAMP 2 (Branch 1): Pin Chon-ni. Approximately seventy miles north-east of Sinuiju. Established as an officers camp in October 1951.

CAMP 2 (Branch 2): Ogye-dong. Ten miles east of Pin Chon-ni. A penal camp established in August 1952 for other ranks only.

CAMP 2 (Branch 3): Chang-ni. On the Yalu River, ten miles north of Ogye-dong. Established in March 1952 for officers and aircrew.

CAMP 3 (Branch 1): Changsong. Near the Yalu River, north of Camp 1. Established in August 1951 for other ranks.

CAMP 3 (Branch 2): Songsa-dong. Ten miles south-west of Camp 2 (Branch 1) and about sixty miles north-east of Sinuiju. Established in August 1952 for new other ranks prisoners.

CAMP 4: Kuup-tong. Approximately 100 miles north-east of Sinuiju. Established in August 1952 for sergeants.

CAMP 5: Pyoktong. Approximately 120 miles north-east of Sinuiju, on the banks of the Yalu River. The very first prisoner-of-war camp, established in January 1951. After October 1951 it was for other ranks only and contained about 180 British.

CAMP 9: Kangdong. Eight miles south-east of Pyongyang. Known as 'The Caves' because it consisted of a series of tunnels and caves in the

117

hillside. Controlled by the North Koreans. Small parties of British prisoners were held here at various times.

CAMP 10: Kanggye. About ninety miles north-west of Hungnam. A temporary camp and indoctrination centre established in October 1950 for UN troops captured in north-east Korea. A small number of prisoners from 41 Independent Commando, Royal Marines, spent three months there at the beginning of 1951, before being transferred to Camp 5.

CAMP 12: Near Pyongyang. Established in May 1951 as the first 'Peace Camp' with fifty-three British and American prisoners recruited from 'The Caves' and other forward transit camps. Administered by the North Koreans, it was closed in November 1951 when the prisoners were transferred to Chinese custody at Pyoktong (Camp 5).

Pak's Palace, also known as Pak's Death House. Located in the northernmost area near the capital Pyongyang. North Korean-administered. Named after the camp commandant Colonel Pak and notorious for its high death rate and the tortures inflicted on prisoners of war. Close to several other camps including Camp 12.

The Bean Camp. At Suan, about forty-five miles south-east of Pyongyang, where beans were the main diet. A Chinese-controlled transit camp, also known as the 'Gold Mine Camp' due to the existence of a gold mine nearby.

This list of camps appears in the booklet 'Treatment of British Prisoners of War in Korea' produced by the British Ministry of Defence in 1956. Unfortunately it does not tell the whole story. Other camps existed, and the British and American governments were well aware of that fact. However, to acknowledge the existence of those camps would have laid the governments open to awkward questions such as 'What happened to our POWs who were imprisoned in Hankow, China or Harbin, Manchuria?' The answer, of course, is that they did not come home.

For the record, the following is the full list of camp locations and holding centres that were known to the British and American governments at the end of December 1951. It can be found in file reference WO208/3477 in the Public Record Office in Kew. The message was sent on 3 December 1951 from the British Joint Service Mission (Air Force Staff Washington) to the Air Ministry, London, addressed 'For Poynt AI.9 info Stephen MI.1 from Fillingham'. The PRO copy bears the stamp of the Director of Military Intelligence.

'SECRET. Most recent information on PW camp locations Korea and China received in Washington from Commanding General Far East Air

Force 24th July 1951. Report states determination of locations has been entirely dependent on interrogations due to fact enemy has no standard method of handling PW and does not mark camps. Photo recce has revealed little. Mines, civilian homes and prisons normally used as opposed to normal hutted camps. Following locations likely. Sinuiju (XE1839) or 1939 civil prison. Sakchu hot spring area (XE7372). Pyoktong (YE0699). Manpojin (BA7358). Chasong (CA0392). Kanggye (BA9837) five miles north of city. Hoeryong (EB6298). Najin (FB0873) one mile north of railway station. Aoju-Dong (FC1508) coal mines. Unggi (FB1587). Musan (EB1672) coal mine. Chongjin (EB6825) coal mine. Namjong-Ni barracks and gold mine (BT7195). Samdung (BT5620). Changsongjin (XE5574) or 5524. Changho-Myon (BU5433).

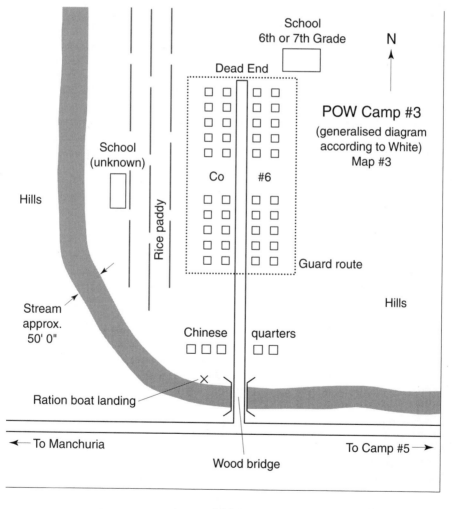

POW Camp #3
(generalised diagram according to White)
Map #3

Sunan (YD3242). Camp five miles east of Yonghung (CU5982). Chungganjin (CB2427). Koksam (BT9795) tobacco factory. Mukden Manchuria. Kirin Manchuria. Antung Manchuria. Tiehling 35 miles NE Mukden, Manchuria. Canton China. Hankow China. Harbin Manchuria. Following are likely staging areas: Pakchong school house (YD193899). Amjong-Ni (YD3074). Monghuidong (XE3237). Sukchon (YD2665). Mundung-Ni (DT1142). Sunchon (YD5267). Korangpor-Ri (CT1106). Chongju (XD9095). Karchon abandoned mine at YD5799. Kujangdong (BU4607). Unsan schoolhouse (YE3928). Hapung iron mine Pukchin (YE3453). Taedong coal mine 15 miles NE Pyongyang. Chomtangni (DT0214) or 0454. Efforts are being made to confirm Korean locations by photo recon. Any additional locations you can definitely confirm will be appreciated here.'

Despite the numerous references to locations inside China, the only prisoners of war to come home from China were a B-29 crew and a couple of F-86 pilots and they were returned long after the war ended in 1955. It is interesting to note that they were all captured after December 1951, so the prisoners of war referred to above as being imprisoned in China must have been other men who did not come home.

FOUR

AGAINST ALL ODDS

THE BATTLE OF HAPPY VALLEY

Three weeks prior to the Chinese offensive at the Chosin Reservoir, on 5 November 1950, the men of the Royal Ulster Rifles lined the rail of the troopship *Empire Pride* and caught their first glimpse of the bleak Pusan harbour and the dark mountains in the distance. They had been on board for five weeks and were looking forward to setting foot on dry land again. Seven troopships and two dozen stores and vehicle-carrying ships bore the men of the British 29th Independent Infantry Brigade Group to Korea. They were led by Brigadier Tom Brodie, who had commanded one of the six brigades of Chindits behind Japanese lines in Burma in 1944. Apart from the 1st Battalion Royal Ulster Rifles, the 29th Brigade infantry contingent also comprised the 1st Battalion, the Gloucester Regiment and the 1st Battalion, Royal Northumberland Fusiliers. The armour was supplied by the 8th King's Royal Irish Hussars with its sixty-four Centurion tanks and a squadron from the 7th Royal Tank Regiment. The Royal Artillery was represented by the II (Sphinx) Light Anti-Aircraft Battery and the 170th Mortar Battery. Supply, signals, engineer and vehicle maintenance units were also in support. As the fifty-five major and minor units began to disembark they prepared to entrain for the 200-mile journey to the forming-up area at Suwon.

While the 29th Brigade moved north to relieve the 27th Brigade which had been caught up in the fighting south of the Chongchon River, the rest of the Eighth Army was moving south. The 'Big Bugout' had begun.

In ten days the men of the Eighth Army retreated 120 miles, and by 15 December they had crossed the 38th Parallel and the Imjin River. Fear drove the men south – fear of Chinese encirclement, of the sound of bugles and whistles in the middle of the night, heralding another attack. Huge supply dumps were destroyed or abandoned, to be pillaged by the retreating troops and eventually salvaged by the approaching Chinese. American sleeping bags were favoured by the Chinese, who suffered more casualties as a result of the extreme weather than American guns.

On New Year's Day 1951 the 29th British Brigade moved up in support of the ROK 1st Division and prepared to go into action for the first time. They found the South Koreans streaming southwards, the enemy not far behind. The snow lay thick on the ground and a bitter wind howled in from Manchuria as the brigade took up their positions. The Royal Ulster Rifles were on the left of the line, adjacent to the US 35th Infantry Regiment. To the right of the Ulstermen were the Glosters and the Northumberland Fusiliers. An armoured force of Cromwell tanks from Cooper Force were in close support of the Rifles.

Early on the morning of 3 January 1951 the Chinese attacked the US 35th Infantry and the British stood-to awaiting their turn. In the light of the mortar flares the Royal Ulster Riflemen saw the enemy approaching, blowing whistles and bugles. A furious fight developed and two platoons were overrun. A counter-attack was launched and hand-to-hand fighting with bayonets, grenades, sten guns, boots and fists spread across the hill. As dawn approached the Chinese withdrew, leaving the area covered with 300 of their dead.

As the day wore on the Northumberland Fusiliers and the Glosters were ordered to withdraw by a different route. By the time orders arrived that evening for the Rifles to pull back, their neighbours, the US 35th Infantry, were long gone and the hills on the withdrawal route were swarming with Chinese.

The Rifles had to negotiate a six-mile-long icy track to join the main highway. The track was adjacent to a river bed and led south over a pass between the hills. High cliffs rose above the road in places and as the Riflemen passed below the cliffs an American aircraft unfortunately dropped parachute flares which lit up the whole scene. Soon machine-gun and mortar fire began to rain down from the hills formerly occupied by the Americans. The Chinese swarmed down from the cliffs on to the road where heavy fighting ensued. At the rear of the column Cooper Force was heavily engaged in the river bed where its tanks hoped to find the going easier. Many men fell at the roadside or staggered through the terraced paddyfields, the able carrying the wounded.

The remnants of the battalion finally fought their way through to the main road where the negro trucking company 'Wags Truckers' bravely waited for them. There were many spaces in the trucks as they bumped across the pontoon bridge over the Han River. A total of 240 officers and men had been lost in the battle of Happy Valley including most of Cooper Force. The Ulstermen were the last unit to cross the river before the bridges were blown up behind them.

THE ONE WHO GOT AWAY

While it was true that the Chinese shot fewer prisoners than the North Koreans, both would do so if the fancy took them. One British soldier was lucky enough to escape death in Happy Valley when those around him were being shot out of hand. Gunner C. Christopher was a member of Cooper Force, an armoured unit of a dozen tanks under the command of Captain Astley-Cooper of the 8th Hussars. He was a hull gunner in Lieutenant Probyn's tank *Huntress* from Number 3 Troop.

The tanks of Cooper Force were tasked to cover the withdrawal of the Royal Ulster Rifles as they pulled out on the evening of 3 January 1951. Around 2200 hours, as the soft-skinned vehicles of the force began to withdraw, enemy machine-gunners opened fire on them. A message came through that the Chinese had blocked the road ahead, and could the tanks try to get through? The tanks moved off one by one, but did not get very far: the Chinese were everywhere. Soon all the tanks were firing their main 77mm guns and their machine-guns, while the infantry clinging to the rear of the tanks joined in with their small arms.

As Lieutenant Probyn's tank neared a broken bridge on the track the firing increased as the Chinese infantry closed in on them. Captain Holman from *Hydra* suddenly appeared at the side of the tank and called Gunner Christopher by name. He opened his door to call Lieutenant Probyn and had started to get out when Captain Holman cried out, 'Oh dear, oh dear,' and sank down to the ground. As Probyn and Christopher lifted the captain on to the rear of the tank, he said, 'I have had my lot,' and lapsed into unconsciousness. Lieutenant Probyn climbed back into the turret, but as Christopher was getting down to the ground a Chinese infantryman advanced to about five yards' range and put a burst of machine-gun fire through his thigh. The battle was reaching its climax as Christopher fell to the ground. Enemy infantry were all around them, although they were suffering heavy casualties to the guns of the tanks and the riflemen.

Holding on to the wire around the ration boxes on the side of the tank, Christopher fired his revolver at the enemy around him. Suddenly Lieutenant Probyn appeared at his side again and said, 'This is a bad show, we had better get out of it!' In the meantime the crew of the tank in front of them, which had slipped off the track, climbed into their tank and began to drive it away. Captain Holman's driver, Gunner England, who was now sitting on the front track guard, suddenly cried out, 'I've got it!' and pitched forward to the ground. By now the Chinese were throwing hand grenades into the tank tracks and Christopher was being peppered with shrapnel. As the tank gathered speed he let go of the wire and rolled clear, dropping into the ditch at the side of the road.

The last the gunner saw of Lieutenant Probyn, he had his revolver levelled and was crying out to the Chinese about a yard away from him, 'Drop that gun or I'll shoot!' He never saw the officer again. As Christopher fell, the Chinese infantry stepped over him and made for the tank, firing as they went. He heard them shouting in English: 'Don't shoot, don't shoot, we are friends,' and 'Don't shoot, I am an American,' and 'Give us a lift.'

The tank drove for about two hundred yards, but then the engine started labouring and stalled as if it was bellied in the mud. There was a great deal of firing where it had stopped, and five minutes later everything went quiet. Chinese bugles were blowing all the time and about 200 infantry ran past, heading south. Gunner Christopher lay in the ditch for about an hour. While he was there he heard two English soldiers coming along. One sounded like a Scotsman. He heard him say to the other one, 'Throw your gun down Jimmy, we will give ourselves up. We have no chance behind their lines.' Christopher was about to get up and join them when he heard them say, 'We are giving ourselves up, we are English!' A burst of machine-gun fire rang out and another voice said, 'What did you do that for?' There was yet another shot and Christopher looked over the top of the ditch. The two men were lying on the ground and six Chinese were walking away laughing. He decided that he had better go.

When the road was empty, Christopher began to crawl along the road towards his now silent tank. He had not gone far when a score of Chinese appeared ahead of him. He turned away and started crawling through the paddyfields towards the hills. Before long he came across two scout cars and a bren-carrier which was overturned beside the track. Captain Fleming and two others lay dead beside one of the scout cars, which was on its side in a ditch.

The Chinese began to make their way back from the south and the sound of a Chinese bugle, presumably sounding the recall, rang out across the paddyfields. Christopher lay down in the middle of the field and the men passed within a few yards of him. They began to congregate by the first tank that had been put out of action, and eventually the gunner heard it start up. He decided to crawl into another ditch and follow it in the direction of the road to the south.

When he was within a couple of yards of the road, Christopher stood up and found himself about four yards away from five North Koreans. As soon as they saw him they opened fire with their machine-guns. They missed with the first burst and he threw himself to the ground pretending that he had been hit. They kept firing and he felt his arm move as a bullet hit him. They walked over, looked at him and then moved on. He lay there for some time, not daring to move, and saw two Chinese soldiers approaching him. They were scavenging, searching all the British and Chinese dead. When they reached the prone gunner he held his breath as they lifted his arms and checked him for watches or rings. Finding none, they kicked him in the ribs and continued their journey.

When Christopher got to his feet he found that he could not move his leg. He picked up a stick and started to limp along when suddenly he heard someone whistle. Looking around he saw someone waving a stick at the back of one of the tanks. He hobbled over and found a Scotsman from the Royal Ulster Rifles. He said that he had been shot that morning and had a broken leg. Another Rifleman was lying on the other side of the tank with a broken leg and a bullet wound through his chest. Christopher helped the first man around to join his friend and broke open a tin of milk for them.

They told him that there were two more Riflemen at the top of the hill. He said that he would go up to them and also look for more men around the abandoned tanks. When he reached the second tank he saw Gunner Yates on the back of the tank. He had been shot through the head. The driver who he believed to be Gunner Clinton and the hull gunner, Gunner Slade, were also lying dead inside the tank. About twenty British dead lay around the four now silent tanks.

It was now about 0830 hours on 4 January. An American spotter plane circled overhead, followed by six jet planes. Christopher waved as he thought they might be intending to bomb the tanks. The spotter plane came in very low and the pilot waved and went off.

On the nearby hill Christopher found two more men of the Royal Ulster Rifles. One was Rifleman Thompson who could still walk, despite being wounded in the neck, arm and both knees. The other had a broken thigh and could not be moved. The spotter plane then returned and the pilot dropped a sheet of paper which Christopher retrieved. On it was written: 'Go west to Seoul river bed'. He called out to the men at the bottom of the hill that he and Thompson would go off and get help.

The two men had covered about a mile and a half when two American helicopters came over. They waved to them and they started circling around. They pointed northwards to where the others were and one of the helicopters went off in that direction; the other landed two fields away. By the time they hobbled over to the helicopter, a Chinese sniper had opened fire on them. The pilot was very calm. As the helicopter soared into the air he told the two men to look down where they had been picked up. The area was swarming with Chinese.

Cooper Force had been virtually wiped out. Of the sixty-five men in the tank crews, only eleven regained friendly lines. Gunner W. R. Slade from 45 Field Regiment, Royal Artillery, was one of the lucky ones. Not only did he survive the carnage, he was later sent back to his own lines by the Chinese. He was not dead in his driver's seat, as Christopher had thought. He was captured at 0200 hours on 4 January, given a cursory examination for hidden arms and then, in company with 200 other prisoners, marched away.

The prisoners were formed into groups of about thirty under the command of a senior NCO and marched twelve miles in a northerly direction. Guards were posted at the head and rear of the column and also along the flanks, and they made sure that any North Korean troops they encountered were kept away from the British. This was due to the Chinese distrust of the North Koreans' treatment of prisoners.

The prisoners' meals consisted of one bowl of rice at 0430 hours and another at 1800 hours. This constituted their sole diet during the period of capture, with the exception of Chinese New Year's Day, when meat was provided. They were not issued with blankets, though, or any other means of keeping warm. Slade later reported that the Chinese treatment was courteous and polite and that no threats of violence were made, but added that at Kyongsong, before capture, he had seen three mutilated and dead UN soldiers. One had been shot in the back and had twenty-seven bullet holes, and another had been stripped and castrated.

The interrogation of the prisoners began on the second day after capture. The interrogators comprised three Chinese officers, of whom two spoke English. They were young and of the student type. The interrogation was carried out in a very informal manner, and both interrogators and prisoner sat on the floor. The prisoner was introduced and given tobacco to make a cigarette. The interrogation was carried out at 0300 hours and lasted approximately ten minutes. The questions asked included: Name, rank, number? Brigade? Circumstances of capture? Where captured? Details of cap badge, including motto?

Seven days after capture paybooks and all personal effects were taken from the prisoners, although most of these were returned later. Slade was asked to identify a number of cap badges.

Sixteen days after capture the questions turned to politics, civil occupation and movements. Military questions were also put to the prisoners at spasmodic intervals. The main theme of the military questions centred on the nature and composition of Cooper Force and the type of armoured vehicles and armament used. The aim of the enemy interrogator was obviously to confirm that Slade was a member of the force.

Eighteen days after capture there was more interrogation at the indoctrination centre by two Chinese officers, of which one spoke English. The interrogation began at 0300 hours and lasted two hours, with the prisoner being fed before questioning. The interrogators adopted a friendly attitude throughout and allowed the prisoners to sit down. The questions included such things as father's and mother's occupation, prisoner's school, prisoner's trade and location of home. During the two weeks the prisoners were at the indoctrination centre they were interrogated four times at intervals of three days.

A number of other prisoners were on the same course as Gunner Slade, including a Sergeant Rankin and some British other ranks. Apparently they were Labour Party supporters and this is possibly one of the reasons why they were freed. Gunner Slade was returned to American lines on 9 February 1951. Four members of the Royal Ulster Rifles were also returned to friendly lines: Sergeant Rankin, Lance Corporal Harris and Riflemen Akid and Griffiths (PRO WO162/211).

Some of the prisoners taken on 3 January were not so fortunate, as the American Sergeant Glenn J. Oliver explained:

'I was captured on 3 January 1951 and kept in the vicinity of the front lines until 10 January. On 5 January I was placed in a mud hut with approximately thirty other men. The room we were placed in was windowless and about six feet by six feet in size and inadequate for any of us to lie down. I was taken back to the front lines to drive a US vehicle back, approximately 10 January, but due to heavy bombing and strafing of UN planes returned to enemy rear without the truck. After 10 January we started moving to the rear at night and during the day we were placed in small dugouts and huts of insufficient size for any of us to lie down without lying on top of each other. We marched in this manner until approximately the middle of February, when we stopped in a mining camp in the vicinity of Pyongyang.

During our march we received two meals a day, consisting of either a half or one bowl of rice, whole corn, barley or millet. We lost approximately three men from our group during the march. We started to march north from Pyongyang approximately 20 February and overtook approximately thirty other UN prisoners on the march. They were without sufficient clothing and none had shoes, though a few had grass slippers. I saw at least six of these men dragged by CCF guards, either by their arms or legs, and many were prodded by bayonets. Eventually all thirty prisoners of war we overtook fell out over a period of days and after we passed from their sight we heard shots fired and never saw any of them again.

We marched until about 15 March, covering between fifteen and thirty miles per day with two meals per day of either rice, whole corn, barley or millet. We reached Camp 5 approximately 15 March and were placed in mud huts with three rooms and a kitchen. Each room contained about fifteen prisoners and was from six to eight feet on a side. We had insufficient firewood and had to steal it. On or about 28 March I was caught with some wood and had to hold it over my head for at least an hour in extreme cold. I witnessed at least fifty others do this also.

About 10 April I witnessed a UN prisoner of war being beaten by two CCF soldiers on a shirtless back with heavy leather belts. This soldier had his hands tied behind his back. In August 1952 a man we spoke of as Sergeant — was taken to a brick building we called the jail and kept there for about a week for no apparent reason. The sergeant was in apparent good health when taken into the jail, but I saw him removed and taken to another building approximately a week later and at this time his head was heavily bandaged and he seemed hardly able to walk. We never saw him again.

In approximately June 1951 I was placed in a work squad and attached to the hospital at Camp 5. Here I saw at least 150 men die with insufficient food and covered with lice. Men in poor condition were placed outdoors with little or no clothing and eaten by flies and worms. I saw at least fifty men given injections of an unknown type of fluid and they would die within five minutes. From approximately 15 March to June 1951 I saw at least 300 men die in the hospital or in the camp. I believe it was from exposure and poor food. Approximately mid-April 1951 I worked on a burial detail and counted exactly forty men carried to the burial ground that day.'

THE LOST DIVISION

For the United Nations forces January 1951 was one of the low points of the war. Seoul fell to the communists for the second time, and just before Christmas General Walker, the Eighth Army commander, was killed in a road accident. Paratrooper General Mathew Ridgway took over his job. He soon came to his own conclusions as to the army's lack of success. More training was needed, particularly in the art of all-round defence. The men were too pampered and had to learn to go without some of their creature comforts. Leadership was lacking and the men were poorly motivated. They were also too tied to their trucks and the road networks and had a lot to learn from the British who were used to marching everywhere. Slowly but surely he began to turn the army around.

The Chinese had now overstretched their supply lines and were vulnerable to UN air attack. General Ridgway began to push his units forward again, testing the Chinese resistance. As his seven divisions slowly advanced, backed up with massed artillery and air strikes, they started to cause heavy casualties among the Chinese. But still the atrocities continued.

Ten Marines from the 1st Marine Division went on a reconnaissance patrol near Nakchon Dong on 29 January 1951. They never returned from their mission. In March, checking on a National Police report, a patrol from the ROK 2nd Division found their bodies, together with those of ten ROK Army soldiers, four National Police and one Korean civilian. These corpses were stripped naked with their hands bound behind them, and the physical appearance of the remains revealed that they had either been bayoneted in the back and chest or had their skulls crushed with clubs. Interrogation of native villagers indicated that the Americans were captured about 30 January and held prisoners until their murder on 5 February.

Two North Korean lieutenants, discovered among captured communist prisoners, confessed to participation in this crime. Although their statements were recorded at different times and places, the factual data is the same. They related that their commanding officer told them to prepare to execute the prisoners secretly. For this purpose they decided to use bayonets. Accordingly, the graves were dug in advance, then the victims were led forth individually, stripped and bound, and ordered to sit on the ground. In this position each man was used for bayonet practice, and if death came too slowly or resistance was offered his head was smashed with a rifle butt. Blood stains were swept from the ground and the bodies buried (KWC185).

The Eighth Army began to flex its muscles again, but the Chinese still

These American soldiers had their hands tied behind their backs with communications wire before they were shot by their captors.

had plenty of fight left in them. On 11 February the Chinese launched their fourth phase offensive and three divisions struck the ROK 8th Division at Heongsong. The South Korean division disintegrated with the loss of almost ten thousand men and the American artillery units supporting the ROKs found themselves in the front line. Oscar Cortez recalled the events of 13 February:

'Our Battery "A" of the 15th Field Artillery Battalion, along with the rest of the batteries, was moved right up to the front lines. We arrived early in the evening and our guns were set up pointing almost straight up. There was a big mountain in front of us and we could see the infantry moving the panel to mark their forward positions up and down. I believe the colour of the panel was red that day. We didn't get the chance to fire any rounds at that location.

I was on guard on my gun that evening when a platoon of South Koreans passed by, walking real slow. Not much later, maybe an hour and a half, the South Koreans were passing by in a hurry and right after I heard the Chinese bugles and our quad fifties started firing. All hell broke loose. We got our march order, hooked up our 105s and were ready to move out. It was night and we waited for daylight, but we couldn't move because we were pinned down. We finally broke out and we received machine-gun fire along the way. Bullets came close to my head but I was lucky, they didn't reach me, maybe because the truck was moving pretty fast.

We stopped along the way in an open field and started firing point-blank at the swarm of oncoming Chinese. Since the ground was frozen and we couldn't dig in the trails of our 105, I had to stand on the trail itself and fire the gun. The recoil would send the gun sliding back, so I had to push the gun back into firing position and do it all over again until we ran out of ammo.

The Chinese got close enough to kill a couple of our men. There was a wooden house to our left front and that's where the firing was coming from. I lay in front of our gun and emptied a magazine from my M1 carbine. I guess I got the shooter because the firing stopped. My section chief was wounded on his left leg. We left our 105s behind after disabling them and we started moving out again. Along the way the convoy stopped and we were told that we were going to join the infantry and try to get out. I was helping my section chief, Sergeant Barrett, when the word came that all the wounded would go back to the trucks and they would try to make it out. Since I was helping Sergeant Barrett I went along. Remember that we hadn't had any sleep for about thirty-six hours, so I fell asleep in the back of the truck.

When I awoke, the truck's engine wasn't running. In a low voice I called for the driver and no one answered, so I reached through the rear opening of the canvas cab, thinking they were lying there dead. No one was there, so I jumped out of the back of the truck and saw a bunch of people on the side of the bank of the road. As it was dark and I had just woken up from a deep sleep I couldn't see real well, so I called out the name of the driver, again in a low voice. Those guys just looked up at me, not saying a word. I also saw a bunch of soldiers running towards me from the rear of our convoy. I couldn't tell if they were ours or not, until one of them fired a shot at me.

Right away I knew it was the enemy, so I started firing my carbine at them and at the people on the side of the road. I felt something hit me in the stomach and I knew it was a grenade, so I ran to the other side of the truck and hit the ground as the grenade went off. I heard a tank firing towards the front, so I decided to crawl to the tank and maybe I could make it out. Unfortunately the tank stopped firing. I knew it was out for good.

I was on the side of the road and I crawled about fifty yards before someone took my carbine, thinking I was dead. He stepped on my body, but not before looking to see if I had a watch. Another commie checked me out to see if I had a watch. I was real close to the rear tyres, just lying there playing dead when I heard some men talking about getting the truck started. I thought if they get it going they are going to run over my head. I also thought that if I got up all of a sudden I could be shot. Finally another commie pulled me up, checked my wrist and then turned me over and took out a hand grenade I had in my parka. Well, that's when I wondered what POW life would be like and opened my eyes. He was shining a flashlight at my face.

I've heard that it was the battalion commander's fault that the 15th was annihilated. I've also been told that a medevac helicopter came by and pulled him out. I heard that the Chinese push was about twelve miles long, so I don't think the retreat would have had a chance. We fought all along the way, but the Chinese push was too deep.

We were gathered up by the North Koreans on 13 February 1951. When they started marching us forward we thought they were going to put us in front and use us as a shield, but they took us up a ravine for the night. Over the following months their treatment of us was brutal and there was not enough to eat. By the time we were turned over to the Chinese on 26 October 1951 my weight was down to around eighty pounds.'

Three weeks after the battle US Marines retook the area. Most of the bodies still lay where they fell, although many had been looted for their boots or clothing. Four survivors were found, two Americans and two South Koreans. One GI was wounded and the other was suffering from frostbite. Several of the bodies had been bound and shot in the back.

The bodies of two men lay together about thirty yards from the road. Both were face down. The legs of one GI were tied together and both had been shot in the back of the head with burp-guns.

SEARCH AND RECOVERY

March 1951 saw the recapture of the South Korean capital Seoul and the recrossing of the 38th Parallel by the ROK I Corps. Ridgway planned to establish the KANSAS line along the barriers of the Imjin River in the west and the Hwachon Reservoir in the centre, shortening the line from coast to coast to 115 miles. The Chinese were also making plans, for a spring offensive involving nineteen armies. However, the plans of the two opposing forces were academic to the prisoners of war struggling to survive in the cold depths of North Korea.

On 13 March Dr Gene Lam left the camp at Death Valley. Only about forty of the prisoners were able to walk by then and they were made to transport the others on ox-carts or sleds. It took a week for them to make the ninety-mile trip to Camp 5 at Pyoktong and eight of them died en route. It was on this march that Lam saw his first evidence of brutality: 'The guards seemed to be perturbed about the sick men not moving fast enough, so they started working them over with rifle butts.' Lam remained in the camp until 10 May when the Chinese decided it was time for him to become 'educated' and moved him to the officers' compound where he was unable to practise medicine. In October he was moved to Camp 2, ten miles to the east. There he was forced to attend communist lectures eight hours a day, six days a week until March 1952. 'Then they finally just gave up. I guess they decided they weren't getting anywhere.' The prisoners were required to write themes on communist subjects or reviews on books they were made to read. 'If you didn't do it to suit them, you had to do it over and over until it did suit them. Otherwise they would put you in "the hole", a dark, damp dungeon.'

Corporal Tom Sechrest served with the 293rd Graves Registration Company in 1951 and 1952. The Headquarters was in YongDongPo, South Korea, although Tom spent most of his time as a Search and Recovery team leader. He recalled one incident that involved civilian atrocities:

'I had received word from our company HQ to check out a report of discovered remains at a certain village. Upon arrival at the village the "mayor" directed one of the villagers to lead us to the site, which happened to be a mile or so away from the village proper.

When we arrived at the site we discovered several bodies, perhaps twelve or fourteen of them. There were both men and women, all wearing typical Korean garb, and each had their feet tied together and their hands tied behind backs with "commo wire". I did not notice any gunshot wounds. There may have been some, but we did not examine the bodies too closely because of what I did see. Each of them had a "spike" driven into their skull just above the bridge of the nose. These spikes were made of iron, square-bodied, approximately three-sixteenths of an inch square and about three inches long. The shaft had been twisted, similar to a screw thread but much more coarse, and ended with an "eye" on the one end.

As I stated, when I saw the wire bindings and these spikes I did not examine them any further, but left two of my men there to guard them while I went to the nearest unit I could find and called my company headquarters to have them locate and have dispatched to our area a War Crimes Commission investigation team. When they arrived several hours later I turned the scene over to them and departed. I never did hear anything more about that case.'

THE CHINA CONNECTION

April 1951 saw the first reports of American prisoners of war arriving in southern China. They probably came from Nationalist Chinese spies reporting back to Taiwan, or from travellers making their way to Hong Kong. Based on these reports, the CIA distributed information report SO66740 to interested parties on 27 June and its contents made disturbing reading. The three paragraphs read as follows:

'Item 1. In early April American prisoners of war from Korea began arriving in Hankow, where they were turned over to the Chinese Communist Central and South China Military Command. By 15 April approximately 500 had arrived in Hankow, and on 18 April some of these prisoners were paraded through the streets of Hankow under heavy guard.

Item 2. In mid-April, sixty prisoners of war, most of whom were American and the rest British, arrived in Canton via the Canton–Hankow railway. In early May they were being detained in a foreign-style compound at the corner of Tunghua Road, East, and Kneinichao in Tungshan, Canton. There were barbed-wire barricades around the compounds and a public security division mounted a heavy guard around the area. No one was allowed to enter without permission from high communist authorities. The prisoners were treated fairly well, and were given good food and billets. (see Notes 1 and 2.)

Item 3. In mid-June, fifty-two American prisoners of war from Korea were incarcerated in the Baptist Church on Tunghua Road, Canton. These prisoners were sent to Canton because the Chinese communist authorities hoped to obtain military and medical supplies from the United States government in return for their release. They planned to demand US $100,000 worth of supplies for each prisoner released. The British and Indian governments were to be used as intermediaries. (See Note 3.)

Note 1   According to another informant, there was no indication as of 24 May that American prisoners of war were being sent to Canton. There were no barbed-wire barricades at the end of Tunghua Road, East, Canton.

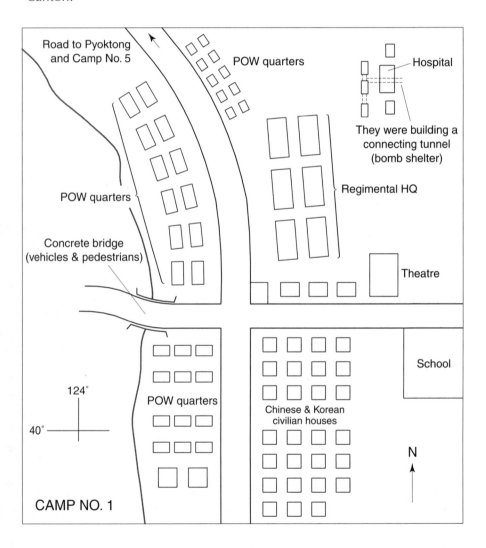

Note 2 Casual informants have stated that as of 20 April twenty-five American prisoners of war who had arrived in Canton were being held in three foreign-style houses at the end of Tunghua Road, East. See SO63715 and SO65066. The latter reports that some of these prisoners were transferred to Kweilin on 2 May.

Note 3 According to some Chinese newsmen in Hong Kong, the presence of United States or United Nations troops in Canton as of mid-June cannot be confirmed. The original report appeared in the Hong Kong newspaper the *Hsing Tao Jih Pao* in late April. The reporter probably based his information on the statement of a traveller from Canton, who stated he had seen prisoners in Tungshan. The *Hsing Tao Jih Pao* would print any news embarrassing to the United States.'

Later reports would include details of American prisoners paraded through towns in southern China. Significantly, none of the prisoners who returned home from North Korea in 1953 took part in such a parade. Clearly China had a use for some of the hundreds of UN prisoners in its hands, and whether they were kept for their technical expertise or for propaganda value, they certainly never came home again.

DEATH MARCH

At least six death marches took place during the first year of the war. After his repatriation in 1953 Sergeant Charles C. Hankey described his march to war crimes investigators:

'On 17 April 1951 we left the Bean prison camp for Camp 1 with 735 men, all Americans except for five who were British. The march went along all right for the first two days; after that the food supply dropped very low, hardly enough to survive on. Then they started to double-time [fast-march] us from fifteen to twenty miles a night. Men who fell out were either beaten to death, shot or pushed over cliffs. Others died of starvation during periods of rest in Korean houses. No one was permitted to lie down during these breaks; we either had to sit or stand up. We were punished for begging food from Korean civilians by being beaten with a club. One day two of the prisoners were accused of signalling airplanes with a mirror. These men were tied and beaten with a bayonet by Wong, Fnu and four guards. When the marched started again these two dropped out. I heard two shots fired. I looked back and saw two men lying alongside the road in a ditch and two guards running to catch up with the rear of the column. The next evening so many men were unable to walk that the rest were unable to carry them all. I saw Wong and Fnu push two of the men over a cliff because they could not go on.

Men had dysentery and when they had to defecate they did it in their pants, not being allowed to fall out of column. Some men did fall out of column to defecate; immediately they were beaten and told to fall back into the column. Some didn't and I never saw them again.

When we arrived at Camp 1 we had a roll call. There were 325 men left out of the original 735. As many as two to five men died each day during the first three weeks in Camp 1 and thereafter the mortality rate dropped slightly to one to five men a week.

When the peace negotiations began in July 1951 we started getting better food, and those of us left survived. When the armistice was signed we who were on the death march got together; we could only account for 155 men alive out of the original 735. At one time during this march the Chinese officer who was in charge said, "I will march you American son-of-a-bitches until you die!" His rank is unknown to me; his name is Wong; he is about 6'2" tall and weighs about 165 pounds.'

By April 1951 Harry Gennaro had already reached his prison camp.

'The death rate was dropping. We began adjusting to being POWs. The ration now was two bowls of barley each day. It was full of small rocks that remained after blowing out the husks. This raised havoc with our teeth as several would be broken or chipped when biting down on a rock. With the winter thaw barges were able to come in on the Yalu. Once a pig weighing maybe eighty-five pounds was brought in for the platoon. Our people scraped and cleaned it. A fifteen-foot tapeworm was removed from its stomach. The pig was butchered, boiled and served up to 350 POWs.

We were issued a lightweight blue uniform of pants, jacket and cap for summer and a padded uniform of jacket, pants and a cap with ear flaps for winter. The summer and winter periods each lasted six months.

The Chinese sent in their political cadre and began the start of brain washing. First they would break you down, as was evident with the conditions suffered during winter captivity and the death of our fellow POWs. The Chinese would pretend to be your friend and say that their only wish for you was a safe return home to your loved ones. They would blame America for intruding into a Korean civil war.

They segregated the troops. All officers were removed to Camp 1. The NCOs were put in a separate camp. The blacks were put in the 1st Platoon. The British were placed in a separate platoon. The Turks were placed in a separate platoon. The enlisted whites were placed in the 3rd Platoon. This practice removed leadership from our ranks.

A Marine general named Squabble announced over the speaker system to cooperate. Two air force pilots were brought in and announced that they had dropped germ warfare on the Koreans. Most of us knew these confessions were forced and paid no heed.

All prisoners were initially brought into Camp 5. With massive overcrowding, the Chinese began opening a couple of new camps. Almost half the POWs from our platoon were loaded on to barges. They were taken to a camp a short distance away on the Yalu.

Classes were intensified. We were forced-marched daily to a large meeting area to listen to Instructor Linn. We referred to him as the Screaming Skull. Other Chinese aides would patrol the aisles and crack you across the head or back if it appeared that you were not paying complete attention. Having to listen was most stressing.

Another ploy to get you on board was to hold back incoming mail from home. It was twenty-two months before I got my first letter. In all, maybe I received six letters over the thirty-three months of captivity. A big turn-off on sending letters home was the way they demanded that you give the return address: "People's Republic of China for World Peace Against American Aggression".

A stressful situation occurred daily, when each morning at roll call we were forced to sing songs about Mao Tse-tung and Stalin. No one under-stood it as it was sung in Chinese. We were forced to sign several peace petitions. There were a lot of Batman, Mickey Mouse and Roy Rogers names which appeared on those petitions. I got so fed up that I, foolishly, passed a petition that we not be forced to sing songs of praise to the enemy. Circulation netted about twenty-five signatures before it landed up at HQ on the hill, along with me. Instructor Linn accused me of being an agent of the CID, CIA, FBI etc., a reactionary and against peace. I merely stated that we were POWs and should be treated accordingly. He got very angry and condemned me to confinement. The holding tank was a potato cellar. It was just outside their HQ compound. It was about seven feet deep, four by four wide and contained some contaminated water on the floor. When the cover was put on only a faint stream of light could be seen. I was stripped nude. I could get out only by writing a letter of self-criticism and repentance. They provided me with pencil and paper. I was fed only at evening meal. The next day I passed them two pages of 'I'm sorry'. Soon the instructor informed me that it was not sincere and provided more paper. By this time, after killing a huge rat and having to stand and sleep in my own waste and urine, I was ready to get out of this confinement. They came for my handiwork about three days later. I gave them seven pages. The following day I was told it did not float. Do it again. The worst part of this was they did not give you back the original. Each time you started from scratch.

I spent fifteen days in solitary confinement and wrote twenty-two pages of "I'm sorry". This one was accepted. Mainly I wrote my life story, about the hardships of growing up on a poor farm that could not produce enough food to survive. I missed my mama and wanted to go home. That was accepted! The next morning at roll call I read my confession in front of the platoon.

The brainwashing lectures lasted about ten months. They figured they had done as much as could be done. We were also wiser having turned the tables by redirecting their questions back to them. We were classified as reactionary and progressive. Only a handful of POWs embraced their teaching.'

All the while reports of atrocities continued to come in, many of them from captured enemy troops. Some of the 'confessions' could be checked out, others could not because of their location. Korean War Crimes case number 1287 is one of those. A captured Chinese soldier, Lee Hai-peng, prisoner of war number 703475, of the 573rd Regiment, 191st Division, 64th Army, Chinese Communist Forces, stated that forty or fifty of his 1st Battalion members, including himself, shot and killed forty-two British prisoners at the foot of a mountain two kilometres north of Seoul (CS2556) on 17 April 1951. The bodies were not buried. A sketch was made of the site.

Korean War Crimes case number 865 took place less than a week later, on 23 April. One wounded British soldier was executed by the side of a road approximately twenty kilometres south of the Imjin River in the vicinity of Sangsu-ri (CS2393). Private Jang Ing shot the prisoner on the orders of Company Commander Jung In Tang and Shee Jeun Swa (prisoner of war number 717009), who was platoon leader of the 1st Platoon, 5th Company, 2nd Battalion, 564th Regiment, 118th Division, 63rd Army, Chinese Communist Forces. The body was not buried. A sketch is included in the case file, showing the approximate location of the execution.

FIVE

STEMMING THE TIDE

THE GLORIOUS GLOSTERS

Early in April 1951 the 29th British Independent Brigade under the command of Brigadier Tom Brodie took up positions along the line of the Imjin River. The four infantry battalions – the 1st Battalion, Royal Northumberland Fusiliers; 1st Battalion, the Gloucester Regiment; 1st Battalion, Royal Ulster Rifles; and an attached Belgian battalion – had a nine-mile-wide front to cover and would be stretched very thinly. They were astride one of the traditional invasion routes from the north to Seoul, thirty miles to the south.

The Glosters were placed to cover the road which ran south from the Imjin River. To their right were the Royal Northumberland Fusiliers, and to their right, on high ground just north of the river, was the Belgian battalion. The Royal Ulster Rifles were in reserve. To the left of the brigade stood the ROK 1st Division, covering the land running down to the sea.

After the battles during the winter of 1950–51 the Chinese and North Koreans had withdrawn north of the river to refit and reorganise. A spring offensive was expected, but no one knew when or where. Heavy fighting patrols had crossed the river in search of the enemy formations, but none had been found. They were there though, but well hidden. Across the river the Chinese 63rd Army was waiting for the order to unleash its soldiers on the 29th Brigade sector. Three divisions would take part in the attack, each comprising around 10,000 men, with orders to destroy the British brigade and push on to Seoul to cut off and destroy the United Nations forces to the east.

On the night of 22 April an ambush patrol from the Glosters took up position overlooking a ford across the Imjin River, later known as Gloster Crossing. On the other side of the river the Chinese were approaching after a twenty-mile march in full battle order. As the leading elements began to wade across the 150-yard-wide river, the men of C Company opened fire and began to call in mortar and artillery fire. The trip-wire had been snagged; now the brigade knew that the Chinese were coming in force.

After their ammunition was exhausted the patrol withdrew and the Chinese swarmed across the river towards Castle Hill, defended by A Company. Some 1,500 yards to the south-east D Company held Point 182, and further to the east was B Company. A two-mile gap separated B Company from the Northumberland Fusiliers. During the night the main attack fell on A and D Companies, both of which were at a disadvantage due to lack of defensive stores such as barbed wire and mines. However, they could call upon fire support from the 170th Mortar Battery, 45 Field Regiment and the battalion mortars.

By 0830 hours the next morning A Company was down to one officer and fifty-three men still on their feet and they pulled back to Hill 235 overlooking battalion headquarters. They were soon joined by the survivors of D Company. For a time the wounded could be evacuated to the rear, but soon the news came that the Chinese were behind them and had blocked the road.

There was no air support for the Glosters that day. Presumably they had customers elsewhere as the Rifles, Fusiliers and Belgians were all under attack, as were other neighbouring units. After another night's heavy fighting the enemy gained a foothold in C Company's position early on the morning of 24 April, from which they could dominate the battalion headquarters and the mortars. Colonel Carne immediately moved his headquarters and the mortars to the top of Hill 235 and ordered C Company to join them there.

A pictorial view of the battle area of Solma-ri. Hill 235 – Gloster Hill, is to the right.

After C Company's departure, attacks continued against B Company for the rest of the night. For Private Graham Bailey, it was the day of reckoning. The previous day Bailey had been in a patrol sent out to no-man's land in front of B Company's position to try to bring back a prisoner. In the distance they could see the shallow ford at Gloster Crossing which was now swarming with Chinese. Returning hot-foot to the comparative safety of their platoon position they could only wait with trepidation for the enemy to begin his attack.

The following morning Bailey sat in a foxhole halfway down the hill. Together with two others they formed a listening post, a trip-wire to alert the rest of the men to the approach of the Chinese. As the sound of Chinese bugles echoed through the valley their platoon commander, Lieutenant Gael, summoned the men back and they raced uphill, one after another. Soon the hill became a maelstrom of fire, explosions and flying lead as the overwhelming numbers of Chinese fought their way into the company positions. Eventually Major Harding, the company commander, ordered the survivors to pull back and abandon the positions.

It was too late for Private Bailey. Shot through the lung, he lay gasping as a Chinese armed with a burp-gun appeared at the edge of his foxhole. Seconds passed as he waited for the final bullet. As realisation dawned that for the moment his life was to be spared, he reached for his shell dressing and tried to plug the holes in the front and rear of his chest.

Soon British artillery began to shell the enemy now occupying B Company's old position. Fortunately Bailey was not hit, but he spent an uncomfortable night until he was taken to the rear in the morning.

Colonel Carne and the 400 unwounded men of his battalion consolidated their positions on what was thereafter known as Gloster Hill. Brigade commander Tom Brodie later faced criticism for not apprising his superiors of the seriousness of the Glosters' predicament. By the time American General Milburn issued orders for a general withdrawal early on the morning of 25 April, the Glosters were surrounded. They had fought all through the night and were now running short of ammunition. Their artillery was in danger of being overrun and gave notice that they had to withdraw. Colonel Carne gave the order for his men to try to break out. It was every man for himself.

The medical officer, Bob Hickey, and the padre, Sam Davies, decided to remain with the wounded. The remainder of the survivors made their way down to the valley where most were captured by the Chinese. Forty men from D Company did make it back to friendly lines, although they lost some of their number to American tank fire.

It was not long before Private Bailey rejoined the survivors of the Gloster battalion. He was put with the wounded and attended by

Captain Hickey, who could do little for him as his medical equipment had been taken by the Chinese. When the two columns of prisoners began their march northwards the wounded were divided into small groups to follow on as best they could. Little did Bailey know it then, but he would cheat death on two more occasions before he finally reached the prisoner-of-war camp on the Yalu River. The first time, an American bomb landed in a cesspit near the house where they were imprisoned, and on the second a fifty-calibre bullet from an American night-fighter came through the roof of the hut and hit the ground between Bailey and his sleeping neighbour. It should be mentioned that the Americans were attacking the enemy's main supply route at that time and had no idea that the Chinese had prisoners of war in the buildings nearby.

Eventually, when the Chinese were ready, the columns of prisoners set off northwards. During the night, as they waded the Imjin River at Gloster Crossing, the adjutant, Captain Farrar-Hockley, sank under the

Hill 235, the scene of the last stand of the Glosters. The area was retaken by UN forces five weeks after the battle.

water and struck off downstream. The first of his many escapes had begun.

Two of the Glosters' officers were taken away for special treatment shortly after capture. Lieutenant G. F. B. Temple was the signal officer and Lieutenant Cabral the intelligence officer. Their Chinese captors wanted certain technical information from the officers, but they refused to cooperate. They also tried to escape and were consequently tightly bound with strong wire and left in this condition for some days. They had to perform their bodily functions in this manner and were forced to eat food like dogs. Soon both were suffering bad attacks of dysentery and beri beri. When the two officers were finally released from their bonds and sent northwards separately, Lieutenant Cabral died as a result of ill-treatment, disease and malnutrition and his body was thrown into the ditch by the side of the road and left for the locals to bury. Lieutenant Temple recovered but was left with deep scars on his upper arms from where the wire was bound so tightly.

The Fusiliers, Riflemen and Belgians also lost many of their number during the fighting between 22 and 25 April, including some to a Chinese atrocity (KWC639). The day 23 April 1951 was only a few minutes old when a battle patrol from S Company, 1st Battalion, Royal

This mass of men are British prisoners, mostly Glosters, taken prisoner at the battle of the Imjin River in April 1951. Armed Chinese guards stand in the background.

Ulster Rifles, was sent out to help the Belgian battalion which was under heavy attack. The men waded across the Imjin River and had advanced about a hundred yards on the other side when they were attacked by the enemy. They decided to withdraw and a party of about ten were left to cover the retreat of the others. By the time they made it back across the river and had withdrawn to a position about a mile south of the crossing, they realised they were surrounded by Chinese. Lieutenant Thomas H. R. Craig of the Royal Ulster Rifles later described the events:

'At approximately 0630 hours on 23 April 1951 I, together with eight Riflemen and an RAMC corporal, was concealed behind the enemy forward position on the south bank of the Imjin River. We were attempting to make our way back to our own lines, having been ambushed by the enemy north of the river at 0110 hours that morning. The enemy having spotted us and mortared our location, I told the men to scatter to the cover of a nearby gully. Five of us reached the gully, to which the enemy switched the mortar fire, while their soldiers moved down and captured us.

We were taken back across the river to a nearby hill and held prisoner there. Some hours later five Belgians, two more British soldiers and a British Royal Engineer officer were brought in. We were held here until approximately 1600 hours that day. At this time American jets attacked the hill with napalm. This landed about thirty to fifty yards from our party who, together with our four guards, commenced to move away from the blaze. Our party had been completely disarmed and made absolutely no attempt to escape on that or any other previous occasion. The enemy, seeing us move, fired on us and the prisoners went straight down to earth. I had not moved from my original position with the others since I had removed my boot to attend to a poisoned foot. When the fire started I took cover in a nearby bush with some Chinese soldiers. I lay there and saw two of the enemy come round from the sides of the party and fire bursts into them from close range. One Rifleman raised his hands and stood up, but was not spared.

When the first burst of fire came, Rifleman Geach and a Belgian soldier made a break, and seemed to get clear. After the enemy had finished shooting they looked down the slope but did not see me. I waited until they had gone and then moved quietly away from the bush and the two Chinese with whom I had been sharing it. They for some peculiar reason made no effort to stop me. They seemed fearful of the air attack and also, I think, the small-arms fire. I reached Rifleman Geach and the Belgian soldier and crossed the Imjin River without trouble, having seen some American tanks fairly close, which we were trying to reach. Unfortunately, to reach them we had to cross the river again since it looped. The enemy fired a few mortar bombs in our direction which fell short. We moved well upstream and attempted to ford the river. Before we entered the water the Belgian told me he was wounded, but apparently only slightly. We took him between us into the water, and about fifteen yards out he said he wished to go back and could not swim. The water was up to our armpits, but nearby there was a rocky ledge which seemed to go well over towards the other side. I told Geach to stay with the Belgian and proceeded along the ledge to see if the way was fordable. I was some two thirds of the way out when Geach yelled to me for help. I turned round and told him to strike for the near shore. The Belgian at this time was thrashing a little further downstream and I finally reached the opposite bank to find that Geach had reached the bank, but there was no sign of the Belgian. I then went to the American tanks for help to get Geach across. They said they would arrange for the Belgians to bring him out as they retreated. However, Geach shortly reached us, having managed to recross the stream.'

On 31 May the bodies of one British officer (Lieutenant Eastgate, Royal Engineers), two British soldiers (believed to be Private Tucker of the Glosters, attached to the Royal Ulster Rifles, and Rifleman McNaughton) and five Belgian soldiers (including Premier Sergeant Lemouche and Privates Deganb, Claeys and Cornette) were recovered. Two of the British had been shot in the back of the head. They were next to each other and the hand of one was clasped in the hand of the other. One of the Belgians had been shot or bayoneted in the back. All bodies indicated that they had been killed by small-arms fire. There was no evidence that the soldiers' hands had been tied behind their backs or that they had otherwise been mistreated. Whether they were shot because the Chinese panicked or because they were under orders to shoot the prisoners if recapture seemed imminent will never be known. The enemy unit was part of the 187th Division, 63rd Army, 19th Chinese Army Group.

EVERY MAN FOR HIMSELF

By the morning of 25 April the 64th Chinese Shock Army had penetrated the western sector of the defence and were in a position to encircle the brigade. The outlying companies of the Glosters had been overrun and the survivors had joined battalion headquarters on Hill 235, to be known for ever as Gloster Hill. They were now surrounded and fighting for their lives.

On Hill 398, north-east of the Glosters' position, C Company, 1st Royal Ulster Rifles, were preparing to withdraw. They were told to make for their old positions to the south, where transport would be waiting for them. B Company was also waiting for them there, in a blocking position near the slopes of Kamak San (Hill 675), the peak of which was now held by the enemy.

The men had four miles to cover – not far under normal circumstances, but now they were tired, thirsty and hungry and they viewed the withdrawal with trepidation. As they began to advance down the road it was quiet, the silence punctuated by the sound of their three-inch mortars firing off the last of their bombs. The Riflemen in the leading platoon were unusually subdued as they scanned the countryside ahead of them. History seemed to be repeating itself as they left their relatively safe defensive positions to advance into the unknown. Comments such as 'We've done this all before' and 'We're going down the road again' caused the men to grip their rifles more tightly. The thoughts of some of the older members of the company returned to the terrible night retreat of 3/4 January at Happy Valley, where 240 of their comrades had been lost. Now the men would run the gauntlet again, this time in broad daylight.

As the men began to lengthen their stride the sound of firing increased all around them. Ominously, most of it seemed to be coming from ahead of them. The men knew which tactics to use: stop and fire, then move on. The firing became more intense and mortar bombs began to explode around them. Henry O'Kane in the leading platoon felt a blow to his leg and tumbled to the ground. In the shelter of a rice paddy bund he pulled off his webbing and pack, checked his rifle and staggered to his feet again. More men began to fall as they ran from cover to cover, but they were now committed to a race for their lives. They passed a group of Royal Engineers sheltering behind a Centurion tank that had shed a track and were yelling at them to get down. They just put their heads down and kept running, past two more burning tanks and an RUR Oxford carrier with the name *Billy McCabb* on its side, its crew now lifeless.

Eventually those still alive reached their old positions and what was left of B Company. The majority of the battalion behind them turned south-east towards the hills, trying to break through the enemy surrounding them. O'Kane and the other wounded were loaded onto a couple of tanks from the 8th King's Royal Irish Hussars, which were trying to keep the road open for the infantry. The tanks moved off in a cloud of dust, the wounded crying out as they were hit again and again. Suddenly the road was swamped with Chinese, many carrying Molotov cocktails and explosive charges on poles. The machine-guns on the tanks and their grinding tracks killed many of them, but still they came on. Clinging to the swaying tank, Henry O'Kane's world suddenly exploded.

The Rifleman slowly opened his eyes and looked around him. He was lying in a ditch at the side of the road, the tank a few yards further on, burning fiercely. He was covered in blood and his nose and ears were bleeding from concussion. As he groped around in the water in search of his rifle he realised he was not alone. Small groups of men were lying along the banks, many wounded, some dead. The ebb and flow of battle continued around them as Chinese troops ran across the road in pursuit of the battalion.

As the men realised summary execution was not their fate that day, they began to move about and help one another. Someone removed O'Kane's camouflage smock, splashed some water over him, bandaged his head and gave him a drink of rum. The noise of the battle began to fade as the fighting moved away from the road. Three Chinese wearing tatty cotton uniforms appeared and began to hand out safe conduct passes, saying 'Good fight' and 'The war is over for you now'. The prisoners, about forty in all, were formed into a line with hands on their heads and marched down the road. The wounded who were unable to walk were left behind. They were never seen again.

Every man has his own reason for joining the army. Derek Kinne's reason was different to most. He had made a pact with his brother Raymond in 1947 that if one or the other ever went missing the other would come to find him. A telegram arrived from the War Office in October 1950: Raymond had been killed while serving with the Argyll's in Korea. April 1951 saw Derek himself in Korea, serving with the 1st Battalion, Royal Northumberland Fusiliers – the Fifth Fusiliers, in the British 29th Infantry Brigade.

The sound of firing had increased by the time Captain De Quidt gave the order to follow the tank. The men liked and trusted the captain; he had fought behind Japanese lines in Burma with Wingate's Chindits and was a cool professional. Fusilier Kinne and eight others had been providing cover for the tank crew while they changed the damaged track. Now, in a cloud of smoke and a rattle of tracks, the Centurion lumbered on down the road. Kinne noticed that there were men from the Royal Ulster Rifles coming across the paddy and others were hurrying along the road from the north. Among the pines, below the hills and crawling along the paddy bunds towards them came the yellow-clad Chinese.

A group of Ulster Riflemen ran across the road in front of Kinne. One of them, a young officer, jumped up on to the eastern bund then suddenly swung round and jumped back into the ditch. He looked at Kinne questioningly: 'Aren't you the man I gave fourteen days' CB to on the ship coming out?' 'Yes sir!' Kinne replied. 'I thought I recognised you,' he grinned. 'Well, best of luck.' With that he turned and jumped back on to the bund and crossed the paddy, dodging the bullets that swept to and fro across the open space.

The Fusilier colonel stood by the side of the road and watched the brigadier's scout car coming up from the south. The brigadier was sitting on the top, dressed in his white sheepskin coat and red peaked hat, looking as cool as if he was watching a training exercise. 'Where are the Chinese?' he asked the colonel. 'All around sir, and they're pushing along the hilltops as fast as they can.' 'I think I'll go a bit further down,' he said. 'I want to see what's happening to the Rifles.' And he drove on towards the north.

The colonel came over to Kinne and the other Fusiliers. 'Not much further to go lads, about another mile or so and you're home.' They shouldered their packs and trudged on down the road, following in the wake of the tank. Some time in the next hour the colonel passed the Fusiliers travelling in a half-track from the 8th Hussars. It stopped and the colonel got out, so more wounded could be loaded aboard. He took over an empty artillery jeep and sat in it as Kinne passed him again.

Everyone was enveloped in clouds of dust as the Centurions drove along. Suddenly a tank halted and an Oxford carrier pulled over and tried to squeeze by on the narrow roadway. It half-slid into the ditch and was pushed aside by the next tank which came past. Ahead of them, on the S-bend, lay a Chinese roadblock.

A few of Kinne's original group of Fusiliers were still on their feet and trying to work their way around the flanks. About fifty yards away a little group of Riflemen, identified by their green head-dress, were lying in the ditch to the left of the road. Whether they were prisoners or not, he could not be sure. But immediately above them the Chinese were lying along the bund firing their weapons. Kinne decided that the road was the quick way out, if only he could find some cover to pass the crucial points. He decided to try to walk out alongside one of the tanks as the sound of battle reached its peak around him.

'I could only stumble forward, hoping that I could judge the right moment to take cover on one side or the other of the tank. Now I was on the eastern side and the dust was clearing. There, fifteen yards away, were the Riflemen in the ditch. I called out to them to warn them of their peril and flung a grenade over their heads at the little domed helmets, dodging back to the west side of the tank to take cover from the answering Chinese fire. This was a mistake. The tank moved quickly away up the road as I came round, leaving me exposed with the dust settling around me. I dived into a ditch and began crawling.

Nearby, lying on its side in a ditch, was the medical half-track of the 8th Hussars. It had suffered the same fate as the Oxford carrier. Round it lay wounded and unwounded men under the eye of Chinese firing from the bank a foot or two above. A small dried-up stream bed led me away from the half-track and I began to crawl up it. No one seemed to have spotted me as there was a renewed outbreak of firing at a jeep that flashed past on the road. The Fusilier colonel was behind the wheel. I watched it reach the S-bend, turn safely and turn again, slowing slightly for the last bend. Then there was a flash and a puff of smoke, and the jeep stopped, its windscreen shattered and the driver now dead.

I continued to scuttle along the stream bed. Perhaps – one man – I would manage to dodge through the mass of enemy soldiers lying all around. Perhaps not. Round the next bend sat a Chinese soldier pointing a burp-gun at me. He made no sound, sitting there, expressionless as we watched one another for two or three seconds. Then he made a movement with his head and pointed with his hand in the direction of the half-track on the road. The barrel trained on my back, I retraced my steps to it. Only another mile.'

Back at the half-track Kinne met Captain Patchett, the medical officer of the 8th Hussars. It was his half-track that had gone into the ditch while he was hurrying to get some of the wounded out. He pulled a bottle of whisky out of his medical bag and passed it around.

A MONTH IN THE WILDERNESS

One member of B Company, 1st Glosters, was to endure twenty-seven days behind enemy lines before help finally reached him. Private Lionel Essex was hit in the head during the bitter fighting on the night of 23 April. Just after dawn the 4th Platoon commander, Lieutenant Costello, told Essex to make his way down the reverse side of the hill. The company was about to be overrun and it would soon be every man for himself. Halfway down the hill Essex was hit again, in the left leg. As he lay there he was hit yet again, the bullet breaking his right leg. Another wounded Gloster, Sergeant Robinson, came across Essex and stayed with him as the company withdrew and the Chinese swarmed around the hill. Later in the day Robinson left to seek help, but he was captured and taken away. The young private was on his own.

The Chinese found Essex the next morning and interrogated him. Although he was kicked and punched, he would only give his name, rank and number. The infuriated Chinese threw a hand grenade at the helpless man, wounding him in his eye, and then they departed.

Two days later Essex crawled down the hill to the village of Paegun, where three weeks previously B Company had given food to the young children of the village. The villagers decided to repay the kindness and brought food and water to the wounded man. It was not long before the Chinese discovered what was going on and caught and shot one of the villagers. Despite this a seventeen-year-old Korean boy continued to bring food and water to Essex during the hours of darkness.

A week later some Chinese soldiers came to the trench where Essex was lying, looked at him and then moved away. He decided to move in case they came back and crawled to another trench a hundred yards away. It was a fortunate decision, for not long afterwards a number of Chinese mortar bombs exploded on his old trench.

The villagers took Essex to a house in the village and here he stayed until an air strike on nearby Chinese troops caused his helpers to move the private to another village nearby. Finally, on 20 May a patrol from a Greek battalion came to the village and took Essex back with them to a field hospital. At the end of the month the re-formed Gloster battalion reoccupied its old positions and was able to reward the villagers for their help.

As for the other prisoners from the brigade, they had weeks of hard marching ahead of them before they finally left the road and climbed to the top of a long, high mountain. As far as they could see there were mountain ranges, stretching into China. Down in the valley lay their future home for the duration: Chongsong town. The brigade lost some of its men on the march due to lack of medical treatment, inadequate food, sickness and ill-treatment and others were to die after they reached the prison camp.

A captured Chinese soldier, Lee Zeu Win, prisoner of war number 704110 from the 579th Regiment, 193rd Division, 65th Army, Chinese communist forces, claimed that on 8 May he and two unnamed others shot and killed two captured British prisoners in the vicinity of the Imjin River. The prisoners were not bound but were required to sit on the ground and were shot in the back. The bodies were not buried. A sketch was made of the place of execution (KWC1282).

FOR VALOUR

Lieutenant Terrence Edward Waters was an officer in the West Yorkshire Regiment, attached to the Gloucestershire Regiment. He was a young, relatively inexperienced officer who had not long graduated from the Royal Military Academy, Sandhurst. He was soon to earn the award of the George Cross, one of only two British officers to do so during three long years of fighting.

At the battle of the Imjin River Lieutenant Waters sustained a serious wound to the top of his head and another wound to his arm. Taken prisoner during the battle, he remained with the wounded other ranks and set them an example of courage and fortitude as they were all marched north to Pyongyang. Eventually, after a long and hard march, the party arrived at an area west of Pyongyang, adjacent to Camp 12 and known generally as 'The Caves'. They were imprisoned in a tunnel cut into the side of a hill, through which a stream of water flowed continuously, flooding the floor. In this hell hole the ragged South Korean, British and American prisoners struggled to stay alive. Their North Korean captors did not tend to their wounds and sickness was rife. The food was totally inadequate and the men grew weaker daily through malnutrition. Before long, men were dying daily from untreated wounds, sickness or starvation.

A North Korean political officer visited the caves and tried to persuade the prisoners to volunteer to go to a 'peace camp' where they would learn the errors of their ways and be taught to criticise their government and its values. In return they would receive better food and medical treatment. The men refused to go. Lieutenant Waters realised that if they remained in the caves they would all die. He ordered his men to volunteer to go to the peace camp and pretend to go along with the enemy's wishes, in order to survive. Waters himself refused to accompany the men. The North Koreans made a concerted effort to persuade the young officer to go with his men, but he steadfastly refused. He was an officer in the British Army and realised that honour, duty and British prestige was at stake. A short time later he died.

On 2 May 1951 Flight Lieutenant Gordon Harvey of the Royal Australian Air Force and two American officers, Major Magee and Lieutenant Simpson, escaped from the notorious Pak's Death House north of Pyongyang. The escapees were assisted by Captain Gibbon of the Royal Artillery. The North Koreans decided to torture Gibbon to discover the escape route and plans of the three men. Captain Zachary Dean, USAF, related the events which took place in the camp shortly afterwards:

'The Korean guards came in and took Captain Gibbon outside the camp and tied his hands behind his back. They then threw a rope from his hands up over the limb of a tree and pulled him up until his toes were just touching the ground. Major Pak and two Korean soldiers loosened his trouser belt buckle and brutally pulled and twisted his testicles and beat him, asking him to tell them the direction in which the escapees had gone. He replied the he did not know, and even if he did he would not tell them. They then pulled and twisted his testicles some more and he screamed in agony. This continued until he fainted. He was then taken down and water was thrown in his face. When he came to again they tied a rope around his neck. Then they pulled him up and put a pistol at the back of his neck and said, "We are going to give you thirty seconds to tell us which way these men escaped." Again he said, "I don't know, and if I did I wouldn't tell you." Then they came out with some sharpened bamboo shoots, tied his hands to a board and started driving the sharpened bamboo under his fingernails. Again he fainted from pain. Then they brought him back. His fingernails came off later and grew back crookedly, but that is not important. He never did tell anything and they brought him back, assuming he didn't know anything, but he did know.'

Captain Acton Henry Gordon Gibbon was the only officer apart from Lieutenant Waters to be awarded the George Cross for conduct during the Korean War.

The flow of American prisoners of war continued northwards throughout the summer of 1951. Corporal James Prewitt was one of them.

'My outfit got to Korea in August 1950. I drove a truck from then to 17 May 1951 when the Chinese overran my outfit. There were twenty-one of us, trying to fight and help the wounded at hand near us. We were in a valley with these hills around us. Eventually we ran out of ammo and had to clear away from the area. As darkness fell the three of us found ourselves near a small tunnel, so we lay down to rest. We fell asleep and were woken up by a Chinese pointing a gun in our faces. The place was nothing but Chinese all around us outside the tunnel. At this point I dropped my weapon on the ground and gave up. We were taken to another tunnel where we met the rest of the men who were also captured.

It was the morning of 18 May. We were given a hot bowl of rice and were then taken one at a time to a high-ranking officer who asked us who we were and what our job was. I told them my name, rank and that I was a cook. A few days later we began the long walk to North Korea.

The Chinese were scared to death when our planes came over. We lay low and prayed they would not mistake us for the enemy, which they did much of the time. But when they did shoot at us, they would miss – God was with us there.

We ate what the Chinese could find for us, but there was very little. Usually rice, or more rice. Sometimes we had greens of some kind mixed with grass and boiled. It tasted bad but we ate it. Muddy water tasted bad too but after a few drinks of it one did not care. We walked over every hill there was going north towards the Yellow [Yalu] River. A few items were always on my mind: Has our government forgotten us? How far do we have to walk? Is there hope we will get away from these guards? Is there hope, or will they kill us?

There were twenty-one of us on the march, including our second lieutenant who was wounded. We dropped him off at a make-shift hospital. One night we found ourselves marching alongside some mules with supplies on them. Our planes dropped everything at us, but they missed us and hit a few mules. It was good for us and bad for them. Old mule meat is tough, but young mule meat is tender. They gave us some after it was cooked. They would push us to the limit to get us going all the time. Those that passed out we would drag and carry until they came to. Two buddies carried me for a mile or better when I passed out.

Items of food we ate on the way to North Korea: cornfield corn, uncooked peas, half-cooked potatoes or rice, mule meat. Any water we saw we drank. Forty-seven days and forty-seven nights later we got to the camp where we found things as bad or worse than on the march. A whole town was where we were, not far from the Yellow River. We were sad to see so many people sick.

We helped bury people on boot hill. Some had just quit eating and others still had wounds from the front, but we had no way of treating them. There were ten men to one small room with just straw on the floor to sleep on. Nothing except what we could make do with. The bathroom was just rails over the river to sit on. If your buddy was weak you had to hold him to keep him from falling in. No toilet paper, just find what you could. All of us lost weight and we had body lice from the straw. We killed them by boiling our clothes in a rice bowl that we cooked in. Items we needed but did not have at all: soap, toothpaste, proper food.

One thing we did have that saved a lot of us: a willingness to help each other all the time. Several men were beaten bad and just left to get well. Nothing we could do but bathe them with water from the river. I was taken to the headquarters many times and they would try everything to get you to tell about your outfit. I just gave name, rank and serial number. Then, one time, the officer in charge came up behind me and pulled the trigger on his pistol several times to get me to talk. Then when that didn't work he hit my chair out from under me and told me to crawl to the door. I got up and walked to the door which he pushed me out of and then the guard took me back to the room where I came from.

One time, after a year, they let us have our own man to cook the rice. All the ranks at this point, sergeants and above, and coloured men as well, were in other camps. One day ten of us went with three guards to a town about ten miles from us to draw what they called food. Before we got to the other side of this town we were attacked by people who threw rocks and spat at us. Where we got the food from was a dirty building with bugs all over the place. Round loaves of bread that were hard with bugs in them. Meat that had bugs in it also. We took it all back to the cooks, and they boiled the meat to get the bugs out of it and then when it was well-cooked we ate it. To this day I don't know what it was, but it was good.

There were good Chinese and bad ones. The good ones were few at our place. I have seen guards hit someone for no reason at all. We could steal food on wood detail if we had good guards.

My weight at capture time was 181 pounds. When I got released on

19 August 1953 my weight was seventy-five pounds. In July 1953 they said over the loudspeakers that the peace talks were over and we would get out of the forgotten hell hole of Korea soon. There were quite a few of us who would not agree with the Chinese so we would be left to last to be released. Wounded went out first with sick. Those who didn't give the Chinese any trouble at all also went. Then there was the rest of us. We got taken to near where we were to be released. After a few days we were taken by truck to the release point. Ten a.m., 19 August 1953: a deep feeling, a gay feeling and a happy feeling to see Old Glory flying high and pretty. Freedom at last. No more rotten food, no more Chinese, no more bad feelings towards our army. Prayers, mail, chow, movies, men to talk to, clean clothes, bath. God had helped all of us get through it. Freedom I could talk about all day long.'

CONFESSION

War Crimes case number 242B is a little confusing, but should be mentioned in lieu of further research. The atrocity took place on 22 May 1951 roughly sixteen kilometres west of Ch'unch'on. The victims were listed as seventeen Australians, one New Zealander, one American and one Mongoloid. The suspects were Jeou Ten Wei (later deceased), Wei Jen Shin, Jeo Pei Soo, Su We Jing, Jang Re Ee and Jan Jin Soo.

This incident is based on the confession of Jeou Ten Wei, prisoner of war number 707921, in which he stated that on or about 17 May 1951 his battalion, after engaging American troops, captured twenty American soldiers, five or six of whom were black. Pursuant to the order of the battalion commander all twenty of the prisoners were executed. The reason for this slaughter was the fact that in the battalion commander's opinion it would have been bothersome to take the prisoners to the rear at a time when the battalion was proceeding forward to engage American troops. The execution occurred on 22 May. The twenty prisoners were executed in groups of four, three, three, five, three and two respectively. The suspect personally executed the remaining two with his rifle.

The bodies were left unburied at the alleged execution site but were later recovered, and the Graves Registration report disclosed twenty recoveries within two kilometres of the very general description of the execution sites as described by the suspect. Although these recoveries were scattered over an area approximately two kilometres in area, considering the mode of execution utilised by the Chinese in executing the victims it is very plausible to conclude that these recoveries are the alleged victims of the atrocity in question.

Order of Battle records for the period 25 April to 8 May indicate the

28th British Commonwealth Brigade (renamed from 27th Brigade) was in contact with the suspect enemy unit, the 180th Chinese Communist Forces Division. It is probable that the deceased were Australians from the 3rd Battalion, Royal Australian Regiment, captured around that time. The suspect's error in describing the victims as American is understandable in view of the communist propaganda line at that time, which described all UN forces in Korea as 'American aggressors'.

THE DEATH OF FATHER KAPAUN

Father Kapaun rejoined the survivors of his unit at Pyoktong on a backwater of the Yalu River where prisoners from many units were being assembled. They had not been there long when the town was bombed and the prisoners were forced to move on. The Chinese, for once, had not killed all the wounded and the prisoners were given the task of carrying them on litters made of straw sacks and rough pine branches. Father Kapaun took one end of a pole and helped carry the load, along with the rest.

Eventually they reached a village, a scattering of huts along a narrow valley, from which the Chinese quickly evicted the occupants. The wounded were placed in one of the houses and the other prisoners in houses further along the valley. Father Kapaun and Dr Anderson protested at being separated from the wounded, but one can only argue so much when a loaded gun is pointed at you.

During the first week in the valley the Chinese gave the prisoners a food allowance of 500 grams of millet or cracked corn per man per day. It was a starvation ration, and when it was reduced to 450 grams the situation became desperate. The solution was obvious: the men had to steal more food or slowly starve. Father Kapaun announced to the others that in such a dangerous undertaking they would need the help of a power beyond themselves. Standing in front of the men he said a prayer to St Dismas, the Good Thief, who was crucified at the right hand of Jesus, asking for his aid.

Despite the risk of being shot by the guards, Father Kapaun would sneak at night into the cornfields and search for potatoes and grain hidden by the Koreans beneath the corn shocks. He moved out of the crowded room where nineteen men slept, spoon-fashion on the dirt floor, to sleep in an open shed in the compound, where he discovered that the shed backed on to a crib full of Korean corn, which he proceeded to steal, surreptitiously, ear by ear.

His most daring thefts were carried out in daylight, right under the noses of the guards. The prisoners now cooked their own food, which was stored in an open supply shed a couple of miles down the valley.

When a group of men was being assembled to collect the rations, Father Kapaun would slip in at the end of the line. Before the detail reached the supply shed, he would slip away again into the bushes and make his way to the back of the shed. The men would cause a diversion to attract the attention of the Chinese and the priest would sneak in, snatch up a sack of corn and stealthily make off with his load.

While Father Kapaun stole food for the common good, there were others who stole food to eat themselves. He would not reproach them directly, but at night, after a successful foray, he would say a prayer of thanks to God for providing food 'which all can equally share'. Perhaps this shamed some of them, for the private hoarding eventually ceased.

One tale told about the priest concerned a small black pig which wandered into the compound after the prisoners had moved back to Pyoktong. The men had not tasted meat for months, so Father Kapaun silently stalked the animal with a large rock in his hand. He struck the pig, but only a glancing blow and the animal let out a terrible squeal. Alerted by the noise a Chinese guard came running, chambering a round in his rifle and shouting, 'Huh? Huh?' The priest fled towards the latrine as the confused guard ran down the road in pursuit of the pig.

Not long after the men reached the valley the wounded began to die, one by one. The Chinese insisted that they be placed in the so-called hospital, merely a hut where the sick men lay unattended, succumbing to their wounds, infection or starvation. Finally the Chinese allowed Dr Anderson to go to the men although he had no medicine or instruments with which to attend them. Father Kapaun asked if he could go too. This was refused: 'What these men need is medicine, not prayer,' the Chinese told him. 'Since they aren't getting any medicine, a little prayer would not hurt,' the Father replied. 'No,' the Chinese said, 'you will not be permitted to spread your poisonous Christian propaganda here.'

It was a challenge the brave priest could not refuse. He would sneak along the creek that ran through the valley to the sick house and tend to the forgotten souls lying there. He would bring them food and wash their old bandages and pick the lice from their bodies. In some he instilled the will to live and to others he read the last rites when their time came. The conditions in this camp were the same as in the camp known as Death Valley, but there the death rate was ten times higher. Much of the credit for this must go to Father Kapaun.

The prisoners buried their own dead on a hillside near the village and later, in Pyoktong, on a small island where they dug the graves in the frozen, stony ground. The men were buried naked, their clothing needed for the living, and as the earth was thrown over them the priest would recite: 'Eternal rest grant unto him, O Lord, and let perpetual light shine upon him.'

He worked hard to keep the men's spirits up, stepping through the entrance to their huts and greeting them quietly with, 'The Lord be with you.' The tired, hungry men would stir and reply, as he had taught them, 'And with thy Spirit.' He would then say a quick general service, starting with a prayer for those who had died in Korea, in battle and in prison, and for the sick and wounded. He would remind them of the folks back home and urge them to hold on – they would soon be free. To those who were succumbing to the communist teachings he would quote, 'Be not afraid of them who kill the body. Fear ye him, who after he hath killed, hath power to cast into Hell!'

The devoted priest tended his flock in many other ways. He traded his watch for a blanket with which to make socks for men whose feet were freezing. He washed the clothes of men suffering from dysentery who were too weak to move. When the latrines had to be cleaned the men would argue about whose turn it was to carry out this loathsome chore. While they argued he would slip out quietly and do the job himself.

In the middle of January the prisoners were marched eight miles back into Pyoktong, into houses still shattered by the bombing and subsequent fires. Nine of the sick and wounded died that day and many of the others were on the point of giving up. Father Kapaun led a scrounging party to search the ruins for materials to patch up the huts. He was caught one day stealing pickets from a fence and was made to stand for hours, stripped of his outer garments, in the bitter cold. Despite this he stole the materials to make a fireplace in the yard of the officers' compound and every morning he would heat water in pans made from tin he had stolen and beaten into shape with a rock. He would bring the steaming water into the hut, calling cheerfully, 'Coffee, everybody.'

By mid-March 1951 the food situation was becoming desperate. The men were becoming weaker, their strength drained by pellagra, beriberi and the perpetual diet of millet and corn which became so nauseating they could hardly bring themselves to swallow it. They searched everywhere for green weeds to boil in their hunt for vitamins. Their bodies began to swell as the first stage of death by starvation approached. The night before St Patrick's Day Father Kapaun called the men together and prayed to St Patrick, asking him to help them in their hour of need. The next day the Chinese brought them a case of liver, the first meat they had had, and issued koliang instead of millet. The liver was spoiled and koliang is sorghum seed, used as cattle feed in the States, but to the prisoners the food was a Godsend. Later he prayed for tobacco and that night a guard walked by and threw a little bag of dry, straw-like Korean tobacco into their room.

As the men grew weaker the communist propaganda assault increased and they were forced to attend lectures given by 'instructors' such as Comrade Sun, a fanatical Chinese with a hatred of all things American. Some men rebelled against this brainwashing and were thrown into freezing holes or subjected to other tortures. A few died. Others would repeat what the Chinese wanted to hear – they were only words after all. Father Kapaun would listen to the lectures and then without losing his temper or raising his voice would answer the lecturer point by point, with a calm logic that caused Comrade Sun to shout and leap on the platform like an angry ape. 'When our Lord told us to love our enemies,' he once said, 'I'm sure He did not have Comrade Sun in mind.'

Although they did not punish him directly, the Chinese took two of his close friends away and tortured them. Their hands were tied behind their backs and they were hoisted by ropes until their wrist joints were dislocated. They were forced to make statements accusing the Father of slandering the Chinese and advocating resistance to their study programme. When they were returned to the hut, unsure of their reception, the two officers were greeted by Father Kapaun, who told them, 'You never should have suffered a moment, trying to protect me.' The expected public trial never took place. It became clear that the Chinese were afraid of the priest and were worried that if he was maltreated the whole camp of 4,000 men would rise up against them.

Eventually his strength began to fail him. A week after Easter he began to limp, hobbling along with the aid of a stick. Soon his leg was dreadfully swollen and discoloured, a mass of purple, blue and yellow flesh. Dr Anderson and his medical companion, Captain Sidney Esensten, diagnosed a blood clot, which was blocking the circulation in the leg. They applied hot packs and slowly the swelling subsided. Then dysentery struck, but the men cared for him as he had often done for them and he recovered. Finally he came down with pneumonia and became delirious, laughing and talking to friends from the past. Again, after a deep and quiet sleep he awoke; the crisis had passed. But then the Chinese arrived with a litter and orders that he must be taken to the so-called hospital. The doctors and others in the room protested, but it was clear that the Chinese did not want him to live and insisted, 'He goes! He goes!'

Father Kapaun made no protest. He looked around the room and smiled at the others. 'Tell them back home that I died a happy death,' he said and began to say his goodbyes to his friends. To Lieutenant Ralph Nardella he gave his prayer book with the request, 'You know the prayers, Ralph, keep holding the services. Don't let them make you stop.' To a tearful Lieutenant Mike Dowe he said, 'Don't take it so hard, Mike. I'm going where I've always wanted to go. And when I get up there, I'll say a prayer for all of you.' As they carried Father Kapaun down the road, a Turkish lieutenant, Fezi Gurgin, a Mohammedan, promised, 'To Allah, who is my God, I will say a prayer for him.' A few days later the brave priest was dead. Sergeant Walter Bray, one of the few men to survive a long period of time in the 'hospital', stated on his return to America that the Chinese took the priest away one night and then he heard two shots. 'They killed Father Kapaun.'

Father Kapaun was buried in an unmarked grave, a fate shared with 1,600 of his comrades. Perhaps one day, when the world has changed, they will find them and bring them home. (Father Kapaun was posthumously awarded the Bronze Star with the Valour 'V' and, for his heroism at the time of his capture, the Distinguished Service Cross).

MORE BRITISH ATROCITIES

Following his capture by UN forces, Section Leader Lee Jing Jun, prisoner of war number 712180, stated that under the orders of his company commander Jou Chang Ming he and Private Wang Deng Chai at dawn on 18 June 1951 rolled two wounded British prisoners of war over a cliff in the vicinity of Kuhwa-ri (CT0818). Although the bodies could not be seen, Lee Jing Jun believed both to be dead because of the extreme height from which they were dropped. The case file apparently contains a sketch showing the probable position of the atrocity. All three suspects belonged to the 7th Company, 3rd Battalion, 599th Regiment, 187th Division, 63rd Army, Chinese Communist Forces (KWC754).

The remains of another unidentified British soldier were recovered by members of the 293rd Quartermaster's Graves Registration Company on 7 July 1951, approximately three quarters of a mile south-west of Pulmiji (CS152712). Sergeant Harold Hiner, in charge of the recovery team, reported that a rope was found tied around the victim's neck, which led him to believe that the soldier met his death by hanging. Statements were taken from several villagers in the area who stated that the soldier was part of a group of British soldiers who were killed after being captured by unknown Chinese or North Korean soldiers. They further stated that some of the villagers buried the body. The deceased is buried at the Tanggok Cemetery as Unknown X-1481 (WO208/4005).

Another British soldier who did not return home was seen by Corporal Charles G. Pixley, US Army, who later reported: 'During September 1951, while the prisoners were being marched to Camp 3, I observed an English soldier beaten by a Korean guard. I was present when he died two hours later. This incident occurred in a tunnel in the vicinity of an unknown reservoir approximately forty miles from Camp 3' (WO208/4005).

Other British prisoners were luckier. Private Graham Bailey from B Company, Glosters, found himself in a group of wounded, including

Sam Mercer and Bill Street. Mike Walker was also suffering from a lung wound, but whereas Bailey's lung had been punctured by a bullet which went straight through, the velocity of the bullet that hit Walker must have been quite low as it simply broke the wall of the lung and dropped inside. As they slowly made their way northwards several of the more severely wounded men died, including Lieutenant Gael and Private Skoines.

Towards the end of June 1951 the wounded reached the North Korean capital of Pyongyang. By now they were also suffering from severe dysentery and were infested with lice. They had been further broken down into small groups of four, five or six and some of them, including Lieutenant Waters, were sent to The Caves. Bailey and his companions continued for a couple of miles past Pyongyang and then turned off the road and up a track to a house. Their guards left them there for several weeks, during which time a Chinese doctor visited them and tended their wounds. Mike Walker had the bullet in his lung removed and Graham Bailey had a tube inserted in his lung to drain the fluid that had gathered there – all without anaesthetic, of course. The doctor who operated on Bailey and inserted the tube into his back had propped a book up against Bailey's neck and was presumably reading up on the operation as he carried it out. It did not inspire confidence, but in the end the treatment worked.

One day Mike Walker wandered over the hill into the next valley in search of food and found himself a spectator as American F-80 jets attacked a target nearby. He was so close to the action that he was wounded in the arm and then found himself surrounded by North Koreans who thought he was a shot-down American pilot. He was given a good beating before the Chinese found him and took him away.

The group was then moved again and billeted with a North Korean family on a small holding near the Chinese main supply route. This was the place mentioned earlier where American aircraft attacking traffic on the route nearly brought their journey to a premature end. On occasion, when the Papasan (father) was away the Mamasan (mother) would give them extra food such as corn on the cob. It was very brave of her because if she had been discovered she would have been killed.

Their next move was to a bunker built on a hill nearby to house the crews of some anti-aircraft guns. That day the US Air Force B-29s bombed Pyongyang ten miles away and the men sat on the hill and watched as the ack-ack guns went into action, hoping that the fighters escorting the B-29s would not come down to suppress the anti-aircraft fire.

They had two Americans with them, Woods and White, who had one of his feet missing. They were taken away elsewhere and at the end of September the British were put on a truck and taken to Camp 5 at

Pyoktong. Bailey eventually finished up at Camp 3 with other 'reactionaries'. Sam Mercer was one of the thirty-two lucky British prisoners to be sent home during the exchange of sick and wounded in April 1953.

THE COMPOUND AT 52 FU HSING ROAD

It took a month before report SO74807 was distributed to interested parties by the US Central Intelligence Agency, and twenty-five years would elapse before it was finally declassified. The source was probably a Chinese Nationalist spy or sympathiser and the report concerned UN prisoners inside China. The source stated that on 13 September 1951 Chao Enh-lu, a staff member of the Central and South China military Area Headquarters, after inspecting a camp for American and British prisoners of war at 52 Fu Hsing Road, Canton, issued an order prohibiting prisoners from speaking to people outside the compound. He was too late, because some of the men had already passed their names to the outside. The report listed twelve Americans and eight British, four each from the Argyll and Sutherland Highlanders and the Gloucester Regiment. Unfortunately the names were written in Cantonese and the author has yet to tie up the translations with the lists of those men still missing. The CIA, on the other hand, with its vast resources, must have done this back in 1951 and should know perfectly well who the unlucky prisoners were in the compound in Canton. British Intelligence should also be aware of the names. One thing is for sure: they never came home.

Six

Life in the Camps

Escape

There were a number of problems inherent in escaping in North Korea. This was recognised by the escape and evasion schools and a number of suggestions were made to improve the chances of anyone finding themselves behind enemy lines. A reliable compass would be ideal, although prisoners were capable of manufacturing such an item. Halezone tablets or some other water purifier were necessary. Some type of highly concentrated food would be essential to limit the need to forage for food. Some means of darkening the skin to a bronze colour may have increased the evader's chances of avoiding capture, but disguising one's height was another matter. Good maps would also be desirable, and why not mark the best escape routes on the maps?

Some of the above ideas would certainly improve the chances of a pilot or stranded infantryman of evading capture, but there were other hazards to consider. Concealment was a big problem: white Caucasians stuck out like a sore thumb and it would be necessary to travel by night and stick to the mountains or thick forests. To descend to the inhabited valleys would invite discovery and the Chinese always used local children to search for escapers. Crops were usually guarded.

Another major factor affecting escape plans was the possibility of disclosure by one of your fellow prisoners. There were always those who sought to improve their position with their captors by informing on others. Captain Farrar-Hockley planned to escape from Camp 2, Branch 2, in the company of three British sergeant-majors, but they were betrayed and caught before they had time to get clear of the camp.

The problems inherent in escaping from the camps were artfully described by two British soldiers, Sergeant 'Knocker' Brisland and Corporal Len Charman, who were recaptured after three days on the run. First they were given two weeks in the local Korean jail, where they had to sit on the floor, bolt upright, for sixteen hours a day. Then they were invited to 'confess' before the assembled camp inmates. Brisland launched into a tirade against the war-mongering Wall Street financiers and apologised for abusing the hospitality of the Chinese

162

People's Volunteers. He informed his audience that escape was impossible, that they had to wade across deep rivers, that their feet always hurt and that by good fortune they were found by a Korean boy who told the police about them. In his own way he was passing on the knowledge gained during his escape: that the bridges were all guarded, that good shoes were vital and at all costs avoid the Korean children. He rambled on in the same vein and imparted the knowledge that food was hard to find, so take your own, together with the means to cook it, and ended his speech with thanks to the Chinese people for liberating them. The Chinese fell for it hook, line and sinker and Brisland received a standing ovation from his fellow Glosters in the audience. The two escapees also received a further seven days in jail, but their punishment could have been a lot worse.

The best time to try to escape from the enemy prison camps was in the summer. With the onset of the ceasefire talks in June 1951 the food also improved as the Chinese finally realised that after the war they would need some prisoners who were still alive to exchange. Captain Zachary Dean, USAF, described his escape attempt:

Camp 5 at Pyoktong on the Yalu River. The bodies of hundreds of American prisoners are buried on the slopes of the hill leading down to the water on the right-hand side of the picture. In the winter the burial parties would carry the dead across the ice, which was so thick it would hold the weight of a tank.

163

'Frank Mills, the Associated Press photographer, and myself decided to escape from Camp 5 in the summer of 1951. We got away from the camp on 20 August after preparing special rations by saving such sugar as we got, collecting rice crusts and grinding up soya beans into a powder. We reckoned that the rations would last fifteen days, by which time we hoped to have reached the west coast. We got out of the camp at 2200 hours. The night was pitch black and it was raining hard. There were no searchlights round the camp at that time, nor wire, so it was only a matter of walking past the sentries.

We walked over to the mountain at the back side of the camp until we reached a reservoir and the Yalu River. We swam about three quarters of a mile to the other side using a waterlogged boat to help us. After walking about two miles along a road we were challenged. Because the night was so black we decided to try to bluff through and walked on after yelling "Chongwa!" which we believed was the word for "Chinese". We walked right past the two men who were posted by the road. They could not follow us because for some reason or other they were hampered by the fact that they were trying to put their trousers on. By the time they had followed us up the road we had got into hiding again.

We went up into the mountain and sat up on the crest out of view during the next day. Our clothes were wet and had been ever since we got away. We tried to find a cave in which to light a fire and dry out. That night we came on to the road and started walking. It was still raining. Because of the rain, every small ravine in the mountains was a rush river and it was impossible for us to make our way across the mountains so we tried to make it along the roads.

That night we walked all night and passed three more checkpoints because we heard the guards talking first and then walked round them in the darkness. On the morning of the twenty-fourth we were still seeking a cave. We found a small abandoned Korean-type hut and went into it. Unfortunately we were seen, it later transpired, by a small child, who informed the security police.

At about dawn three members of the police came in and sat down and carried on a normal conversation. They were in civilian clothes and tried to give the impression they were ordinary civilians, but we were suspicious. Eventually we stood up and wished them goodbye, and then the three pounced on us.

Frank gripped one of them by the arm and broke his hand. I had a razor with me and took it out and slashed one of the security police through the arm. Then the three of them ran away. We chased them a short way and then turned round and ran ourselves. We could not run so quickly because we were in poor physical condition. We ran through a soya bean field and then after about another quarter of a mile we reached another field where the soya beans were growing close to one another. We tried to rub out our tracks and crawled into the vines. We got into good concealment.

After we had been there about three hours we heard a terrific noise and shouting, and about 150 small children started searching the field. Their ages were between eight and fourteen, and they all had knives. Immediately behind them was a group of armed Korean adults. They flushed us out and all the people jumped on us and tied us up. They tied our hands and in this condition we were marched all the way back to the village where we were handed over to two Koreans from whom we tried to escape. At the time we were walking along a river bank and we tried without success to push them in. They then retied us and put a rope round our necks, tying our heads down so that we had to walk in a bending forward position. We walked about twenty-five miles that day. They took the hobbles off our legs so that we could walk.

Eventually, at about five in the afternoon, they turned us back to the Chinese. One of the Chinese approached and asked me why we had escaped. I just stood looking at him saying nothing and he knocked me down. I stood up again and did not rub my chin, or do anything except look at him. All this in front of about 150 enlisted men. That was the only time I was actually hit.

The Chinese then started interrogating us separately. They wanted to know who was the leader of the escape. We each said that we were. For some reason the Chinese assumed that Frank was. We were then put into solitary confinement, Frank in a building and me in an old latrine. I remained there for twenty-six days. There was no smoking allowed and no privileges, but we received the normal food ration: a bowl of rice and a bowl of soup twice a day. I do not know of any person being shot for attempting to escape.

After twenty-six days we were told that we were being tried. They told us to write a self-criticism and stated that it would not be possible to convert us because we were too old and had been too conditioned. They added that the trial would take place that evening. There was no trial. They merely gathered all the people in the camp in one compound and we had to read our self-criticism over the public address equipment. I didn't write anything, I just said that whatever Frank had written went for me too, and we read it together.

After this sentence was announced. Frank as the leader got six months' hard labour and I got three months' hard labour. This was to be served in a Korean jail we were told. Then they took us back to solitary and at the end of seven and a half weeks both of us were released. We never did see the Koreans.'

Captain Dean also described one of the methods used by the Chinese to discourage escape attempts:

'General Ding, the Chinese commandant of Camp 2, had everyone paraded. He told us that he considered it absolutely impossible for us to escape. Anyone who thought otherwise could put his name on a list and he would be given fifteen days' supplies and two hours' start. In total 105 prisoners out of 130 in the camp put their names on the list. Ding immediately withdrew his offer and put twenty people in jail. This was in June 1952.'

One report which came out with some of the prisoners during Operation 'Little Switch', the first prisoner exchange in April 1953, concerned the building of radios.

'There are plenty of radio technicians in the camps who should be able to build a radio receiver and efforts are still being made in this direction. At the present time in Camp 2, Branch 2, efforts are being made to collect all copper wire, and it is being carefully collected and stored. They did manage to obtain a field telephone and an attempt was made to construct a crystal set, but without success as a rough quartz had to be used instead of a proper crystal. The CCF have now started holding Sunday record concerts. At first they had a hand-cranked machine but now they have received an electric gramophone so they may soon have the necessary equipment to build a set. Lieutenant Alan Blundel of the Dorset Regiment is one of the people working on this project. The frequency they will try and work is the broadcast in English from Radio Tokyo and the *Voice of America* programme.'

THE MURDER OF PRISONERS

Without doubt the Chinese did murder prisoners in their camps. It goes without saying that deliberately feeding the prisoners starvation rations, depriving them of adequate shelter and withholding medical treatment is tantamount to murder, and this occurred on hundreds of occasions. Perhaps murder by maltreatment is an appropriate description of these crimes. Beating a man until he dies of his injuries is also murder in anyone's language. After repatriation in 1953, one American prisoner told war crimes investigators:

'Around the end of May 1951, while in Camp 5, Pyoktong, I saw — beaten with fists, belts and clubs, while his hands were tied behind his back, by Chinese soldiers and political instructors for a period of about one hour. He was then taken inside a building in the prison compound. The next morning I saw his body as it was being taken out for burial by other prisoners. His body was all black and blue and blood-stained. He had a blue mark about half an inch wide around his neck [WO208/4005].'

Corporal Floyd C. Christensen from E Company, 19th Regiment, 24th Division, was captured by the Chinese on 25 April 1951. On 13 May he met another twenty-year old soldier who told him a story about three other unnamed American prisoners. Apparently their Chinese captors had placed Soldier X and two other American soldiers in an unused bunker in an area that was soon to be taken by UN forces. They stayed there for one day and when no one arrived they went looking for food. They went inside a house in a nearby Korean village. While inside a Chinese soldier found the three men and tried to take them prisoner again. The three men overpowered him and one man shot the Chinese. The three men then returned to the previously occupied bunker. After contemplating what they had done, they decided to return to the Korean house to bury the body. While attempting to bury the body they were discovered by three Chinese soldiers. The two men with Soldier X escaped, but he had frozen feet and could not run. The three Chinese took him to their unit and he was subsequently taken to 'Peaceful Valley'. About 1 June Soldier X arrived at the 'Mining Camp' where he was placed in the young soldiers' platoon. On 5 June the Chinese came to the platoon area, tied Soldier X's hands behind his back and read his court-martial details to all those present in English. He was charged with a war crime, having killed a Chinese. He was given no opportunity of defence. Soldier X was then taken to a nearby hill and told to run. He took about five steps before the Chinese officer and three guards opened fire. The helpless man dropped to the ground and the officer walked over and shot him in the head. A detail of American prisoners buried the body nearby.

Corporal Robert D. Smith also had a tale of ill-treatment to tell:

'During the winter of 1951, approximately the first week of February, I, along with about fifty other POWs, was marched out on to a frozen parade ground and made to stand for four hours exposed to extreme cold. We were made to do this because the Chinese Reds in charge of the prison camps were punishing us for losing two pamphlets which they had tried to force us to read. As a result of this many of our soldiers suffered exposure and got pneumonia. This camp was Camp 5, Compound 105, near Pyoktong.'

Doctors Without Medicine

Captured on 27 November 1950, Dr Sidney Esensten and his group took ten days to reach their northern destination, a place named Sombakol. Situated in a valley three miles long and half a mile wide, it was surrounded by cliffs 8,000 feet high. All the traditional Korean buildings in which they were housed had been damaged. A few days after they arrived the Chinese commander sent for Esensten.

'He asked me if I wanted to care for the sick and wounded. Of course, I told him yes. He brought in a Dr Anderson who had been captured on 4 November and we were given two unheated buildings to use as a "hospital".

I want to make it perfectly clear that except for the POWs who were wounded at the time of capture, all deaths in the communist prison camps were caused directly or indirectly by starvation, exposure, torture, purposeful killing and harassment by the enemy.

Our sick and wounded consisted mostly of people who had been hurt during the firefights and brought north. Among these we had seven cases of infected compound fractures of legs or arms, many open bullet wounds and one soldier who had a bullet go through his lung and out the other side. Fortunately he lived. We also treated many for dysentery.

The "hospital's" equipment consisted of four hemostats, two of which clamped imperfectly, and two old-fashioned scalpels. We also had two hook retractors, one bone clamp and one old hand bone saw. We were also given an ancient stethoscope. We had no bandages. The medication we had consisted of powders for diarrhoea, which were Japanese in origin. There was no aspirin, but there was a little methiolate.

The Korean doctor was supposed to keep the medicines, and Dr Anderson and I were supposed to go up and down the valley every day visiting all the prisoners to see who was sick. We were then to determine the illness and list the name of the patient and the medication we felt was required. At night we would give the list to the Korean doctor and he doled out the medication to us. Some days we would get all that we asked for, some days we would get none. It took twenty-four hours before we could treat our patients.

In January 1951 all the POWs from five camps were moved to Pyoktong, which became our main camp. Dr Anderson and I were allowed to set up another hospital. Eventually all the POWs in North Korea came into this area. By March we had a total of about 3,500 men. We took care of them in two "hospitals", which were Korean houses such as we had had in the valley. Neither hospital was heated. We used one for surgical conditions and one for medical cases. Most of the medical cases were related to dysentery and pneumonia.

To give you some idea of where we were, Minneapolis is at the 45th Parallel, which goes through Vladivostok, a Russian base in Siberia. We were approximately at the 42nd or 43rd Parallel, so our temperatures were about the same as in Minneapolis. And, as we lived in the mountains, this even made it a bit colder. It was often between twenty and thirty degrees below zero in our unheated buildings.

In February the pneumonia cases kept getting worse. By March we began to see avitaminosis and many other problems. Our death rate didn't change because we didn't have any medicine, food, heat or shelter to offer these people. We did simple procedures such as amputating soldiers' frostbitten and gangrenous toes and fingers, without any anaesthesia. Most of the men who were captured were not equipped to live in the winter. Most of them were captured wearing fatigues and maybe a sweater. Within four months their socks were worn out, their boots began to wear out, we had no blankets and our food was terrible.

We did surgical procedures with knives we made out of the metal arch supports of our combat boots. At first we didn't have any bandages and when we finally got some we were only allowed to change bandages every ten days to two weeks. The Chinese and Korean doctors claimed that changing bandages was not necessary because a great Russian professor had determined that you don't have to change bandages more than every ten days to two weeks because the wound heals better with pus and maggots.

Early on in captivity our food consisted of corn. This is not sweetcorn as we know it, it's field corn, like we used to throw out to the chickens on the farm. We got this to eat twice a day. In order to make it anywhere near soft enough to eat, you'd have to boil it all day long. But we never had any wood to build a fire to boil it. Once we got into Pyoktong the wood had to come across the Yalu River from China, and there was never enough of it. Even if we had enough wood to boil the corn for twenty-four hours, we could never seem to crack the hard shell. If you ate it this way, it would come out exactly as it went in. This produced an irritative diarrhoea.

Beginning in March we got what was called koliang, grown in Manchuria and Russia. It had a little shell on it that was a bit different to rice. This shell must have contained vitamin B1 because it did help some of our avitaminosis. It tasted terrible, but we gulped it down. Sometimes we got millet, which is what bird seed is made of. In April they began to give us rice, but we Americans cooked the food for ourselves and we didn't know how to cook rice. We would get great big paste balls of rice glue, so we used it as a glue instead of eating it. We would steal paper from the Chinese and paste up the doors in our living area. The rice made good glue, good enough to keep the paper on the door and thus keep the wind out.

Until March we had no utensils to eat with. We didn't have any dishes or spoons. Many of the men would tear tiles off the roofs and use these as plates; many used the inside of their hat as their plate; many just dug in with their hands and ate, just like a baby bringing food to its mouth with its hands. In March they finally gave us a tiny bowl about the size of a cereal bowl, and one little Korean spoon.

Korean Atrocity!

What kind of medical diseases did we see? All of us had lice and scabies. Most of us had roundworm, which is about three inches long and probably about the width of a fountain pen. We'd pass these worms, which wasn't so bad. The problem is that one of the cycles of the ascaris is that it also gets into the bloodstream, and it would come through the lungs. We'd cough them up, then have to pull them out of our mouths. We also had tapeworms.

Between the lice and the scabies, we all scratched and ended up with impetigo. This was not the simple impetigo you see in some of the youngsters in your practice or in the hospital, these were very large ulcerated lesions. They wouldn't heal because of the avitaminosis. If they did heal, we got great scarring and abnormal discoloration.

We had three kinds of dysentery. One was infectious, which I am sure was E. coli, salmonella and shigella, characterised by severe diarrhoea, severe cramps, watery and bloody stools and high fever. We also had irritative dysentery, which came from the uncooked corn as well as the uncooked soya beans, which they gave us occasionally. Soya bean has a lot of protein in it, but it must be cooked completely to be of any value. If you don't cook it well enough, you get an irritated diarrhoea. We also had psychogenic diarrhoea. We didn't have diarrhoea in the daytime, but the minute the sun set over the mountains we immediately began to see this dysentery because the fear of night was tremendous. As most of the men would die during the night, everyone went to sleep wondering if they were going to get up in the morning. This dysentery would occur eight to fifteen times a night.

And then we had psychogenic urinary disease, the same sort of thing as psychogenic diarrhoea. Their fear of the night had men going eight to ten times a night. These men had to run out of their rooms without sufficient warm clothing in the thirty-degrees-below-zero temperatures, run to our latrines, which we set about fifty yards away from where lived, and move their bowels or urinate, and then they'd turn round and run back. They were constantly in and out, all night long. This contributed to our pneumonia. It also made our frostbite and gangrenous toes and fingers much worse.

By March we began to see avitaminosis effects, because corn, koliang, rice and millet don't contain very many vitamins. The first one we used to see was cheilosis of the mouth, where the corners of the mouth would crack and bleed. Then we saw beefy red tongues, which is due to vitamin B deficiency. We had bleeding from the gums and urinary tract from vitamin C deficiency, and I'm sure that some of the young men had scurvy due to lack of vitamin C.

We also had night blindness due to vitamin A deficiency. This really gave us trouble because if you had night blindness and you had to run out to the latrine you had to ask a friend who didn't have night blindness to lead you. You went with one hand on his shoulder until you got to the latrine. We'd see people four and five deep, because when the word went out that someone was going who could see, everybody would follow because that was the only way they could get there. They couldn't go by themselves. If they tried they'd fall into the latrine because it was just an open pit with two little boards on it. You squatted on the board and that was it. We did have some people fall into the latrine and they came out pretty messy. We also saw people who were developing permanent blindness due to retrobulbar neuritis as a result of vitamin B deficiency. These people are still blind.

There are two kinds of beriberi. One is called wet and one is called dry. Dry beriberi is characterised by joint pains, bone pains and some peripheral neuropathy and mild oedema [swelling]. Wet beriberi is characterised by huge amounts of oedema. Sometimes a boy's legs would be huge (three or four times the normal size), their scrotums would be full of fluid and would hang down to their knees and their abdomens would fill up with fluid. And then we would have beriberi heart, which occurs because the fluid interposes between the muscle fibres of the heart, weakening it and spreading the mitral and aortic valve. Men would develop murmurs and some would die from heart failure.

Then we had pellagra in which we got blisters all over our body. Pellagra has a triad that's characterised by dermatitis, dysentery and dementia. Some people became markedly demented. This is also from vitamin B deficiency.

Our fracture treatment early in our captivity was nil. We could do nothing but try to push any fractures back into place by touch, without any such thing as X-rays. All we could do is take some rags and try to wrap them up and hold them in place as best we could. After July 1951 we'd get food in wooden boxes. We would use these boxes to enclose fractures. Some of our men were excellent carpenters and they used to whittle these boxes down into shapes we wanted. So we put the arm or leg in the box and wrapped it up, and they walked around in a box.

Then we had a problem due to a Chinese torture which produced nerve injuries – we would see wrist drops. One of the favourite Chinese treatments was, instead of tying your hands behind your back at the wrist, they would tie them way up high on the humerus. They would tie them as tight as they could; of course, that would obstruct the blood vessels and the nerves. If that wasn't bad enough, they would then take a rope and tie it to the rope on your arms, throw it over a rafter, wrap it around your testicles and then yank you up off the ground. That was every time they were mad at you, or any time they wanted to get something out of you. Of course this produced a tremendous number of wrist injuries with a wrist drop. All we could do was find some wire and mould it so we could cock these kids' wrists up in extension. They stayed that way for

months, and most of them fortunately returned just by that simple procedure.

The other times when wrist drop occurred was when the Chinese
would get mad at you and tie you around a tree with your arms behind
you. They usually did this to you in the cold weather. Most of the time
we didn't have to worry about wrist injury because you usually died in
two to three days standing out in the cold that way. The first man who
died that way was an army major. The only crime he committed was
when they started to talk to us about indoctrination. He said, simply,
about their indoctrination, "This isn't worth the paper it is written on,"
which is a very common phrase in America, but the Chinese took it as a
personal affront against Chinese paper. They tied him to a tree and he
died.

We began to see an increased number of pneumonias. By February
1951 we were beginning to see twenty-eight to thirty-five kids dying of
pneumonia every day. The average age of the prisoners of war was nineteen to twenty. We had seventeen-, eighteen- and nineteen-year-old kids
with us and when they died we tried to keep records of their names. The
Chinese destroyed these records because we put down the word "starvation" or "malnutrition" or "pneumonia" and this implied that they
weren't taking care of our people. In their minds they were giving us food
and medicine and shelter.

Every morning I had to get up and do what I called Ghoul Parade. I
would go around the entire camp to get the names of the people who
had died and try to keep the lists. At this time I had to do this alone
because Dr Anderson had developed severe dysentery, pneumonia and
encephalitis. I sat up all night long and took care of him, because he was
too weak even to go to the latrine. I had to pick him up and carry him.
We never had less than 350 cases of pneumonia a day in the camp.

As things got worse we began to see hysteria, all kinds of hysteria from
visual, telescopic vision and inability to move hands and arms to
complete paralysis from the neck down and complete coma. Some men
were actually completely paralysed apart from being able to move their
eyes and talking. They would not respond to usual pain stimulus. There
wasn't much we could do for them, unless we could catch them early in
their paralysis or before coma and get some buddies to get them out and
walk them day and night and force-feed them until they began to eat.

We didn't do too well with that kind of severe hysteria until, suddenly,
one day I got called to see a young second lieutenant who had just been
brought into the camp. I had known the man before we came to Korea
and had struck up quite a friendship with him. When I walked in and
saw him I was so damn mad at him for allowing himself to get into this
hysterical state that I just lost my temper. I hit him in the jaw, and then
I hit him three times, and by God he woke up. I personally fed him, and

he lived, only to die of starvation later on, but he did live through that episode. From then on anybody who got hysterical coma or paralysis got hit in the jaw three times. It's not the kind of medicine you learn in medical school, but it was effective.

In the spring of 1951 we began to see lots of hepatitis. At that time there was a tremendous epidemic in North Korea of typhus and smallpox. The Chinese Army was decimated. They lost about 20 per cent of their troops and were so afraid that we would die that they decided to give us immunisations. However, they only had one syringe and one needle and did not even bother to wipe the needle with alcohol between each injection. The third man who got the shot among the officers was in the process of developing hepatitis and in two weeks 20 per cent of the officers had full-blown hepatitis.

Then we had the most interesting thing of all, called "give-up-itis" or, in psychiatric parlance, "face-the-wall syndrome". The morale of the men was such that whether you were sick or not you felt you were never going to go home and morale began to drop tremendously. To try to give the men a boost we tried to blame everything on their lack of motivation. But it's hard to motivate a seventeen-, eighteen- or nineteen-year-old boy because their fathers and mothers are not enough motivation to go home. We did better with the older men who had wives and children at home. They survived much better than the younger ones. All these kids had been sick with pneumonia, dysentery, hunger or avitaminosis and when their depression set in we had to come up with a name for it, and 'give-up-itis' they would understand.

The first sign of the affliction was that they would not eat their corn or whatever we got without drinking ice-cold water from the stream or well. Then they wouldn't talk to anybody, then finally they would lie down and cover their head with whatever they had and turn their head to the wall. They wouldn't eat at all, they would only drink cold water. From the minute they drank cold water with the corn or rice or koliang, you could accurately predict that in three weeks to the day they would die. It turned out to be true every time. Only two things would help them. First, if they had some very close buddies who noticed this desire to drink water and would be willing to walk them day and night and force-feed them, we could save them. Second, and the best way, was to make them mad at the doctor. If they got mad enough at us for calling them all sorts of names, they would want to get up and eat in order to be able to get enough strength to beat up the doctor.

Another phenomenon was the premonition of death. People who were relatively well would tell the men in their rooms, "Don't bother to wake me up in the morning, because you will not be able to get me up." One hundred per cent of the time they were right.'

INDOCTRINATION

Dr Sidney Esensten again:

'About this time the Chinese began their indoctrination programme to convert people to communism. The young men were resisting their indoctrination because they told the Chinese interpreter, "You don't really want us to stay alive. Look how many men are dying." One day a Chinese general called Dr Anderson and me in and said, "We demand that the death rate be stopped immediately. We will provide you with all the necessary material plus better food, and we demand that within two weeks there be no deaths."

For this tremendous help to stop the death rate we got 1,000 tablets of sulfadiazine, 1,000 tablets of sulfaguanidine and two million units of penicillin. We didn't get the food he promised, the blankets, the heat or anything. Because they were afraid that their indoctrination programme was falling apart they wanted to convince the men they were really interested in them. They woke me up at midnight in a raging snowstorm to tell me that the medicine had arrived. The Chinese doctor wanted to treat thirty men with the two million units of penicillin, but not only was it not enough, they did not want me to treat the sickest in the hospital. They wanted me to go around the five different areas where the enlisted men lived so they would all know the penicillin had arrived.

After a long argument we compromised that I could treat ten men, instead of the three that I really wanted to treat. The three were moderately sick and I thought if I treated them they might stay alive. Forty other men were to be treated with sugar water, to make them think they were receiving penicillin.

We had to go out in the raging snowstorm with a Chinese interpreter and they warned me that if I said anything about who got the penicillin and who got the sugar water they would shoot me the next day. They wanted the people to think it was all penicillin. The worst part about all this was that all ten men who got the penicillin died, as well as the forty men who got the sugar water. I had to play God that night and try and decide to whom I would give whatever little medication we had. I didn't like that and it is one of my common nightmares.

Then there was another peculiar disease we had that made us all afraid that we were abnormal. We lived with life and death so peculiarly that all of us laughed about death and kidded about dying. As more and more people died, the stimulus of the fear of death increased, which was what the Chinese wanted as part of their indoctrination programme.

We could not dig in the frozen ground to bury our dead. Instead we laid them on the next hill from our camp. We covered them with rocks in order to keep the Korean dogs from chewing them up. The Chinese ordered that we put them on the next hill where we could see them from our camp. As the number of rock mounds increased, the stimulus of fear of death increased. When there were enough mounds the Chinese felt we would then be ready for indoctrination.

Indoctrination, or brainwashing as we called it, was an attempt to convert prisoners of war into communists. This was the first time in the history of US military service that American prisoners of war had been political prisoners and not military prisoners.

Indoctrination theory is based on Pavlov's theory of conditioned reflex. Pavlov was a Russian physiologist. His conditioned reflex experiment was done with a dog. He made an opening in the dog's stomach so he could collect gastric acid. He would feed the dog and collect gastric acid, then he would feed the dog and ring a bell at the same time. Eventually he would just ring the bell and the dog, thinking he would get food, would respond by pouring out gastric acid. Therefore, with his conditioned reflex he could guarantee a response by the dog. He could guarantee that a certain stimulus would get a certain response.

The Chinese believed the same thing could happen with people. Their stimulus, of course, was our fear of death, starvation and malnutrition. In other words, if we didn't behave or agree to their philosophy they took away whatever little food we had and denied us what little medical care we had.

As more and more people died and the stimulus of the fear of death increased, we thought it wouldn't be harmful to listen to their indoctrination programme. By this time they had broken us down to the point where none of us could think beyond four-letter-word invectives and none of us was strong enough to walk across the room to say anything to try to resist. At this point they thought we could accept foreign ideology. We would not accept it until we were physically and morally broken down to that point.

They also made it worse by separating all the young soldiers, the privates, the corporals and the sergeants from the officers. The reason for this was that most of us were college graduates and knew something about Marxism, but these young kids were barely out of high school. They didn't have any idea of political history, political economics or anything. The Chinese used Ph.D.s in political science to indoctrinate these kids. How could these young kids argue against these political Ph.D.s? Some of us officers gave them a good run for their money, but the kids couldn't do anything, so they had to listen and believe.

The indoctrination programme consisted of lectures, reading material and discussion groups constantly from when the sun came up until it set. This happened every day from March 1951 until negotiations were finally settled on 27 July 1953. There were four main topics: (1) The wonderful life in Russia and China under the communist regime. But they forgot to mention the fifteen million Chinese the communists killed in the first year they took over China; (2) Political economy and Marxist philosophy. I really enjoyed this because I could sit and argue with them because I knew something about this subject; (3) America was decadent and there was nothing good about the country. They claimed we didn't have democracy in our country – all we had were slums. No one had cars and houses and no one had nice living. The few times we did get some mail (in three years I received seven letters from my wife) our wives would send pictures of our homes and our cars and we'd show them to the Chinese guards. They were impressed and finally told their company commander about it. The next time they would not look at the pictures, just shook their heads in disbelief. Their commander had told them that the American government had sent the letters as propaganda, that the cars and homes and so forth didn't really belong to the wives, they were just being used for the pictures and then were taken back afterwards. Of course the Chinese peasant soldiers believed them; (4) Germ warfare. The history of the Far East, of course, includes recurrent plague, cholera, typhus and smallpox. The Chinese were claiming the Americans were dropping germs that caused all these epidemics. The Chinese actually tried four American air force officers for dropping germs and forced confessions from them.'

OVER THE HILLS AND FAR AWAY

During the three years of fighting there were two major periods of British Army losses. The first occurred in January 1951 when the Royal Ulster Rifles and the 8th Hussars suffered heavy casualties during the Battle of Happy Valley. The next took place in April 1951 when the major part of the 1st Battalion, the Gloucester Regiment and a smaller number of Royal Northumberland Fusiliers were overrun during the battles around Gloucester Hill. During November 1950 a small number of men from 41 Royal Marine Commando were captured while serving with the 1st Marine Division, but prior to that action Commonwealth losses were negligible. After April 1951 the Commonwealth forces suffered small losses at intermittent periods until the cessation of hostilities in July 1953. Of all the British prisoners taken during the war, the most prolific and successful escapee was the adjutant of the 1st Glosters.

Captain Anthony Farrar-Hockley squatted on his haunches and surveyed his new surroundings. He was inside one of two bunkers built halfway up a hillside. The doors were iron bars set in thick pine logs and fastened with padlocks. The walls, ceiling and floor were lined with pine logs, impossible to cut through. Two guards and one NCO were on duty outside. As the captain would soon discover, any movement in the cell at night would provoke instant verbal admonishment by the guards. At the slightest sound from the straw mat on which he lay a flashlight would be shone through the bars, and if he was out of luck a long, sharp, steel rod would be poked at him. Escape was impossible.

However, two days later he was moved to another village and a new bunker and this seemed a better prospect. The doorway was simply an opening into which an oil drum would be rolled. The only light which penetrated the bunker was from a narrow space at the top and down one side of the oil drum in the doorway. The bunker itself was a primitive affair, not built for western guests. It had been dug into the hillside at an angle of about forty-five degrees and the roof was so low that the prisoner could not sit up inside. He could either lie down or half-sit, resting on his elbows. The guard could only see inside the bunker by moving the oil drum aside, thus giving ample warning if one was ignoring the regulations and dozing in the daytime. Or, in Farrar-Hockley's case, digging.

There were no logs lining the new bunker, only straw thrown across the dirt floor. For two days he worked on his tunnel, carefully scattering the dirt across the floor, under the straw. One evening, on returning from a trip to the latrine, he was horrified to see two Chinese officers inspecting the inside of the bunker with flashlights and poking at the walls. One of the Chinese spoke to him in a very angry voice and shook his finger at him. The second officer emerged with a stone in his hand and joined the other man examining the outside of the bunker. Was that one of the stones which concealed the entrance to the tunnel? Eventually the men left and Farrar-Hockley was returned to his new home. Nothing more was heard from the officers and that night the human mole went to work again.

By the fourth night the tunnel was almost finished. As usual the majority of the village garrison had climbed the hill opposite the bunker to sing songs in praise of their leaders or in denunciation of their enemies. Farrar-Hockley crept to the oil drum and put his eye to the crack. The guard was standing by a tree, looking up at the heavens. Now was the time. Crawling to the far end of the bunker he removed the stones and surveyed the end of the short tunnel. It would be a tight squeeze and he would have to remove another foot of earth at the end, before he broke out on to the hillside. He worked quickly and with only a few more inches of mud to clear he wriggled back into the bunker to check on the sentry. He peered through the crack. Twilight was now descending and it was hard to make out the tree. The sentry had gone.

A shadow fell across the oil drum as the sentry halted right outside the bunker. Farrar-Hockley froze and waited with bated breath to see if the sentry would come in and shine his torch around the cell.

Eventually the shadow moved away and minutes passed before he could be seen standing by the tree again. There was no time to lose. He slid back into the tunnel and thrust his hand through the mud at the end, feeling the chill of the night air as he dragged his body through the opening. Peering over the top of the bunker he could see the sentry twenty feet away. He had his back to the bunker and was talking to a friend nearby.

Not daring to breathe, Farrar-Hockley crouched and slowly made his way to the field of maize nearby. He pushed the cold, wet stalks aside and began to crawl up the hill towards the bushes on the upper slopes. Five minutes later he emerged from the bushes and reached a burial clearing just below the crest of the hill. He leapt to his feet and ran across the clearing and down a path that led between the fields beyond. The night air smelt of freedom as he headed for the hill to the north.

Between April and November 1951 Captain Farrar-Hockley made six escape attempts. On his sixth attempt he was accompanied by two other officers, but was caught while his companions continued on their way. The Chinese tortured the captain to try to persuade him to divulge their escape plans. For days he suffered what is known as the Japanese water treatment, during which a towel is placed over the head and shoulders of the person concerned and water is poured on to the towel until it is no longer possible to breath and a sense of drowning is induced. Captain Farrar-Hockley was not permitted to pass out completely and was brought back to awareness by the application of lighted cigarettes to his bare back. At the same time he underwent many periods of severe beating and kicking while bound and blindfolded. After six days of this treatment he had still not disclosed the route or plan of the escapees.

THE KENNEL CLUB

The boxes were five feet long, less than four feet high and just wide enough for the occupant to lie on his back. For some of the men five feet was not enough and they had to sleep on their back with their knees bent. There were five of the wooden boxes in the room. Lance Corporal Mathews was in one, an American medical orderly named 'Doc' McCabe was in another. Tom Cabello, another American, was near the door, from where he could see the approach of the guards, while thinking back to what might have been. He had escaped on his own and covered over 200 miles in nineteen days before he was recaptured, almost within sight of friendly lines. Doc McCabe was being punished for trying to reconvert prisoners who had fallen for the Chinese propaganda. He was also an inveterate chicken thief, with dozens of the tasty fowl to his name. Mathews, one of the Gloucester Regiment, was suspected by the Chinese of being a member of the escape committee and was consigned to the Kennel Club to cool his heels until he confessed.

There were four other rooms adjacent to the main room. In one was US Air Force Master Sergeant Jack Gauldin, an observer in a T-6 Mosquito spotter plane that had been shot down over enemy lines. He had been in the room for nine months. Another room was occupied by Corporal Bob Shanwell of the 1st Cavalry Division. This brave man had been tied to a beam and beaten with wooden staves for two days in an attempt by the Chinese to extract a 'confession'. The third room was empty, but the fourth contained two men: American Sal Conte and Derek Kinne, the Royal Northumberland Fusilier who would not bend and would not quit.

He had previously ruptured himself while using a wooden barbell to train for his escape. Thrown into a storeroom jail for threatening one of the 'progressive' prisoners, he had broken out to join two others in an escape attempt. Richards and Brierley had already left when night fell and Kinne had decided to follow them. He struggled for eighteen miles before his rupture brought him to a halt. He was recaptured the next morning and interrogated by the Chinese who wanted to know who had helped him to escape and what the plans were for the other two escapees. Kinne would not talk.

A rope was thrown over a beam and a noose placed around Kinne's neck. His arms were tied behind his back and one leg pulled clear of the ground, and all three limbs tied to the other end of the rope. The Chinese then left. If Kinne slipped or fell, he would strangle himself. By the time the Chinese returned a couple of hours later Kinne realised that his ruthless captors meant business. He agreed to tell all, or rather write all, on condition that he was left alone to write his confession. Overjoyed that one of their toughest prisoners had agreed to co-operate, the Chinese gave Kinne food and cigarettes and three whole days to complete his literary masterpiece.

Finally the Chinese had the confession in their hands. Entitled 'Goldilocks and the Three Bears', the tome was eighteen pages long and told the story of how Goldilocks had become disillusioned with conditions in her communist motherland and, together with the other bears, had left to sample freedom in the capitalist West. Kinne was beaten, then beaten again and again. Then he was thrown into a hutch in the Kennel Club.

It was now 20 August 1952. Fusilier Derek Kinne had been in the new block for only five days when he had his first real argument with his new guards. The daily diet was two meals of watery rice and on some days it was more water than rice. Being at the end of the line that day the bucket was almost empty when his turn came to collect his ration. The guard dipped the ladle in and filled Kinne's bowl with the watery concoction. He protested and asked for some rice. The guard kicked the grille in the door petulantly and threw the contents of the bowl back into the bucket. When he refilled it a second time there was not a grain of rice to be seen. Kinne lost his temper and the guard lost his also. The guard NCO appeared and ordered the Fusilier to stand to attention. He was about to refuse when he heard fellow prisoner Air Force Master Sergeant Gauldin's wise voice whisper, 'Do it, Kinne.'

Kinne stood at attention for six long hours. Under normal circumstances this was no mean feat, but the ceiling was under five feet in height so he had to stand with his shoulders and neck bent forward as well. Eventually they brought along the next meal, and this time he was given koliang and mouldy turnip tops. Thinking that his punishment had ended, Kinne sat down after the meal. The guard NCO ordered him to stand to attention again. Kinne refused and requested to see the officer known as 'Crab' to complain about his treatment.

The three guards let him out and took him to the rear of a building about a hundred yards away, where they stopped. Nobody moved; they all seemed to be looking at one another. 'Look,' Kinne said to the guard NCO, 'I'll give you five minutes. If no one goes for the instructor by then I'll go myself.' About ten minutes later the position was unchanged and Kinne began walking towards the Crab's office. The guards leapt on him and a fight began. As the guards dragged Kinne back towards his cell, the Crab appeared.

The officer was in a great rage as he ran towards them, strapping on a large Mauser pistol in a wooden holster. He ordered the guards to face Kinne towards the wall and began to beat the back of his neck and shoulders with a greasegun. As Kinne shouted his protests to the officer, the Crab redoubled his efforts, each blow forcing the prisoner against the wall. Suddenly there was a sharp explosion and everything became quiet. The gun had been cocked and, shaken by the blows, the mechanism had come forward, firing the round in the breech.

A terrible change came over the Crab. His muddy eyes turned from Kinne towards the terrified guards, his body gave a convulsive jerk upwards and the ugly, bulging head followed suit. His mouth was thrown open, exposing his gold-filled teeth, and he clasped at the bloody hole in his shirt. As the blood spurted through his clutching fingers he fell at Kinne's feet with a little moan. Death came quickly to the Chinaman.

Kinne was dragged away by the guards and over the next month he was beaten longer and more severely than any other prisoner taken during that long war. But he would not die.

After three months in the Kennel Club, Mathews found himself on his own. The others had all been sentenced for their 'crimes' and moved elsewhere. A note left for Mathews in the latrine by a sympathiser informed him that he may as well confess as the Chinese now had all the information they required on the escape committee. Finally he did so, and spent another freezing month in his hutch before he was taken away for a show trial and sentenced to a year in prison for his 'crime' of being a member of the escape committee.

Seven

Stalemate

More Prisoners Required

By the beginning of 1952 the war had ground to a halt with the opposing armies facing each other roughly on the 38th Parallel, where they had been eighteen months before. In order to counter UN superiority in air power, the Chinese went underground. Vast caverns were built to house tens of thousands of men and the Chinese became experts at camouflaging the thousands of artillery pieces in their armoury, many of them captured earlier from the Americans.

Another year and a half would pass before the peace agreement was finally signed. During that time many more men would die, others would be taken prisoner and some would disappear for ever. The static nature of the war meant a lack of intelligence about the enemy's plans and prisoner 'snatching' became a useful tactic to both sides.

On the afternoon of 29 February 1952 a platoon of ten men from the Royal Norfolk Regiment led by Corporal Ashling went forward into no-man's land to obtain firewood. The corporal was in the lead, with Private Pantrini behind him, when he entered a partially destroyed village. Before the following members of the patrol entered the village firing broke out and some thirty Chinese rose from hiding and over-powered the two leading men and rushed them away. Three Chinese held each prisoner, while one who appeared to be an officer said 'Quickly, quickly' – the only English spoken by the Chinese. A Chinese soldier who had been wounded in the head by Corporal Ashling tried to murder him, or at least injure him, but was stopped by the officer and had his burp-gun removed from him. The incident was being watched by a Royal Artillery forward observer through his field glasses and within seconds British twenty-five-pounders began to engage the fleeing Chinese. In the resulting confusion Corporal Ashling and Private Pantrini both made a dash for their own lines and escaped. The Chinese fired at them as they were running, but scored no hits. The Chinese then made off.

Second Lieutenant Jonathan Wormald, also from the Royal Norfolk Regiment, was wounded during a fighting patrol against a Chinese position on the morning of 30 May 1952. The location was about eighteen kilometres north-east of the town of Chandgan near the village of Kajanhari-Saemal on the west bank of the Imjin River. Despite an intensive search of the ground by his regiment he was not found. It was later learned from an intercepted wireless message that the Chinese claimed to have taken two British prisoners that morning. Lance Corporal Guess was the other prisoner taken that day. He was being held in a Chinese slit trench when the lieutenant was carried past on a stretcher with a three-inch-diameter wound in his left ankle. His head was hanging back, his eyes were closed and he appeared not to be breathing. The Chinese have never given any information about Wormald nor even acknowledged capturing him. On 8 November 1954 an Interim Death Certificate was issued by the War Office.

Atrocities continued to take place on the front lines during 1952. On 21 September an American artillery forward observer team and a squad of South Koreans were in place on Hill 854 near Samchi-yong. Their position was overrun by the enemy but was recovered the next day in a counter-attack. The bodies of two US soldiers, horribly mutilated, together with those of several South Koreans, were discovered. The lieutenant who found them made the following affidavit:

'One of the boys had no head. It seemed to have been mashed or beaten and was lying all over the road. Both of his feet had been cut off about halfway between the knee and the ankle. It appeared as though they had been chopped off with a dull instrument. He had no means of identification on him. I searched him for dog-tags, clothing markings, belt markings, shoes, ID tags and personal effects in his pockets, but nothing was to be found.

The other GI had his eyes gouged out, and nothing remained where his eyes were except holes. He had been bayoneted all over the body with the upper part of his legs completely laid open to the bone. He also had no marks of identification on him.'

Apparently the bodies of the South Korean soldiers had received similar treatment, one of them having had the genitals severed with a sharp instrument – they were lying alongside the corpse. One can only imagine the terrible suffering to which these victims were subjected (KWC1670).

On the night of 22/23 November a reconnaissance patrol of one officer and two men of the 1st Battalion, Durham Light Infantry, were lost in circumstances which indicated that they had been captured by the Chinese while lying up in an observation position, with a radio set, behind enemy lines. As a result of their failure to complete their mission a patrol raid connected with their reconnaissance was abandoned. However, at 2359 hours on 23 November an intercept was obtained from the Chinese commander warning his troops to stand by for an attack between 0300 and 0400 hours. This was the time planned for the patrol raid. It was very unusual for a raid to be carried out at that time and place, and although a similar command was intercepted the following night, it is thought to be more than coincidental. It is probable that the captured patrol were successfully interrogated as to their mission within twenty hours of being captured. They were never seen again. They are still carried on the British Missing in Action list, now buried in the depths of the Public Record Office in Kew.

This incident was noted by the Royal Air Force AI9 liaison officer at British Commonwealth Forces HQ in Korea (AIR40/2642). The intelligence officer wondered if a change in the Chinese attitude towards prisoners of war was indicated. It was thought that the Chinese placed their main emphasis on indoctrinating prisoners with communism and to that end they treated them reasonably well. Now he wondered, was emphasis being placed on obtaining tactical military information as quickly as possible, using force to obtain it?

Another case involved Major P. B. Stephenson of The King's and Second Lieutenant D. A. P. Clark of the Royal Army Service Corps. It was a dark night on Monday, 30 December 1952 when Stephenson set off on a reconnaissance patrol with Clark. While a small patrol can sometimes move around in no-man's land easier than a large one, there is no substitute for firepower when the enemy is encountered. The duo set off around 1700 hours along the bank of the Samauon River and then crossed a creek between Samauon and Point 76, heading up a valley towards the enemy. Lieutenant Clark later reported:

'About 300 yards up the valley we turned back a few yards and stopped to have a rest in a gully. It was then about 2130 hours. While we were in the gully Major Stephenson looked around and then said that he could hear some Chinese on a bank above the gully. I looked round and said that I would see what I could do when the communist patrol leader shouted some orders and I was fired at by a burp-gun. The first burst hit me. The patrol, which was about ten strong, had not seen the major, who was still in the gully, while I was on the opposite bank, and the major was in between me and the enemy. After being hit I lay doggo. I heard a lot of jabbering and about a minute later the enemy patrol pulled out. I waited about three minutes and then crawled over to where I had last seen the major. There was no sign of him. I whispered loudly for some response and got none. I then crawled back to the battalion. I think the enemy patrol snatched Major Stephenson and then went off with him.'

The next day a search was initiated but no sign was found of Major Stephenson, and nothing more was ever heard of him.

Lieutenant Edmund Radcliffe also disappeared in Korea. Trained as a solicitor, he joined the army and went out to Korea with the Durham Light Infantry. He volunteered for every dangerous mission that came his way, and on the night of 16 April 1953, at the age of twenty-eight, he prepared to go out again. His unit was dug in on Hill 355, a key position on the Commonwealth line. Together with an Australian private, J. K. Christie, he set out on a night reconnaissance patrol to spy on the Chinese lines 1,000 yards across the valley. Later, shots were heard and the private radioed back, 'The boss has been wounded in the leg but we are going on.' That message was the last contact the unit had with the men. Patrols were sent out at first light to search for them, but without success. In 1954 Edmund's sister, Georgia, received a letter from the War Office which read: 'The situation about Edmund is that there are roughly 100 officers and other ranks missing in Korea and still not accounted for. Steps are being taken to make another approach to the Chinese with a view to getting more information. I would rather you did not discuss the question of this diplomatic approach to the Chinese, except in confidence, for obvious reasons.'

Edmund never came home.

A Summer's Day

By the spring of 1952 conditions had begun to improve in the prisoner-of-war camps on the Yalu River. The peace talks had begun and the Chinese realised that the men were valuable bargaining chips that should be taken care of. The indoctrination campaign was coming to an end. One school of thought suggests that the Chinese had given up their efforts as a failure; another more likely scenario is that the Chinese now knew which men would continue to resist their captors, who would go along with the Chinese for the sake of peace and quiet and, more importantly, who could be converted to the communist cause.

In 1955 a book was published in the People's Republic of China entitled *Thinking Soldiers – By Men who Fought in Korea*. The editors were former British Royal Marine Andrew Condron and US Army Sergeants Richard Corden and Larance Sullivan – three of the twenty-one soldiers who had elected to remain behind with the enemy at the end of the war. The 250-page book is an eye-opener to anyone carrying out research into the behaviour of British and American prisoners in communist hands during the Korean War. It contains the writings of more than a few prisoners, usually with their names omitted so as not to draw attention to the men who by now were back home in England and America.

One of the pieces from the book is reproduced here so the reader can compare the lot of the resistors such as Derek Kinne and Bob Shanwell with the life led by those who embraced the communist line. It is entitled

Korean Atrocity!

'A Summer's Day' and was written by an unnamed British trooper in the form of a letter to his folks back home.

'Good morning friends! No doubt many of you at home have been wondering just how we POWs manage to while away our time. Well then, why not spend a day with me, on tour of Number Five Camp, North Korea. We will make our day a Saturday in August 1952. Saturday is no particular day; except in a slight variation of games, every summer's day is the same.

The time is six o'clock and the clanging of our company bell has just aroused us from our peaceful slumbers. After roll call and ten or fifteen minutes' brisk exercises, we fall out and return to our rooms. Breakfast is not until eight-thirty, so what shall we do? What's wrong with a stroll down to the sports field, or better still, to the river? If it's to the river we're going, then let us take a towel and soap. What's that! You'd like a swim? Sorry, no swimming until twelve. You see, there's odd jobs to be done in the company area during the morning. But look across the bay – there's some of the boys fishing, and if I'm not mistaken I can see Bob Parker and Albert Spurr. Come on! Albert's just pulled one out. Morning boys! What's your catch? Albert's quite cheerful, but Bob replies with, "Not a bite yet." Well folks, this won't get us a wash!

As we finish washing the sleep from our eyes, we can hear drifting through the misty haze on the river music from the public address system. A sign to us that in five minutes' time world news will take the air. We're all keen for the news and a brisk walk back brings us nearer to the PA. The news is on and once more we are greeted with more disappointments from Panmunjom. Ah well! It cannot last for ever. There's still an hour to go before breakfast, so what about a game of cards, or maybe you would like to finish the book you drew from the library yesterday. Please yourself! The PA system goes quiet, your book is interesting . . .

We are awakened once more to life when breakfast is announced. Breakfast consists of rice, with bean, pork and potato soup, made quite tasty by the cooks. While breakfast is on, the soft strains of the Blue Danube Waltz drift around the camp. A quiet smoke follows and then we are ready once more to continue our tour. By now the sun has taken a warming position in the sky. What's that! You need a shave? I could do with a haircut myself, so let's pop round to the barber's shop. As we step from our house you can see the mist rising rapidly from the river, to be lost in the mountain tops. A sure sign of a scorching day.

The barber shop is fairly full when we arrive. David Fulton and Sid Carr are already on the job. We'll wait a while and listen to the conversation. Yes, it's a typical English barber's. All the latest news is being discussed, and look, there's a lad passing some snaps around. He

186

received them last mail-call. Anyhow, it's your turn for a shave and mine for a haircut.

Well, time is marching on, and with thanks to the barber we take our leave. But where now? What's wrong with the reading room? They tell me there are new papers in, and some new magazines. That's fine, the newspapers put us in touch with home. Of course they're not right up to date, for many miles separate us from our homeland. Just the same, we are very grateful for them.

Having digested the latest "blighty" news, we leave the reading room. We find, confronting us as we leave, the daily news board on which you can read the day's events. Let us step over and see what's on! Why! At twelve-thirty there's a basketball and also a volleyball game. Two o'clock, a whist drive; six o'clock – ah! now we're really getting somewhere – a soccer match, the Rest versus England. And to round off the day, advertised in technicolour, a Grand Open Air Dance. Looks like we're going to have a busy day. Anyhow, what's the time? Twelve o'clock? Just time for us to visit the library and change our books. We find quite a varied selection and, taking our choice, depart with two

By 1953, conditions had begun to improve in the camps. Here four American prisoners read letters from home. Left to right: *Lt Billy B. Foshee, Lt Hayward Cameron, Capt. William McTaggart and Capt. Gerald Fink.*

world-famous novels of Dickens and Hugo. Being twelve o'clock, what about a dip in the river? Oh! But wait a minute, I almost forgot. There's a midday snack and there goes the bell to announce it. Sweet rice doesn't take long to put away and we quickly gather our towels and make for the river.

The basketball and volleyball games are already in progress, but by now the sun has reached its height and the clear blue river calls. The sides of the bay are crowded as we undress and plunge into that cool, refreshing and very soothing water. In half an hour we find ourselves refreshed and cool enough to endure the closing stages of the basketball game. The volleyball players are already in the river after playing a very hard game. The game we're watching finishes, and – hark! there's a familiar voice calling. Yes, it is Jack Green, and he's calling the boys for the whist drive. Would you care to join, or perhaps you'd rather sunbathe? You may prefer the whist drive. For myself, I'll sunbathe, so cheerio until tea-time.

The heat of the sun soon forced me to sleep and that was how you found me after the whist drive. What's that you say? Tea is ready? Well, let's go then! On our way back to the house we see a crowd gathered around the noticeboard. A crowd like that can mean just one thing: a mail list is up. Wonder if we are lucky? A quick glance tells us that we both have letters. But did you notice the many disappointed faces as we came away? Yes. Hope they are luckier next time.

On entering our room we find not only our tea waiting but also our sugar and tobacco issue. Soap is due tomorrow. Putting our tobacco and sugar away, we sit down to tea. A very tasty salad along with steaming bread and pork and potato soup. No sooner have we finished our tea than we hear the voice of Charlie Elliott – "Come and get your mail." A mad rush ends with a letter from the wife and, along with it, four snap-shots. Yours is from the wife too. Good! Our spirits go even higher.

Here, come on, we must hurry, the football match is shortly due to start. As the players take the field, we move to a seat on the "sea" wall. A fast and furious game follows, every man striving to do his best and be one better than his opponent. The sportsmanship is of the highest class, giving our referee a very easy game. After a brilliant last effort the Rest just manage to pull off a 2–1 win and I'm sure that you enjoyed every minute of the game. There is just time now for a wash before the dance. Oh yes, I forgot to ask – how did the whist drive go? You managed to take third place. Not bad! That will be some extra fags anyway.

The evening wears on and the first darkness is now giving way to the moon, as it climbs steadily into the already starlit heavens. A bell sounds in the distance, to be followed by our own. That means it is half an hour to lights out. The band strikes up the Anniversary Waltz – the last waltz. It is now that your thoughts turn back to the letter which you received from the wife, and the memories of the last waltz you had with her. As the band finishes the number the boys make their way slowly back to their rooms. But we've still a little time, so what about a last glimpse of the river? Making our way down to the "sea" wall, we are quiet – our thoughts are at home. Everything is silent, but for the sound of water lapping the shore. Then the silence is broken by the barking of a dog and the distant braying of a mule. The river rolls on to the open sea – to freedom and liberty.

With but five minutes to go before lights out, we must hurry to bed. By the way, are you feeling tired? Yes, but surely not too tired to lie down and dream for a few minutes – it happens every night. Just a few minutes alone with your thoughts, your wife, your children, your sweetheart. You pray that it will not be long before this whole wide world will sleep in a peaceful repose, without that dreaded fear of war.'

RESISTANCE

Private Godwin of the Glosters could not have been aware that such a fairytale kind of life was being planned for him and his fellows by the Chinese in January 1952. They had just instituted a curfew, and when Godwin realised that this would interfere with escape activity he started a protest in which a letter demanding the raising of the curfew was written. As a result he was taken to a Korean jail where he remained from 1 February to 15 March. He was required to sit cross-legged between 0700 and 2300 hours each day, in solitary confinement. The floor was concrete and the room was unheated, and no warm clothing was issued.

On 2 June he was jailed again for 'illegal activity'. He was handcuffed and placed in a wooden coffin-type box three feet by two feet by five feet. This box was not water- or wind-proof and was exposed to the elements. He was allowed to use the latrine five times a day, although in practice this worked out to twice. His food was eaten inside the box. After ten weeks he was interrogated, then put into another box on 4 August. He remained inside the box for four more months before he was released.

Godwin was forced to wear handcuffs from June 1952 to 12 February 1953, with only a ten-day break. His wrists would later bear the scars of where the flesh had grown over the wire. Unwilling to confess to a 'hostile attitude' he was not returned to the camp until 8 June 1953, just before the ceasefire was agreed.

Corporal Holdham of the Glosters also refused to give in. He had won the Military Medal during World War II and planned to make use of his extensive experience of operations behind enemy lines to get him back to friendly lines. On the evening of 14 May 1952 he escaped, together with Privates Devine and Tozer from the Glosters. They lay up in the hills until it was safe to move on; however, on the fifth day Tozer said he could not stand it any longer and Holdham was persuaded against his better judgement to go down to the valley. They were seen by several peasants but none of them was hostile; nevertheless Holdham still felt they were better off in the hills. Tozer refused to return with the other two and subsequently surrendered to the North Korean police, having attracted a large collection of children.

Soon Holdham and Devine were recaptured. It later became apparent that the Chinese had been given information about the escape by a collaborator. They knew the course taken by the men and their destination and that Holdham had a map. The corporal was later beaten with a baseball-type bludgeon for five-and-a-half hours one night by a Chinese guard. He was supposed to remain at attention stripped to the waist while the guard belaboured his back.

Oscar Cortez was another prisoner of war destined to miss the special communist treatment of afternoon tea and whist drives. In the spring of 1952 he and a few other GIs were taken to another part of their camp to join Company 4, where the reactionaries were held. There were approximately fifty Americans of Mexican descent and they usually spoke in Spanish to the Chinese. He told the author:

'Sometimes when we went to bed someone would shout that whoever got up in the morning was a SOB. When morning came the Chinese would come by and holler "Get Uppo!", but we would stay in bed. They never tried to force us to get out of bed. Also, whenever we got the guitars, two guys would play and sing Mexican songs. When the time came for us to go to bed the Chinese would say "Sleepo!" Someone would say that when the song ended we would go to bed. So when that particular song would end, the guys would change tune and continue with another song. That went on until we got tired and then we went to bed. After the armistice was signed a guy by the name of Belhome, one of the twenty-one GIs that stayed behind, told a few of us that the Chinese were afraid of us because we were always united and they didn't know what to do about that.'

MAY DAY

The communists decided that May Day 1952 was to be a special occasion for the prisoners of war in Camp 1 at Chongsong. They would be given special rations, football matches would take place and a concert would be held. In return for this the communists wanted the men to march through the village carrying a number of red flags. This was refused, but a compromise was reached whereby a Chinese colour party would be placed well ahead of the column for the benefit of the official photographers. It was decided that a good feast would be well worth the price of supplying the Chinese with some propaganda photographs.

The concert that day was to end in nothing short of a riot. The master of ceremonies was Sergeant 'Bill' Sykes of the Glosters. A true cockney and possessing the unrelenting wit of his ancestors, Sykes was on top form that night. Assisted by Private Keith Godwin, who acted as his 'stooge' in the audience and heckled repeatedly, Sykes would make such replies as, 'We utterly and absolutely reject the unreasonable demands of your side of the footlights,' and 'This show is still running due to the ceaseless efforts of our side and in the face of frivolous demands by your reactionary side.' This attempt to parody the phrases likely to have been used by the communists at the peace talks at first confused the Chinese interpreters sitting at the back of the audience. It was not long before they caught on.

Sergeant Sykes then told a joke which truly put the cat among the pigeons: 'They tell me that Mao Tse-tung died the other day. When he arrived at the gates of heaven, he met St Peter. "Who are you?" asked St Peter. "I'm Mao Tse-tung." "Who?" "Mao Tse-tung." "Well you can't come in here." "Why not?" "Because we aren't going to the trouble of cooking rice just for one."' The audience erupted in laughter,

Men of the 1st Glosters at church parade, taken by Padre Sam Davies just before the Imjin Battle. Note that in the background an urgent conference is beginning at battalion HQ.

191

but the interpreters at the back understood the joke and were livid. Then Sykes followed up with a poem: 'They seek him here, they seek him there, they seek for Mao everywhere. Should he be shot, or should he be hung? That damned, elusive Mao Tse-tung.'

The sergeant was dragged off the stage by the Chinese, but the resulting uproar was so great that he was released and the concert ended in chaos. Yet again it demonstrated that if the prisoners presented a united front to the Chinese they would back down rather than cause a riot with its unpredictable consequences.

RELIGIOUS INTOLERANCE

The communists ignored the provisions of the Geneva Convention for the duration of the war, including Article 34 which states that prisoners of war 'shall enjoy complete latitude in the exercise of their religious duties, including attendance at the service of their faith'. Furthermore, Article 35 says that 'chaplains who fall into the hands of the enemy power . . . shall be allowed to minister to the prisoners and to exercise freely their ministry among prisoners of the same religion'.

What was the reaction of the Chinese to the chaplains and the religious rights of the prisoners of war? During 1951 three American chaplains arrived at Camp 5 and two died within a short time. The third, Father Kapaun, whom we have met before, was not permitted to take part in any religious activity, but he did anyway, despite being branded by the Chinese as a troublemaker and reactionary. He too died in the summer of 1951.

In October 1951 Padre Sam Davies of the Glosters arrived at Camp 2, Branch 1. By then the peace talks were underway and as a result the Chinese were allowing religious services. The vacuum which had existed earlier had been partially filled by Captain James Majury from the Royal Ulster Rifles, who carried on religious activities as best he could. He had previously been threatened with death for reading the burial service over men who had died on the long march north to the camp.

In February 1952 Padre Davies was forbidden to visit the sick and found himself in hot water with the Chinese for allowing 'God Save the King' and the 'Star Spangled Banner' to be sung after the Easter Sunday service. Although he had been holding them for six months, the services he held in the middle of the week were banned by the Chinese as an 'illegal political activity'. His captors insisted that Sunday was the 'holy day' for Christians and the padre would have to confine his religious activities to that day only.

The Chinese gradually increased their pressure on the padre and from the summer of 1952 until he was released in September 1953 Sam Davies underwent a long series of threatening interrogations and an eighteen-day period of solitary confinement. Thrown into a cell six feet long by four feet wide, Padre Davies wrapped himself in his outer coat and blanket and lay down to sleep. The next morning he discovered that he had two neighbours, Captain Farrar-Hockley and Corporal Abbot, a young US Air Force NCO who had been in solitary for months because he would not 'confess to germ warfare'. He was extremely pleased to learn that a chaplain was in the next cell, and Padre Davies was able to give him both moral and spiritual consolation during their conversations through a hole in the wall.

On his first Sunday in jail Padre Davies waited anxiously for some sign that a church service was being held, despite his absence. Suddenly the faint sound reached his ears of 300 men singing 'Holy, Holy, Holy, Lord God Almighty'. The men had crowded the lecture room to overflowing and made a mass defiant protest against the removal of their padre. On 28 August he was returned to his parishioners.

PRISONERS OF THE UNITED NATIONS

By the time the peace talks began in July 1952 the United Nations held 170,000 North Korean and Chinese prisoners of war. What was to be done with them all? Many clearly did not want to fight for their communist masters, but they had no choice in the matter. The decision was made to screen the prisoners and ask them whether or not they wanted to return home. Surprisingly four out of five Chinese and three out of five North Korean prisoners of war declared that they would forcibly resist any attempt to return them to their homelands.

From a strategic point of view, if the war spread to other lands, including Europe, how many Asian and European troops would rally to freedom and turn their guns towards Moscow? The Chinese prisoners had only known civil war in their country and the North Koreans had suffered four decades of foreign domination, first by the Japanese and then by communists. They had never experienced life in a democracy, nor exercised the right to make decisions which would affect their future well-being.

The possibility that in future wars the communists might lose vast numbers of men to the call of democracy could severely inhibit the war plans of the leaders in the Kremlin and Peking (Peiping). It was too good an opportunity to miss. Two million North Korean civilians had chosen to flee to the south when the Chinese invaded at the end of 1950. How many of the prisoners of war could be converted to democracy?

The reader might pause here and compare the treatment of the prisoners in both communist and UN hands. The Chinese began by starving UN prisoners and increasing the food ration in relation to the amount of attention paid to their indoctrination instructors. 'You feed, we listen' was a common phrase mentioned to the author. On the whole communism had little to offer the American or British prisoners, and although many would sign peace petitions or parrot communist phrases, how much was due to the better food and treatment given to these converts? There were others who embraced the communist cause because of persuasion or genuine belief and collaborated or informed on their comrades to improve their standing with their captors. But when the final count was made, only twenty-one American and one British prisoner decided to remain in North Korea at the end of the war.

The treatment given to the 'reactionaries' and those who resisted communist indoctrination has been recorded on earlier pages in this book. In contrast, those Chinese and North Koreans who declared their wish to return home were spared ill-treatment by their UN captors. Why waste time and effort trying to convert these men to democracy when there were so many others queuing to see what was on the other side of the fence?

Communist prisoners of war digging a drainage ditch in their new compound on Kye-do Island, under the supervision of men from the 1st Battalion, King's Shropshire Light Infantry.

In October 1952 the decision was made to release 38,000 of the prisoners on the grounds that they were really civilian internees, rather than prisoners of war. Many were South Koreans who had been impressed into the North Korean Army against their wishes and who had surrendered at the first opportunity. This reduced the prisoner population to around 130,000.

A pilot rehabilitation project had begun at the end of 1950. By the time the Chinese decided to enter the war there were 80,000 North Koreans in the UN POW compounds and 500 were picked to represent a cross-section of the prisoners. Their participation was voluntary and anyone could return to his quarters if he desired, without reprisal. For the first time in their lives many of the men were taught to read and write. Others were taught skills which would be useful to them, such as carpentry and blacksmithing. This in itself was a revelation to the prisoners, for such skills are usually handed down from father to son in a society where apprenticeships do not exist. It took a while to persuade the blacksmiths and other skilled men to share what they knew, but when they did and realised that they had now been elevated to the position of teacher as well, their enthusiasm knew no bounds.

For once the North Korean and Chinese prisoners of war could appreciate two of the mainstays of democracy: the right of free speech and the right of choice. The programme was then extended to all prisoners and directed by psychological warfare experts, but the prisoners themselves knew first-hand what brainwashing was about and could tell the difference between that and what the Americans were trying to do. As the days went by more and more of them resolved to fight to the death to resist being returned to North Korea or China.

One cannot help but wonder whether the number of UN prisoners of war returned by the Chinese would have been larger if the Americans had taken the decision to return the majority of the communist prisoners following the ceasefire, regardless of whether they wanted to go or stay. It is clear that UN prisoners were being taken across the border into China long before the peace talks began, but were the numbers subsequently increased when the communists realised that the majority of their men would not be returning home? More to the point, did the UN commanders know this was a possibility when they rubber-stamped the rehabilitation programme? Did anyone consciously decide that the loss of perhaps two or three thousand extra American prisoners was worth the conversion to democracy of 50,000 communist soldiers?

THE SON-YI HOLE

It was 22 December 1952. Lance Corporal Mathews was cold and stiff as he walked out to the truck. It was time to leave the Kennel Club and begin his one-year 'jail' sentence for being a member of an escape committee. His spirits rose as his old friends Sal Conte and Richard Upjohn climbed aboard, followed by an American named Joe Hammond, one of the original reactionaries. The journey took two days and ended at Son-Yi, a penal camp for the worst reactionaries. The new guys were taken to a small thatched house and ordered inside. This was The Hole. Sleeping figures stirred as the newcomers stepped across the crowded floor. Old friends appeared from the darkness: Doc McCabe and, surprisingly, Derek Kinne.

The next day was Christmas Day. The men were fed boiled rice and soya beans. There were seventeen men now in the hole, twelve Americans and five British, crowded into one ten by ten room with a small charcoal burner in the centre. These men were the toughest of the tough. Ed Osborne was a tough hill-billy from North Carolina who took it upon himself to re-educate those men who embraced the communist cause. He formed a one-man rock-throwing committee and found many victims among the progressives with his unerring aim, before the Chinese arrested him. Bob Shanwell and three of the others were of a similar mind and tried to beat some sense into those who were turning their coats. They eventually suffered terrible beatings themselves at the hands of the Chinese interrogators.

Life at Son-Yi was hard. The 130 men in the penal camp were there to be punished. They were beyond conversion to the communist cause. For the men in the hole, lack of food was the worst privation, with just two buckets of rice or sorghum per day between seventeen men.

In February the spectre of death hovered close again. It was the birthday of one of the Americans and the men in the hole had a sing-song to celebrate. Unfortunately they chose to include a verse along the lines of 'hanging Mao Tse-tung' and incurred the wrath of the camp commander. As a punishment their food ration was decreased and the fuel for their stove was stopped. This was serious. They were in the middle of a cold, hard winter and the temperature at night fell as low as forty degrees below zero. Inside the hole a layer of frost built up on the inside of the walls and the men's breath froze on their beards.

Drastic steps were required and the men began to take the outside latrine apart, stick by stick, hiding the pieces of wood in their clothing. When that was nearly gone they took apart the wall which divided the two rooms in the house and some of the ceiling rafters.

Two weeks passed and the Chinese refused to reinstate the wood allowance. The men in the hole put their heads together and came up with a plan. 'Doc' Frazier thought of it first. 'If someone was really ill with pneumonia or something like that, the Chink doctor would have to tell the camp commander. If he has been ordered to keep us alive and we can scare him enough, we may get the wood back!' They decided to give it a try. John Hartigan, the first British prisoner in the hole, was selected to be the patient. He was tall and thin and after charcoal had been used to produce shadows under his eyes and DDT powder applied to his face, he looked like death itself. Soap rubbed under his armpits would produce a fever and a cigarette made out of shom, a narcotic weed, temporarily increased his heartbeat.

After the unfortunate Hartigan was shown to the guard, the camp commander and the doctor appeared, together with an interpreter. As the patient lay shivering and gurgling on the floor, Doc Frazier briefed the Chinese doctor on his symptoms. The Chinese doctor knelt down and examined Hartigan 'Severe pleurisy,' he announced. 'You must keep him warm.' Doc Frazier pointed out that this was impossible since there was no wood, and when the man died it would be the fault of the Chinese People's Volunteers. A hasty discussion followed and the camp commander left, promising to do what he could.

Hartigan was playing cards when the doctor returned and just had time to resume his position on the floor. The doctor placed a hot water bottle at his feet and announced that the wood ration would be restored in the morning. That evening they were given a large bucket of rice instead of the nauseating sorghum. They were even given a few apples.

Life became a little more bearable as the peace talks ground slowly to their conclusion.

EIGHT

HOPE AT LAST

OPERATION 'LITTLE SWITCH'

On 13 December 1952 the Executive Committee of the League of Red Cross Societies, meeting in Geneva, adopted a resolution proposed by the Indian delegate that recommended the sick and wounded prisoners be exchanged in advance of a truce. The proposal was put directly to the communists in February 1953, but no reply was received. Then, on 5 March, Joseph Stalin died and China and North Korea realised they could make their own decisions without looking over their shoulder at Big Brother in Moscow. On 28 March the communists not only agreed to exchange sick and wounded prisoners, but proposed a resumption of the truce negotiations which had been suspended six months previously.

The communists used Operation 'Little Switch' for all the propaganda value they could obtain. Not only did they withhold the most seriously sick and wounded UN prisoners, in order to make the world believe that they had been treating the prisoners well, but they also sent back many prisoners who they thought had been won over by communism – so-called 'progressives'.

The exchange took place in April 1953 at Panmunjom, where communist ambulances would drive to a chalk line fronting a series of reception tents. The sick and wounded were counted and a receipt given for their delivery. A brief medical check followed to ascertain whether each man could stand the forty-five minute ambulance ride to Freedom Village, or whether he should be taken by helicopter. The two Freedom Villages, one for ROKs and the other for American and UN POWs, were huge compounds with processing and hospital tents. General Mark Clark, then the Commander in Chief of the United Nations Command, was there to welcome each of the 149 American prisoners home. A total of 684 UN prisoners were returned, including thirty-two British, and in exchange 6,670 North Koreans and Chinese were sent home. It later transpired that an additional 234 sick and wounded non-Korean POWs and 141 South Korean POWs that should have been repatriated were kept back by the communists.

The first US airman prisoner of war to be exchanged by the communists was A/2C Robert L. Weinbrandt. Handed over on 24 April, he was flown to the Tokyo Army Hospital in Japan for treatment. The twenty-year-old was a tail gunner on a B-29 bomber, taking part in a bombing run on supply and billeting installations in the vicinity of Pyongyang on the night of 28 January 1953. After the bombs were dropped the aircraft turned for home, but it was intercepted minutes later by enemy MiG fighters. It was night, and the only targets the gunners could aim for were the gun flashes from the incoming fighters. After four or five passes the bomber caught fire with all four engines and gas tanks burning furiously. When the aircraft commander ordered a bail-out Weinbrandt had to crawl from the tail gun position to the rear escape hatch. Three others went through the hatch first and Weinbrandt was the last man out. Once on the ground the airman was captured within a few hours. He had sustained shrapnel wounds to both feet during the attack, but the enemy would not treat his wounds. For the eighteen days during which the airman was moved to the rear areas and interrogated, his wounds were neglected. Finally he was taken to an enemy prisoner-of-war hospital and his feet were amputated by Chinese doctors (AIR40/2642).

On their way home during Operation 'Little Switch' in April 1953, 1st Cavalry Division platoon leader First Lieutenant Roy Jones (left) and Sgt Gerald Neighbors (right).

As he waited for his turn to be called forward to the Freedom Gate, Sergeant Walter E. Bray Jr thought about the things that had happened to him during his thirty-seven months in Korea. The first four months were spent fighting with the 34th Infantry Regiment and later the 19th Infantry Regiment after the 34th had suffered so many casualties they had actually retired their colours on the battlefield. The last thirty-three months had been spent as a prisoner of war. On his return to New Jersey he would speak of his experiences.

'We were among the first soldiers to fight the North Koreans. We only had 2,000 men when we should have had 12,000. Our vehicles kept breaking down. I had a rifle that did not fire and had to take one off a dead soldier. We were experienced soldiers, but we did not have the equipment to back us up. The country was tired of war. After thirty days of battle just 160 of the original 2,000 soldiers remained. We were slaughtered. We were running out of ammo and were not supplied with food. We had to eat out of the fields to stay alive. If you saw a comrade dead the first thing you had to do was take his ammunition. After re-inforcements arrived, the United Nations forces started winning until the Chinese entered the war. By then I was a platoon sergeant.

I was severely wounded on 4 November 1950. After my unit was overrun I was left behind because I could not walk. Two hundred others were captured with me. We were forced on a death march to North Korea. Fellow American soldiers helped me; I hopped on one leg and sometimes was carried piggy-back style. If you fell down you were shot and left on the side of the road. My foot swelled up and I had to cut off my boot. Chinese soldiers took the other boot and I had to walk bare-foot. The clothes on my body froze. It took us three weeks to reach a small village at the end of North Korea. We lost a man a mile on the way. They fed us just a few ears of raw corn and no water. We ate snow to survive.

In the prison camp we were dumped into small mud huts. It was fifty degrees below zero and we still wore summer uniforms – no jackets or coats. Survival was an agonising, painful existence. I could not walk for fourteen months and my weight dropped to eighty pounds. At Camp 5 I saw over 1,800 comrades die that winter. Friends died lying alongside me during the night, while we huddled to keep warm. Some just gave up because of the pain and the meagre existence we lived. Others, including myself, were tortured, some maimed for life; part of my ankle was blown off on 4 November and my big toe was cut off at the camp with shears. There was no medical treatment in the camp, nor any Red Cross.

One day in the middle of winter they took my clothes away and threw me into a hole on the edge of the mountain and put boards and rocks on top. When I came to my buddies were trying to restore my circulation – I had been in the hole for ten days without food or water. I don't know how I made it out of the prison camp alive. It must have been my willpower to live and my hatred for the enemy. My life has been one of remembering those left behind and what they gave on behalf of their country.'

When his turn came Walter Bray was escorted forward by two Chinese guards. Two American military police walked towards them. 'Am I free now?' Bray asked. 'You sure are son,' replied the MP. At that, Bray stripped off all his Chinese prison clothes and threw them at the Chinese guards. Then he went for the forty-five-calibre pistol on the MP's belt and wrestled him to the ground in an attempt to obtain the weapon and settle the score. The eighty-pound soldier was overpowered by other MPs and led away to freedom. On 29 April 1998 Sergeant Walter E. Bray Jr passed away. He was sixty-seven years old and the recipient of four Purple Hearts.

As the returning prisoners were debriefed, the war crimes investigators began to plot charts and gather statistics in an attempt to establish the

Bravest of the brave. General Myong Song, a Korean veteran, and Staff Sergeant Walter Bray, pay their respects during the ceremony to dedicate Interstate 287 as the Korean War Veterans Memorial Highway in June 1995.

fate of many of the missing men. Much of the information received from prisoners of war returned under Operation 'Little Switch' was very difficult to evaluate since it was taken at a time when many of the prisoners were in a state of shock and exhaustion and their memories were not too reliable. Also, many of the men suffered from deprivation, exposure, neglect and hardship to such an extent that they were physically incapable of observing what went on around them. However, the information was still of great value, if considered with reservations.

The prisoners of war who came back from 'Little Switch' had much to say about death marches and deaths in the prisoner-of-war camps. A

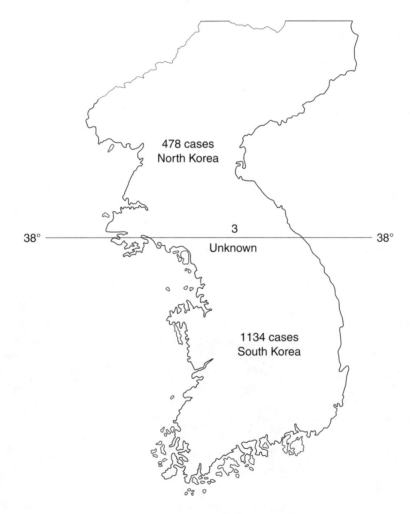

478 cases
North Korea

3
Unknown

38°

38°

1134 cases
South Korea

Sites of reported war crimes

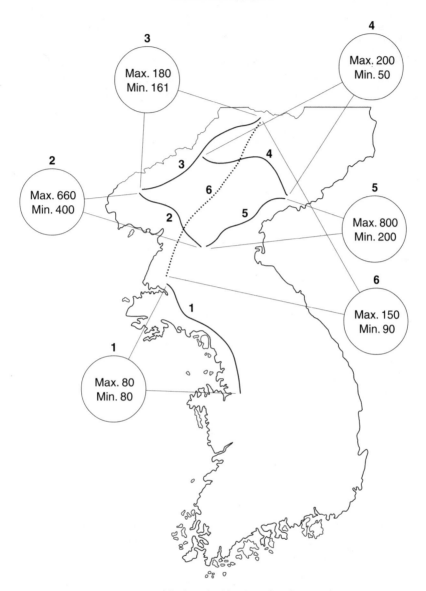

Victims in Korean death marches

Key

Death march 1. Suwon to Pyongyang
2. Tokch'on to Pyoktong
3. Pyoktong to Singalpajin
4. Death Valley to Manpojin
5. Tokch'on to Death Valley
6. Pyongyang to Singalpajin

chart was compiled to reflect the American casualties, based on a few lists that were smuggled out and the memories of those who returned. Maximum and minimum figures were established, and as at the end of June 1953 the death toll known of up to that time amounted to 2,384 maximum and 1,057 minimum. The statistics were based on six death marches.

At this time the reader should pause and be made aware that these facts appear in the Korea War Crimes Division Extract of Interim Historical Report cumulative to 30 June 1953, i.e. four months before the bulk of the prisoners came home to add their stories to the files. A

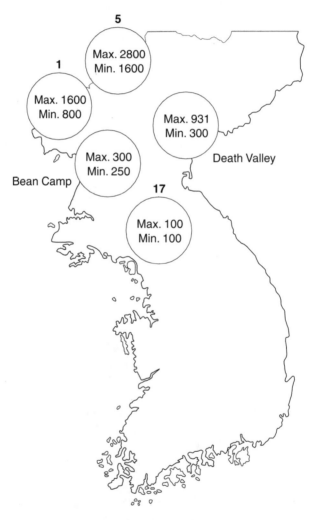

Victims in POW camps

later and more updated report has yet to be found. The report itself did not list the various death marches by location or date and the topographical map 'Exhibit P' supplied with the report is poorly drawn and annotated. It also seems to have missed some of the death marches previously mentioned, including that of the poor men who died in the Sunchon Tunnel. However, for the moment we will deal with what we have.

According to the report, the six main marches which saw the demise of the greatest number of men were: Death March One, from Suwon to Pyongyang which was given a maximum and minimum figure of eighty men dead, reflecting the accuracy of the reports on that incident; Death March Two, from Tokch'on to Pyoktong, was one of the worst, with a maximum of 660 and a minimum of 400 dead; Death March Three, from Pyoktong to Singalpajin along the line of the border of North Korea and China, cost a maximum of 180 and a minimum of 161 deaths recorded; Death March Four, from Death Valley to Manpojin, led to a maximum of 200 deaths and a minimum of fifty; Death March Five, from Tokch'on to Death Valley, was responsible for a maximum of 800 and a minimum of 200 deaths; the longest march of them all, Death March Six, from Pyongyang to Singalpajin, was 150 maximum and ninety minimum.

The death rates in the prisoner-of-war camps were equally shocking. A maximum of 5,731 and a minimum of 3,050 were recorded. Most, if not all, could have been saved if their captors had fed them adequately and treated their wounds. It was estimated that in Camp 1 a maximum of 1,600 and a minimum of 800 had died; in Camp 5 a maximum of 2,800 and a minimum of 1,600. In the Bean Camp the figures of those who died were a little more exact with a maximum of 300 and a minimum of 250. In Death Valley a maximum of 931 and a minimum of 300 reflected the conditions in that awful place. Lastly, at Camp 17 the maximum and minimum were both set at a hundred, reflecting the certainty about the fate of the men who died there.

While the information on the death marches and camp deaths was comparatively new to the investigators due to the fact that they had taken place deep inside North Korea, the information on the atrocities was more detailed, many taking place in the south. On 30 June 1953 the War Crimes Division files contained 1,615 alleged atrocity cases. The sites were plotted on 1:250,000 maps of Korea. This revealed that 1,134 incidents occurred in South Korea, 478 in North Korea and in three cases the location was too indefinite to be determined as either North or South Korea.

The cases were then screened to ascertain the nationality of the perpetrators. This revealed that the North Korean People's Army was responsible for 1,164 while the Chinese Communist Forces were the instigators of 439. In twelve cases it was impossible to affix nationality on the basis of the available evidence.

In the summer of 1952 the War Crimes Division requested 1,082 investigations through the Home Ministry of the Republic of Korea, forwarded 574 check forms to the Graves Registration Office and ordered its own investigators to make 525 field trips. The search was on to build up as many war crimes case files as possible and to reinvestigate the sites of such crimes that were still accessible to the United Nations.

Altogether, 57,559 atrocity victims had been reported in war crimes case files and of these it was the opinion of the legal officers that 29,815 was the 'probable' accurate figure. The bodies of 10,032 known victims had been recovered, and 533 survivors had returned to provide living proof of the acts. From approximately 57,000 atrocity victims there were 10,233 reported American victims, of which 6,113 were listed as 'probable'. Only 511 bodies had been recovered and 216 survivors returned to tell the tale, excluding any returnees in Operations 'Little Switch' and 'Big Switch'.

One interesting paragraph which followed the above items on page thirty-six of the report went as follows: 'Three primary causes have resulted in the release from restriction or confinement of Chinese or North Korean individuals implicated in war crimes. They are closure of cases, Operation 'Little Switch' and the mass break-outs from UN POW camps of June 1953.' In the absence of any other clarification the author can only assume what is being suggested here. Remember the confessions made by surrendering enemy personnel? 'Closure of cases' presumably means that some were let off the hook when perhaps the site of the alleged atrocity could not be located. Operation 'Little Switch' suggests that some of the suspected war criminals were among the thousands of communist POWs exchanged for the small number of UN POWs who came home in April 1953. Rather careless perhaps, in view of their alleged crimes. And the mass break-outs of June 1953 may also have accounted for the disappearance of some subjects. Again, rather careless. Surely of all the communist prisoners of war those involved in war crimes were the most valuable, to be separated and guarded at all costs?

The report from which this material was taken was dated 30 June 1953 and no updated or revised report has been located as of the time of writing. A report was compiled for presentation to the United Nations General Assembly by Henry Cabot Lodge Jr in December 1953 (reference no. A/2563 dated 26 November 1953) but it consisted mainly of statements from survivors and investigators and contained little in the way of statistics. It is very likely that, since war crimes trials could not be held as there was no clear victor in the war and many of the perpetrators once in custody had flown the coop, the files and any later reports would have been consigned to a dusty storage basement some-where in Washington DC.

Operation 'Big Switch'

The final four months before the ceasefire was agreed saw one crisis after another. In May the communists gave such indications of bad faith and evasiveness that General Clark was given authority from Washington to terminate the talks and continue with the war. All the while South Korean President Syngman Rhee was threatening to wreck the peace talks. One can understand his resentment: Korea was still divided in two, but now he had over a million Chinese facing him across the 38th Parallel.

The main issue blocking the signing of the armistice was the communists' insistence that all prisoners of war be exchanged, whether they wanted to return home or not. It was becoming clear that not all Chinese or North Koreans wanted to return home, with a consequent loss of face for their governments. Should the UN force them to go back? At the

Free at last. Corporal Harry C. Gennaro of the 8th Cavalry at Freedom Village on the 38th Parallel on 12th August 1953.

end of World War II the Allies forcibly repatriated tens of thousands of Russian soldiers who had been captured by the Nazis. Stalin wanted them back, but they knew he planned to punish them for being captured in the first place – a bullet in the head for the officers and ten years in a Siberian labour camp for other ranks. The ill-feeling that this created behind the Iron Curtain caused the supply of enemy defectors to dry up for some years after the end of the war. Why defect or surrender to the Americans if they only send you back, they asked?

Eventually it was agreed that any prisoners who did not want to return home would be handed over to representatives from a neutral country, in this case India, where they would remain for ninety days while their governments subjected them to 'explanations' and tried to persuade them to come home. Thereafter they would revert to civilian status and the neutral Commission would help them relocate to a new home. President Rhee did not agree with this, though; as far as he was concerned on the day the armistice was to be signed any North Korean who did not want to return home would be set free to live in the south.

Just after midnight on 18 June the ROK guards at the four main POW camps threw open the gates and the first of 25,000 North Koreans who did not want to be repatriated walked out into the night. Outside the gates they were met by ROK soldiers and police and given civilian clothes and directions to hiding places in private homes. By the time US troops took over the camps the North Korean POW population had dropped from 34,500 to less than 9,000.

The Chinese response was not slow in coming. The Chinese launched their most violent offensive in two years and fired so much artillery at the UN lines that they appeared to be using up all the shells they had stockpiled during the two years since the front had stabilised. The Chinese threw three armies totalling almost 100,000 men against five ROK divisions of half that number and pushed them back several miles until UN artillery stalled the offensive. The fighting continued into the early days of July and clearly shook President Rhee's determination to continue the war without the UN if necessary.

The armistice was finally signed on 27 July 1953, and on 5 August Operation 'Big Switch' began with the first exchange of prisoners of war 'desiring repatriation' by both sides. The United Nations Command began the transfer of 75,823 enemy POWs (70,183 North Koreans and 5,640 Chinese) directly to the communists in the de-militarised zone (DMZ) and the communists began the transfer of 12,773 Allied POWs, including 7,862 South Koreans, 3,597 Americans and 1,000 British, in return.

The following day the Commander in Chief of the United Nations Command, General Mark Clark, flew back to the United States and held a news conference in the Pentagon. *The New York Times* reported his concern regarding the true number of prisoners believed to be in communist hands: 'General Clark pledged to press the communists for further information on the additional troops he believed they held and for a possible exchange. He said that he pointed out the wide discrepancy between his information and that supplied by the communists on prisoners during the truce negotiations. He had been advised by his superiors in the Pentagon, he said, not to delay the armistice negotiations over the discrepancy but to reserve the privilege of later protest.' As far as General Clark was concerned the only way of obtaining any results on the missing prisoners of war question was by the application of force, and in that respect his hands were tied. It was with great reluctance that he announced at the press conference that he would retire from the army on 31 October 1953.

One of the men still missing was the son of General James A. Van Fleet, commander of the US Eighth Army in Korea. On the day after General Clark's press conference he stated: 'A large percentage of the 8,000 American soldiers listed as missing in action in Korea are still alive.' His statement was confirmed by a 10 August 1953 Combined Command for Reconnaissance Activity Korea (CCRAK) memo, which

Going home. UN prisoners queue at Freedom Gate for processing.

stated that a compilation of reports indicated that during the past two years several POWs had been transferred from POW camps in North Korea to points in Manchuria, China and Siberia. These points included Mukden, Harbin, Antung, Yench'eng, Chiamusso, Miensien, Peking, Shanghai, Chungking, Timesin, Canton etc. Figures also showed that the total number of MIAs, plus known captured, minus those to be repatriated, left a balance of over 8,000 unaccounted for.

By 27 August it became obvious that very few officers were being returned by the Chinese. It was encouraging to see that some of the men who had long been thorns in the side of the communists, such as Kinne, Hartigan and Godwin, had been released, even though they had been given jail sentences by their captors for their 'crimes'. But as of the twenty-seventh not one British officer had been released.

On that day General Clark sent a message from his headquarters in Tokyo to the Joint Chiefs of Staff (ref. no. CX64657). In the four-page message Clark wrote that the communists had not yet given a clear indication as to whether they would return all UN captured personnel, including those they alleged were guilty of post-capture offences. On the other hand the UN still held a number of enemy officers, war crimes suspects and post-capture suspects and witnesses – mainly fanatical communists who had taken part in riots, murders and other such disturbances in the poorly policed UN prisoner-of-war camps.

The war crimes and post-capture suspects could have been held indefinitely by the UN, but there were disadvantages in pursuing that course of action. The value of a hostage depends on the desire of his masters to secure his return. If the communists had their reasons for keeping UN prisoners of war, the fate of the communist prisoners in UN hands would have been of no concern to them. From a practical point of view, of the 418 enemy war crimes suspects then still in UN hands it was considered that a successful prosecution for war crimes would be assured in only thirty-nine cases, all of them North Korean soldiers. In addition General Clark assumed that any war trials crimes would be conducted by a United Nations Command military commission rather than a US military court, and that in the post-armistice period they could not guarantee their allies would be represented on the court. In other words any non-American or non-British judges and juries at any war crimes trials may show a great deal more leniency towards the suspects than those from the nations who had lost so many men in the atrocities.

One of the suggestions in Clark's report was that the UN made a 'flat offer for a one-time exchange of all remaining POWs, including pre- and post-capture offenders. If the communists refuse, we would convene the trials'. Another suggestion was that after 23 September, the last day open for repatriations, they 'make a public announcement here, with simultaneous release in Washington, to the effect that the communists have flagrantly violated the solemn pledge to return all POWs as specified by the armistice agreement, but the UNC will not be a party to such action and, therefore, will return all communist POWs, including war crimes and post-capture personnel'.

It was quite clear that General Clark was trying hard to find a way to persuade the enemy to return all prisoners of war still in their hands, even if it meant returning the remaining war crimes suspects as well. Indeed the Joint Chiefs of Staff also discussed at that time other methods including a blockade of Chinese ports. However, the UN prisoners of war the Chinese had earmarked to be kept for ever were of more value to them for internal propaganda and intelligence purposes and they had no intention of sending them back. Nor, for that matter, had the Russians, who had already collected their share of the prisoners of war. It eventually became clear to the Joint Chiefs of staff that, short of renewing the war, there was no way they could persuade the communists to return all their men. Surprisingly, though, in the first week of September the British officers began to return from Camp 2, Branch 1. Forty army officers returned in all, although ten others remained on the missing list.

On 6 September the United Nations Command and the communists announced that Operation 'Big Switch' had been completed for all individuals who had elected to be returned to their own side. When the figures were compiled it appeared that 38 per cent of American prisoners of war died in captivity – 2,730 out of a total of 7,190.

Three days later the UNC presented a list to the communists of 3,404 UN and South Korean personnel who were still unaccounted for. The list included the names of 944 US personnel, of which 610 were from the army. The list was compiled from statements made by the communists themselves, radio broadcasts originating in Peking, letters written from prison camps or from the observations of former UN prisoners of war while in the enemy prison camps. On 16 September Peking radio stated that the list was 'fake' and designed to obscure the fact that the Allies were forcibly detaining Chinese and North Korean prisoners of war. And at this point an impasse was reached. The UN Command knew the enemy was holding back Allied soldiers and had no intention of returning them. On the other hand the propaganda value of tens of thousands of communist soldiers refusing to return to their homelands was not to be underestimated.

According to the terms of the armistice any prisoner of war who did want to return to his own country would be turned over to the Neutral Nations Repatriation Commission. Under the protection of the Indian Army these men would be interviewed by representatives of their own side, who would 'explain' the reasons why they should return home.

211

The men would then make their own choice – to return whence they came or stay with their new patrons. On 23 September the United Nations Command handed over 22,604 Chinese and North Korean non-repatriates to the Indians, and the following day the communists delivered 359 UN non-repatriates. The majority of the UN non-repatriates were South Koreans, but a score of Americans and one Briton, Royal Marine Andrew Condron, elected to stay in North Korea. As the 'explainers' of both sides began their task, it became obvious they had a great deal of work ahead of them.

One message discovered by the author illustrated the problems that faced the explainers of both sides as they prepared to try to persuade their men to return home.

MESSAGE 23014/LTC Received by Secure Means on 17th September 1953. From BRPWIU BRICOSAT JAPAN. To Air Ministry London. Operational Immediate – Secret. For A19 from McNabb Explainer.

Para 1. Appears possible that some of UK PW listed in paragraph 2 below may appear before Explainers having remained behind or having been detained. Due to fact that in conduct of interview PW will not be obliged to give name to Explainer and may for one reason or another be unwilling to do so grateful if photographs of those listed below could be sent urgently to me via BRPWIU care of Britcom Sub Area Tokyo. Photograph

Two Indian Army officers from the Neutral Nations Repatriation Commission, with four communist Chinese 'explainers'.

of Tondror [presumably a misspelling of Royal Marine stay-behind Condron] already held here.

Para 2. List of PW as follows. W/Cdr Baldwin RAF, S/Ldr Hulse RAF, 414991 2/Lt St.Clair Morford P.A. KSLI, 99741 Major Stephenson P.B. Kings, 22492807 Pte Dellow P. BW, CH/X60670 Marine Nicholls R. RM, 22463590 Pte Perfect R.M.Royal Norfolk, 22493860 Fus Pryor AR. RFus, 22689480 Pte Smith D. DWR, 22787802 Pte Wright F.W. DWR.

British Air Intelligence obviously had good reason to think that those men may have been alive, either forcibly detained or possibly staying behind of their own accord, in September 1953. The sad fact is, though, that none of them was ever seen again.

Propaganda was also on the minds of the Chinese leadership as the prisoner exchange came to an end. They made it known through communist correspondent Wilfred Burchett that they were retaining certain USAF personnel who had allegedly flown over Chinese territory in a 'non-prisoner of war' status. To secure the release of these men – the crew of a B-29 bomber and a handful of F-86 pilots – the United States would have to negotiate through diplomatic channels.

On 21 November three former members of the ROK Army escaped through the demilitarised zone and reported to the United Nations Command that the communists still held large numbers of prisoners of war. However, the Neutral Nations Armistice Supervisory Commission declined to conduct an investigation into the claims. Despite the arrival of two more escapees on 14 December telling the same story, the only real option open to the United Nations Command was to complain at the Armistice Commission meetings. It would do no good.

When the dust had settled the numbers were counted. During the war the United States had lost 23,196 killed in action and a further 105,871 wounded, of whom 2,495 subsequently died of their wounds. In total 13,108 had been listed as missing in action, although 5,131 had returned during the prisoner exchanges. Twenty-one men had turned their coats and refused to return to the United States. That left a figure of 7,956 still missing, of which 944 were known to have been alive in enemy hands at one time or another. Just what had the communists done with almost 8,000 American soldiers?

As far as the British were concerned, their missing in action numbered around 150. The thousand men who did return home were sent questionnaires together with a list of names and a request for information. The fates of fifty of the men were more or less agreed thereafter, leaving a hundred whose true fate is known only to the North Koreans, the Chinese or possibly the Russians.

The War Memorial at Pusan. The plaque in the top right-hand picture *is dedicated to the men of the Royal Navy, Royal Marines and 8th Hussars who never came home. The first Marine name is that of Gerald Ahern, who died during the 'Tiger' death march due to lack of medical attention and starvation.*

War Crimes or not War Crimes?

In November 1953 a discussion took place in the Air Ministry in London regarding the atrocity reports concerning British troops that had been sent over by the US State Department. Could the various incidents be classed as war crimes? Miss Joyce Gutteridge, an expert on prisoner of war conventions, stated her opinion as follows:

'Prima facie, all the incidents in the attached reports constitute "war crimes". They are offences against the laws of war which, quite apart from anything in an international convention, prohibit the killing of prisoners of war and the wounded and sick. They are also acts which are specifically enumerated as constituting "grave breaches" of the 1949 Geneva Convention.

The 1949 Geneva Convention did not apply de jure during the Korean conflict, but at the outset of those hostilities the Supreme Commander of the United Nations forces declared that persons taken into custody by or falling into the hands of the forces under his operational control in connection with hostilities in Korea would be "treated in accordance with the humanitarian principles applied by and recognised by civilised nations involved in armed conflict", and the North Koreans made a declaration to the effect that their forces would abide by the principles of the Geneva Convention.

The 1949 Geneva Convention has therefore been regarded as applicable de facto, although not de jure, during the Korean conflict. For instance, the lengthy discussions about the repatriation of prisoners of War were conducted by both sides with reference to Article 118(i) of the 1949 Prisoners of War Convention, although different interpretations of that provision were put forward by the opposing sides.

If it were decided to bring to trial the persons responsible for the incidents described in the attached lists, they could, however, without any reference to the 1949 Geneva Convention, be tried for the "war crimes" constituted by these violations of the customary laws of war.'

The discussions were largely academic. Successful convictions would depend on the evidence available, much of which comprised confessions by the participants. They in turn had either been repatriated to their communist masters or were planning to begin a new life in South Korea or Taiwan. If a long-drawn-out war crimes trial had been held, how many North Korean or Chinese prisoners would have stuck to their confessions in court, knowing that the hangman's noose awaited those found guilty? It was much simpler to let the problem disappear with the enemy prisoners.

Some trials did take place after the war, but these were not war crimes trials, these were court-martial trials of American servicemen who had

215

WAR CRIMES VICTIMS

	Reported	Probable	Bodies Recovered	Survivors
American	10,233	6,113	511	216
Republic of Korea Army	10,334	5,460	1,004	14
Turkish	135	13	0	0
British	57	10	3	2
Belgian	6	6	6	0
Australian	20	20	0	0
Total Military Victims	20,785	11,622	1,524	232
South Korean Police	260	176	5	0
South Korean Civilians	26,487	12,777	7,334	292
North Korean Civilians	8,600	4,399	1,163	9
Irish Priest	1	1	1	0
German Priest	1	1	1	0
Total Civilian Victims	35,349	17,354	8,504	301
Unknown	1,425	839	4	0
Grand Total	57,559	29,815	10,032	533

disgraced their country while prisoners of war. The British did things differently and preferred not to wash their dirty laundry in public. Unlike the American POW debriefing files, the 1,000 British files currently stored in the Public Record Office are kept secret. The author requested their release but was told that they contain information on collaborators and would remain closed in order to protect the men concerned. Such is the British way of doing things. A list of almost a hundred British political collaborators can be found in one of the files in the Public Record Office and it does make interesting reading. The author has decided that the list has no place in this book – those who were not there do not have the right to judge the actions of those who were.

As for the Americans, all returning prisoners were debriefed in great depth and the skilled interrogators soon came to the conclusion that at least 425 of the POWs were guilty of serious collaboration with the enemy, that is roughly one man in seven or 13 per cent of the whole. So great was the concern over the conduct of many of the American prisoners of war that President Eisenhower authorised a Code of Conduct for members of the Armed Forces of the United States. The document was unprecedented; never before had it been deemed necessary to remind American soldiers of their duty. The six articles of the code read as follows: (1) I am an American fighting man. I serve in the forces which guard my country and our way of life. I am prepared to give my life in their defence; (2) I will never surrender of my own free will. If in command I will never surrender my men while they have the means to resist; (3) If I am captured I will continue to resist by all means available. I will make every effort to escape and aid others to escape. I will accept neither parole nor special favours from the enemy; (4) If I become a prisoner of war I will keep faith with my fellow prisoners. I will give no information or take part in any action which might be harmful to my comrades. If I am senior, I will take command. If not, I will obey the lawful orders of those appointed over me and will back them up in every way; (5) When questioned, should I become a prisoner of war, I am bound to give only name, rank, service number and date of birth. I will evade answering further questions to the utmost of my ability. I will make no oral or written statements disloyal to my country and its allies or harmful to their cause; (6) I will never forget that I am an American fighting man, responsible for my actions, and dedicated to the principles which made my country free. I will trust in my God and in the United States of America.

Of the 425 files on collaborators eighty-two of them were referred to the Army Board on Prisoners of War Collaboration and forty-seven were finally approved for general court-martial. The crimes of which the accused men were charged included informing on fellow prisoners, collaborating with the communist enemy, misconduct as a prisoner of war, assault on an officer, larceny and murder. Thirty-five of the forty-seven cases did not go to trial. Of those that did, there were eleven convictions and the sentences ranged from life imprisonment to a mere reprimand with freezing in rank for two years. Under later review the life sentence was reduced to twenty years, one sentence of eight years reduced to two and a half and one sentence of fifteen years reduced to one year.

The most notorious offender was probably Sergeant James C.

Gallagher who was convicted by a court-martial of killing two seriously ill fellow prisoners in February 1951 by throwing them out into the snow. At the time the men were suffering from dysentery and unable to help themselves. A third fellow prisoner also died as a result of ill-treatment by Gallagher, who was sentenced to life imprisonment for his crimes.

If that was not bad enough, it was alleged that at least seventy-five others had been so thoroughly indoctrinated that they had agreed to work as espionage agents for the communists. They had codes with them and explicit instructions as to how to reach and recognise future contacts. In many cases the men were to act as 'sleepers' and not make contact until at least five years had passed. Interestingly most of the men had never committed any acts in the prison camps that would have marked them as being pro-communist.

THE DISAPPEARANCE OF WING COMMANDER BALDWIN

On 18 December 1953 the British government offered to make on behalf of the Unified Command an approach to the Chinese communists in Peking to seek the return of United Nations Command personnel who might still be in communist custody. The details of the approach cannot be studied at this time, but it was presumably a failure. The United Kingdom does not have a Freedom of Information Act and successive governments can keep information out of the public domain for as long as they wish. The files on Foreign Office communication with communist China in 1953 and 1954 will remain closed to the public until at least 2003 and 2004.

Were there other prisoners under communist control in North Korea, China or Russia? Surely they all came home or died from ill-treatment or were killed by their captors? Possibly. Could some of them still be alive, destined to spend the rest of their days in a lonely cell or knee-deep in a rice paddy?

Twenty-one-year-old Johnny Baldwin joined the Royal Air Force as an airman in the dark days of September 1939. He was soon sent to France and worked as a ground crewman until the RAF was forced to flee back across the Channel, just prior to the retreat to Dunkirk. During the Blitz he was employed in bomb disposal, but he wanted to fly and in 1941 he volunteered for pilot training. Posted to 609 Squadron in November 1942 he was soon flying Typhoons and shot down his first enemy aircraft after only four hours in the new rocket-firing machine.

During the next two years Baldwin progressed in rank and the number of decorations on his chest grew in proportion to his number of 'kills'.

In 1944 the Allies found themselves back in France with the Typhoons ranging far and wide searching for targets. One day Baldwin led his flight of eight Typhoons in an attack on a road convoy, wounding Field Marshal Erwin Rommel. By the time the war ended he had sixteen enemy aircraft to his credit.

When the United States Air Force received the new North American F-86 Sabre, Baldwin, by now wearing the rank of wing commander, was one of four RAF pilots sent to Korea on an exchange tour to fly the new jet. Not long after arriving Baldwin went out on a four-aircraft reconnaissance mission over North Korean territory. He was flying as number two to First Lieutenant Robert L. Larsh Jr when he disappeared while they were making a turn in dense cloud at 12,000 feet. A search and rescue operation was launched, but they could find no sign of the RAF pilot.

At the time of her husband's disappearance in March 1952, Mrs Baldwin was awaiting the birth of her second son, Michael. On a number of occasions she was unofficially called up to London by the RAF, who thought that her husband was still alive. However, when the armistice was signed and the prisoners came home, Johnny Baldwin was not among them. In 1954 Mrs Baldwin was officially informed that her husband had died in the crash. But had he?

Forty years later Michael Baldwin decided to try to discover just what had happened to his father. He made contact with Royal Canadian Air Force Squadron Leader Andrew MacKenzie, who had been released by the Chinese in December 1954, over a year after the war came to an end. In 1998 Michael Baldwin received a letter from Andy Mackenzie:

'I will say at the outset that I didn't have the pleasure of meeting your father. However, sometime in January 1953 I was being held in solitary confinement in a North Korean house when something very unusual happened. I was visited by a young Korean, who spoke good English, and said he was a North Korean fighter pilot. The only thing I can remember about the conversation is that he made a special effort to tell me that "they had" Wing Commander "Johnnie" Baldwin. I got the impression that your father was also a POW, presumably because he called him "Johnnie". Later I tried a couple of abortive escape attempts and ended up in a prison in China until my release on 5 December 1954.'

In 1955, almost two years after the fighting had ended in Korea, four more American F-86 pilots were released by China. One of them, Lieutenant Roland Parks, later stated that he believed he would not have been released if it were not for the pressure applied by the Canadian government over MacKenzie. How much pressure did the British government apply over Wing Commander Baldwin? They certainly had good enough reason to believe he was still alive.

On 9 November 1953 the US Embassy in London sent a telegram to the Secretary of State in Washington (number 2019, National Archives, ref. 641.95A24/11-953). It read:

British armed services have asked Foreign Office what, if anything, can be done through diplomatic channel for RAF Wing Commander and Canadian Squadron Leader reported to be still held as POWs by Communists in Korea.

Foreign Office notes some 16 USAF pilots still reportedly detained by Communists and is of opinion all these officers should be handled as a group. Preliminary view is question might be handled at Panmunjom, at least in first instance, and only after other measures have been tried would Foreign Office recommend asking Raghavan make representations on their behalf at Peiping [Peking].

Eight days later a second telegram was sent from the US Embassy to the Secretary of State (number 2118, National Archives, ref. 641.95A24/11-1753):

(A) Names of officers concerned are Wing Commander J. R. Baldwin, RAF and Squadron Leader A. R. MacKenzie, RCAF. Former reported missing March 1952 and latter December 1952. Neither listed by Communists as POWs but definite information re. both obtained from repatriated POWs who saw them while still in captivity. (B) MacKenzie case leaves no (repeat no) room for doubt. He [was] seen by at least three former POWs on separate occasions, and on one occasion he passed note to a POW asking that if he ever repatriated he forward it to his wife. MacKenzie said to be held in solitary confinement and undergoing detailed interrogation. This information has been passed to RCAF. (C) Baldwin reportedly seen by two USAF officers separately and fuller information being sought through USAF Washington. (D) It may endanger lives [of] these officers if their names re-submitted separately.

Another report suggested that Baldwin was being held in a tungsten mine together with thirty-five American officers.

Despite these reports, anyone making enquiries nowadays about Wing Commander Baldwin is referred by the RAF to the Army Historical Branch. This department at the Ministry of Defence is the keeper of British POW/MIA secrets and they will tell you that Baldwin died in the crash of his aircraft. They do not mention tungsten mines, reports from USAF officers or the fact that the wing commander was on the explainers' list in September 1953.

LAST TRAIN TO MANCHOULI

The message was dated 23 March 1954. The subject was American prisoners of war reported en route to Siberia. Although the event had taken
place a couple of years earlier and the war was now over, the refugee
had only just managed to gain his freedom. He went straight to the US
Embassy in Hong Kong. His story was contained in Despatch Number
1716. Classified SECRET from AMCONGEN, Hong Kong to the
Department of State, Washington, it read:

'A recently arrived Greek [actually a Polish-Russian according to Lt-Col
Simpson, originator of this report] refugee from Manchuria has reported
seeing several hundred American prisoners of war being transferred from
Chinese trains to Russian trains at Manchouli near the border of
Manchuria and Siberia. The POWs were seen late in 1951 and in the
spring of 1952 by the informant and a Russian friend of his. The informant was interrogated on two occasions by the Assistant Air Liaison
Officer and the Consulate General agrees with his evaluation of the information as probably true and the source as of unknown reliability. The
full text of the initial Air Liaison Office report follows:

First report dated 16th March 1954, from Air Liaison Office, Hong Kong,
to USAF, Washington, C2.

This office has interviewed refugee source who states that he observed
hundreds of prisoners of war in American uniforms being sent into
Siberia in late 1951 and 1952. Observations were made at Manchouli
(Lupin), 49°/50' – 117°/30' Manchuria Road Map, AMSL 201 First
Edition, on USSR–Manchurian border. Source observed POWs on
railway station platform loading into trains for movement into Siberia. In
railway restaurant source closely observed three POWs who were under
guard and were conversing in English. POWs wore sleeve insignia which
indicated POWs were Air Force non-commissioned officers. Source
states that there were a great number of negroes among POW shipments
and also states that at no time later were any POWs observed returning
from Siberia. Source does not wish to be identified for fear of reprisals
against friends in Manchuria, however is willing to cooperate in
answering further questions and will be available [in] Hong Kong for
questioning for the next four days.'

Upon receipt of this information, USAF, Washington, requested
elaboration of the following points:

'(1)   Description of uniforms or clothing worn by POWs including orna-
       ments.
(2)   Physical condition of POWs.

221

(3)   Nationality of guards.
(4)   Specific date of observations.
(5)   Destination in Siberia.
(6)   Presence of Russians in uniform or civilian clothing accompanying movement of POWs.
(7)   Complete description of three POWs specifically mentioned.'

The Air Liaison Office complied by submitting this telegram:

'From USAIRLO Sgn Lackey. CITE C 4. REUR 53737 following answers submitted to seven questions.

1.   POWs wore OD outer clothing described as not heavy inasmuch as weather considered early spring. Source identified from pictures service jacket, field, M1943. No belongings except canteen. No ornaments observed.
2   Condition appeared good, no wounded, all ambulatory.
3.   Station divided into two sections with tracks on each side of loading platform. On Chinese side POWs accompanied by Chinese guards. POWs passed through gate bisecting platform to Russian train manned and operated by Russians. Russian trainmen wore dark blue or black tunic with silver-coloured shoulder boards. Source says this regular train uniform but he knows the trainmen are military and wearing regular train uniforms.
4.   Interrogation with aid of more fluent interpreter reveals source first observed POWs in railroad station in spring 1951. Second observation was outside city of Manchouli about three months later with POW train headed towards station where he observed POW transfer. Source was impressed with second observation because of large number of negroes among POWs. Source states that he was told by a very close Russian friend whose job was numbering railroad cars at Manchouli, every time subsequent POW shipments passed through Manchouli. Source says these shipments were reported often and occurred when United Nations forces in Korea were on the offensive.
5.   Unknown.
6.   Only Russians accompanying POWs were those who manned train.
7.   Three POWs observed in station restaurant appeared to be 30 to 35. Source identified Air Force non-commissioned officer sleeve insignia of Staff Sergeant rank, stated that several inches above insignia there was a propeller but says that all three did not have propeller. Three POWs accompanied by Chinese guard. POWs appeared thin but in good health and spirits, were being given what source described as good food. POWs were talking in English but

did not converse with guard. Further information as to number of POWs observed, source states that first observation filled a seven passenger car train and second observation about the same. Source continues to emphasise the number of negro troops, which evidently impressed him because he had seen so few negroes before. Source further states that his Russian railroad worker friend was attempting to obtain a visa to Canada and that he could furnish more information. The railroad worker's name is Leon Strelnikov [phonetic] whose mother's sister lives in Canada and is applying for a visa for Strelnikov. Comment Reporting Officer: Source is very careful not to exaggerate information and is positive of identification of American POWs. In view of information contained in Charity Interrogation Report Number 619 dated 5th February 1954, Reporting Officer gives above rating of F-2. Source departing Hong Kong today by ship. Future address on file this office.

In this connection the Department's attention is called to Charity Interrogation Report Number 619, forwarded to the Department under cover of a letter dated 1st March 1954 to Mr A. Savin Chase, DRP. Section 6 of this report states "On another occasion source saw several coaches full of Europeans who were also taken to USSR. They were not Russians. Source passed the coaches several times and heard them talk in a language unknown to him."
Signed Julian F. Harrington, American Consul General.
Copies to: Taipei, Moscow, London, Paris.'

On 5 May 1954 the US Embassy in Moscow sent the following note to the Russians:

'The Embassy of the United States of America presents its compliments to the Ministry of Foreign Affairs of the Union of Soviet Socialist Republics and has the honour to request the Ministry's assistance in the following matter.
The United States Government has recently received reports which support earlier indications that American prisoners of war who had seen action in Korea have been transported to the Union of Soviet Socialist Republics and that they are now in Soviet custody. The United States Government desires to receive urgently all information available to the Soviet Government concerning these American personnel and to arrange their repatriation at the earliest possible time [note number 947, copy in National Archives].'

The reply came on 13 May:

'The United States Government assertion contained in the indicated note, that American prisoners of war who participated in military action in Korea have allegedly been transferred to the Soviet Union and at the present time are being kept under Soviet guard is devoid of any foundation whatsoever and is clearly far-fetched, since there are not, and have not been any such persons in the Soviet Union.'

The report of the American prisoners being transported from Manchouli, China, into Siberia had initially landed on the desk of Colonel D. K. Simpson, the US air attaché in Hong Kong. Seven years later, in 1961, Simpson retired from the air force. In the intervening years he heard nothing more about the men; certainly they had not returned home to America. A man with a conscience, he began to make enquiries and tried to generate some action.

Flanked by British military police, Colonel Delk Simpson, the US air attaché in Hong Kong, escorts Colonel Arnold and the rest of his crew back to freedom.

'I have visited offices of Senators and a member of the House of Representatives. I have given interviews to the *Washington Post* and the *Wall Street Journal*. I have visited with the officer in charge of MIAs in the White House, and I have been interviewed by the Director of Intelligence in the Pentagon, where it was later said, I am told, that I was senile and the prisoners I reported were French from the French–Indo-Chinese War, being taken to Siberia for return to the French.

It was not until May 1992 that I came to understand the possibility of why I received such official inaction. At that time I met Colonel Corso. He told me that in 1953 he was the author of a policy while on the White House staff, to abandon all prisoners held by the Russians. He said the policy was approved by President Eisenhower.'

THE LUCKY SABRE PILOT

It was 4 September 1952, 1630 hours. The lone F-86 was in trouble. Four enemy MiGs were after him and his buddies were nowhere to be seen. One of the MiGs began his attack just as Lieutenant Roland Parks came on the scene. Separated from his flight leader in a dogfight in the clouds, he was heading south to rendezvous near Cho Do Island, a friendly island off North Korea. He immediately opened fire on the MiG and saw pieces fly off as he pressed his attack.

'Then some of the other MiGs moved in on me and I felt some hits on my plane, so I broke off. I had made about a 180-degree turn in attacking the MiG, so I turned back and picked up on my compass a general heading of south. I had to keep zigzagging. I was keeping my eye on the compass, flying through soup. Some of my other instruments already had been knocked out, I could see. Soon I found out that my compass had also been damaged. When I broke out of the overcast and could see the coastline, I realised that I had been flying west into the sun and must be considerably west of Korea.

Shortly after breaking out of the overcast, at an altitude of about 42,000 feet, my engine quit. I knew from this altitude I could easily glide a hundred miles and planned to glide back south-east as far as I could and then bail out over the water. At this point, though, I ran into more MiGs and got bounced again. With my engine dead, my only alternative was to get out. I had the choice of bailing out over the sea or over the land in the vicinity of Port Arthur. I elected to bail out over the land, with the hope, ridiculous though it may sound, of hiking my way back. I thought I could walk further than I could swim. So I just rolled my plane over on to its back and went down as fast as I could. During this time I had got into radio contact with one of our own craft, briefly explained the situation, and said I was bailing out.

I tried to pick a place that was thinly populated, but every place was thickly populated. At about 10,000 feet I headed the plane for the water and ejected. Everything was going perfectly, just like I'd been told to do. But after my parachute opened I saw the plane starting to circle back, heading right towards me. It went underneath me by about 200 feet.

While I floated down the plane circled again and hit the side of a mountain. I could see people watching me from the ground. I lit on a rock-covered side of a mountain and rolled a good way down it, but fortunately I was not even bruised. I headed for some trees, hunting cover, climbing this mountain like a goat. Finally I made it to a valley on the other side and hid in some woods until dark. I still had my pistol and some emergency rations, but had lost my knife and my escape kit. After dark I headed for the highest point of land in the vicinity to get my bearings. I could see water on three sides, and I was between Port Arthur and Darien.

I wanted to get back to where I had lost my escape kit and recover it and set out in that direction. But I ran into a bunch of Chinese and turned back before they spotted me. It was just about midnight when I ran into these Chinese and started to sneak around them. While trying to circle them, I ran smack into another Chinaman. He was so scared he shook. I tried to make him understand that I wouldn't hurt him, and only wanted him to help me. I was just grasping at a straw, hoping I might have found one Chinese friendly to us. I followed him into a small village, then, just as we reached the village square, he grabbed me and started yelling. Chinese came from everywhere. They were armed with iron spears that must have been four feet long. Here I was with just one pistol, surrounded by all these Chinese.

I just said to myself, "Parks, you've had it." I threw my forty-five on the ground and put my hands up. One kid tried to run me through with his spear, and they all converged on me. I think they would have killed me right there if one old man hadn't driven them off. He brought me a drink of water that I really needed badly.

Pretty soon two Russian soldiers walked up, just sightseeing apparently. Then came several Russian officers, one of whom could speak English, and several armed Russian soldiers. They put me in the back of an old truck and drove about thirty minutes. We stopped in the middle of a cornfield and I began to sweat. I was expecting a bullet in the back of the head. But apparently this was a camouflaged airfield, for a MiG flew in and landed nearby. We went through a gate into a camouflaged area of tents, occupied by Russian soldiers. The Russians seemed friendly and treated me well. They fed me. Then they questioned me, but only generally, and gave me back the watch and pen from my escape kit that had been found. I gave them the general information that we were permitted to give, but gave them the wrong air base that I had flown from. I explained that I had got lost, and that's how I came to be near Port Arthur.

In the morning a Russian Army doctor came to examine me. He was accompanied by a beautiful young Russian woman who spoke perfect English. They brought in a bottle of lemonade. They were surprised to find that I, a jet pilot, was only twenty-two years old. The real questioning got under way later in the day. It was done by Russian officers. They seemed especially interested in our radar equipment, but I told them I didn't know anything about it. The place we were in was a military compound in a residential area of Port Arthur. I spent the next thirteen days in this compound.

Between 6 and 9 September they questioned me about everything, especially equipment, and wanted me to draw maps of our airfields. On the eleventh a Russian officer questioned me about American politics, asked what party I belonged to. Sometimes I was embarrassed, because

The Lucky Sabre Pilot – First Lieutenant Roland Parks in his F-86 Sabre jet at airfield K-13 Suwon in July 1952. Very possibly his young age and relative experience may have saved him from a one-way ticket to Siberia.

he asked me some questions about the details of the American governmental system that I just plain couldn't answer.

On the seventeenth the Russians told me they were taking me to Russia where I would be with other Americans. I had told them I did not want to be turned over to the Chinese and that's probably why they told me they were taking me to Russia. I thought they were taking me to the Siberian salt mines. I had made up my mind that if we kept going north towards Siberia I was going to go over the hill at all costs. We stopped in Darien for food and supplies for the trip. My Russian guards on this trip were dressed in civilian clothes until we crossed the border between the Russian zone of Port Arthur and China proper. Then they put on uniforms. We drove until late that night.

I saw a number of American GIs riding in American 6 × 6 GI trucks on my way from Port Arthur to Antung. They appeared to be hauling firewood and there were two Americans in the back of one truck and one in another. I was rather shocked; they were heading west and moving right along. When I recovered I said to myself, "Did you really see that?" The GIs were well dressed in typical winter garb: GI field jackets, wool sweaters and typical GI winter hat with flaps. I did not see any guards, although I do not know who was driving or who was riding in the cab. Also where I was held in or outside of Antung, I was aware of other Americans held there. Who they were I will probably never know.

We finally arrived in Antung about three p.m. and stopped near the airfield. A Russian officer went away and came back in about an hour with some Chinese officers. Then I was blindfolded while we drove about thirty minutes more, stopping at what I learned later was a Chinese military base, where I was taken into a room and the blindfold was removed. The Russians took away from me everything Russian they had given me, destroying the evidence that I had been in Russian hands.

The Chinese immediately started questioning me, with the interpreting being done by a Chinese named Lue who spoke perfect English and said he had taken pilot training in the United States during World War II. Lue turned out later in my imprisonment to be the man they used as a sort of "pacifier" to soothe you and try to trick you into telling something when things didn't go to suit them in their long interrogations. Lieutenant-Colonel Edwin L. Heller and Captain E. Fischer, who were later imprisoned, also encountered this character Lue. I really learned to hate this Lue. He thought he was such a slick operator. Finally it became so obvious that I disliked him that they kept him away from me.

On 21 September another American was brought into the room next to mine, under guard. He moaned constantly for the day and a half he was there, apparently wounded.

During the last half of September I was questioned repeatedly, hour after hour, sometimes nine hours at a stretch. They tried to get me to say that I had flown into Manchuria many times. They showed me a pamphlet accusing the Americans of atrocities and I wouldn't look at it. Some guards gave me apples, candy, nuts and butter and some clothing. They tried to get me to write a description of American air-to-air combat tactics. When I refused they kept questioning me far into the night. They always held out the promise that if I cooperated I would go to a North Korean prison camp, and threatened that if I didn't cooperate things would be very bad for me.'

On 4 October Parks was taken by train from Antung to Mukden. The journey, which lasted almost seven hours, took the American further into China to a town where the occupying Japanese had housed American and British prisoners during World War II. His cell was cold and damp and the food was pretty inadequate. On the thirtieth of the month he received three meals instead of two. He later learned that this was the day Lieutenant Lyle W. Cameron arrived at the prison. Eighteen days later Cameron joined his fellow pilot in his cell.

One day Cameron jokingly told the guard that for a drink of whisky and some apples he would give him his watch. That night the guard came in and woke them up and offered some Chinese wine and two apples. They drank the wine, ate the apples and then demanded two more bottles of wine and more apples before they gave him the watch. During the next few nights the guard paid up and got his watch. The Chinese were really strict about guards taking prisoners' watches and if he had been caught he would have been in trouble.

In February 1953 the pair found themselves in trouble with their jailers. All the food they were served was bad, but the least bad was the cold Chinese sausage called 'chong char'. They decided the sausage would taste better if it was hot and started heating it with their candles. One of the guards intervened and tried to take their candles, but Lyle just pushed him out of the cell. The guard called for reinforcements and then they took away the candles. After a while they found a new way to heat their food. They started hoarding toilet paper and would build a small fire in the latrine, where one would cook the sausage while the other stood watch for the guards. They got by with this method for weeks.

In April 1953, while the 'Little Switch' prisoner exchange was taking place in Korea, Parks and Cameron were moved to a new jail and put in separate cells. Within a few days they realised there were other Americans in the prison, when they heard them talking to the guards. One of them was Captain Harold E. Fischer, who was two cells away from Parks. Another resident was Andy MacKenzie, the Canadian F-86 pilot.

August 1953 came and went, with the interrogators insisting that the prisoners write confessions that they had repeatedly flown across the Yalu River into Chinese territory. Across the border in Korea Operation 'Big Switch' began and the repatriation of prisoners of war commenced. However, there was to be no going home for the prisoners in Mukden jail. Their solitary confinement did come to an end, though, and Parks, Fischer and Cameron were all put in the same cell.

The months dragged on until June 1954. It was almost a year since the guns had fallen silent in Korea. On the twenty-eighth of that month Parks received a cablegram from his family, the first news from home in twenty-two months. That month one of the interpreters returned to the prison and mentioned that he had been spending time with Lieutenant-Colonel Edwin L. Heller in a hospital in Mukden. He had been in the hospital for almost two years and had had four operations on his injured leg.

During the winter of 1953/54 the pilots were separated following some infraction of the rules. Captain Fischer was blamed and sent to

Left to right: F-86 Sabre pilots MacKenzie, Cameron, Fischer and Parks, prisoners in China until 1955. Here they pose in a prison cell converted into a 'library' for propaganda purposes. Note the finger gestures.

another wing of the prison. After a week or two he had had enough. He dug a hole through the wall and went out into the night in freezing weather. He had no plan and no provisions. He walked for several hours, wading across a small stream on his journey. With wet feet and becoming colder by the hour, he saw a guard shack on a bridge. He decided to turn himself in and was soon brought back to the prison.

In January 1955 United Nations representative Dag Hammarskjold visited China to try to obtain their release, but the wheels of diplomacy turn slowly. In May 1955 the men were taken to Peking and put on trial on charges of violating Chinese territory. After a show trial they were pronounced 'guilty' and ordered to be deported immediately. On the afternoon of 31 May they crossed the border into Hong Kong. After thirty-three months of imprisonment, twenty-one of them after the war in Korea had ended, Roland Parks was free.

Why was this story entitled 'The Lucky Sabre Pilot'? Well, Roland Parks was lucky, and so for that matter were MacKenzie, Fischer, Cameron and Heller. Unlike many of the other F-86 pilots downed in battles near the Yalu River, they came home.

THE RUSSIAN DEFECTOR

It was not long before other sources began to confirm the presence of American prisoners of war in Russia. In January 1954 Yuri A. Rastvorov, ostensibly a Foreign Ministry official but in fact a member of the MVD, the forerunner to the KGB, defected to the United States from his post at the Soviet Mission in Tokyo. On 28 January 1955 he met with officials of the Eisenhower administration. Three days later a memo was circulated summarising the event. The memo was discovered on file in the Dwight D. Eisenhower Library in Abilene, Kansas, but requests for its declassification in 1991 were refused. Five years later, following requests from Associated Press and others, it was released. The memo, written by Special Projects Staff member Dr Craig, was sent to Mr Elmer B. Staats, who was executive officer of the Operations Coordinating Board, a White House group charged with implementing national security policies, including some related to accounting for Korean War POWs.

'SUBJECT: Interview with Rastvorov (former MVD) concerning US Prisoners of War in the USSR. Date 31st January 1955.

On Friday, 28th January 1955, a meeting was arranged between members of the Special Projects Staff and Mr Rastvorov. General Dale O. Smith was also present. The interview was on the subject of US prisoners of war being held by the Soviets. Mr Rastvorov made the following important points bearing upon the subject:

1. He was told by recent arrivals [1950–53] from the Soviet Union to the USSR's Tokyo mission that US and other UN POWs were being held in Siberia.
2. The POWs will be screened by the Soviets and trained to be illegal residents in US or other countries where they can live as Americans.
3. Selected POWs will be used in propaganda work.
4. Use will be made of the identities and biographies of dead POWs in preparing legends for new Soviet agents.
5. The mechanism for POW control in Korea was headed by the Soviets.
6. The sentencing of the eleven US POWs charged with espionage by the Chinese Communists was conceived and directed by the Soviets. The release of other Americans in Europe was part of this plot.'

This memo, marked SECRET when it was written on 31 January 1955, was finally declassified on 9 April 1996, forty-one years later. How many more such documents are buried in dusty vaults? And who decided that such things were to be kept from the eyes of the American people? The buck started, but did not stop, with the then President of the United States, Dwight D. Eisenhower.

THE EISENHOWER BRIEFING

Colonel Philip Corso, a former army intelligence officer who was a National Security Council staff member in the mid-1950s, arranged and conducted the interrogation of Rastvorov that is described in the above memo. He was later summoned to meet President Eisenhower to discuss the subject of American prisoners in the Soviet Union.

During the Korean War Colonel Corso was head of the Special Projects Division in the G-2 Section of the Far East Command. One of his primary duties was to keep track of enemy prisoner-of-war camps in North Korea – their locations, the conditions in the camps, estimated numbers of American and Allied prisoners of war in each camp and the treatment these prisoners received at the hands of the enemy. Corso also served as a member of the UN truce delegation at Panmunjom during the closing days of the war, and he assisted and participated in the discussions on Operation 'Little Switch', the exchange of sick and wounded prisoners of war. He stayed on for Operation 'Big Switch' and was actually present at the time when the prisoners were brought in.

At the end of 'Little Switch' he prepared a document showing that

not all the sick and wounded were returned. Intelligence reports estimated that there were between 1,700 and 2,000 sick, seriously ill or
wounded men in the camps. Around 1,200 were eventually repatriated
and Corso estimated that another 500 prisoners would not survive long
unless they were handed over for treatment. The statement was read out
at the negotiating table by Rear Admiral John C. Daniel, who was
deputy chairman of the truce delegation at the time. When the statement was read the presiding Chinese general, Lin Zang-woo, snapped
in half the pencil he was holding at the time. Four more months would
elapse before any more UN prisoners were released.

After 'Big Switch' Colonel Corso went back to the United States and
was assigned to President Eisenhower's National Security Council
operations coordinating board as a member of the staff. His primary
duties were prisoner-of-war matters on the National Security Council
level, because he had compiled and worked on this data in the Far East
Command and in Korea. Following the end of 'Big Switch' Colonel
Corso and his colleagues concluded that about 8,000 prisoners of war
had not been returned. Corso was directed to prepare a statement on
the subject for Henry Cabot Lodge to read out at the meeting of the
United Nations in New York. At the same time it was discovered that
the Chinese, under Russian tutelage, were conducting detailed and
scientific Pavlovian-type experiments on UN prisoners. Although they
knew about the information, they were hindered from sending agents
to the north to find out more about this because it was being handled
mostly by OPC, which was a unit of the Central Intelligence Agency.

During his tour of duty in Korea Corso received evidence daily that
prisoners had not been returned from North Korea and had been sent,
in fact, to the Soviet Union. The war was still going on at the time and
the reports came from prisoner-of-war interrogation reports of North
Korean and Chinese prisoners, defectors and photographs from reconnaissance aircraft. He had between 300 and 400 reports indicating that
UN prisoners of war had been sent up through Manchuria to
Manchouli, where they changed trains because of the difference in the
rail line gauges and went on to the Soviet Union. At least two train loads
of prisoners, and a possible third, were involved.

One day Colonel Corso was called to brief President Eisenhower on
the reports about prisoners being transferred to the Soviet Union. He
was required to make his briefing short because Eisenhower had a
saying: 'If you can't say it in one paragraph, don't say it.' The report
stated that between 900 and 1,200 American prisoners had been transferred from North Korea to the Soviet Union. The President had a very
serious look on his face and he asked the colonel for his recommenda-
tions. Corso said, 'These men will never come back alive because they
will get in the hands of the NKVD [later the KGB] who will use them

for their purposes. Espionage, play-backs, or whatever. This is not uncommon in the intelligence business. Once they fall into their hands, there's little hope of them coming back. My recommendation is not to make it public to protect the families.'

Colonel Corso appeared at the 1992 Senate Hearings on prisoners of war and related his story to the chairman and other committee members. Senator Grassley asked Corso if he knew how many amputees came back during the prisoner exchanges. Apparently not one amputee came home during the prisoner exchanges at the end of the Vietnam War in 1972. Strange, considering the serious injuries that could be sustained by many pilots who bailed out of damaged or burning aircraft during the long war. Colonel Corso recalled that he was present when the 1,200 sick and wounded were exchanged during 'Big Switch' and he could not recall seeing any amputees. Did the communists decide not to release such men, in case it reflected badly on their treatment of prisoners of war? Were all men with such serious injuries killed out of hand on capture or did they die from neglect? Or could another fate have befallen them?

Prisoner in Peking

Item number six in the Rastvorov briefing memo referred to eleven US POWs who were charged with espionage by the Chinese communists. During much of their imprisonment they actually shared the same prisons as Roland Parks and the other F-86 pilots. Rastvorov confirmed that the scenario was conceived and directed by the Soviets. The whole affair was extremely embarrassing for the United States and when the men were finally released the CIA debriefed them and warned them to keep quiet about their incarceration in China. For some of the men it was easy to comply – they had a bad experience to put behind them and lots of freedom to catch up with. For others it was not so easy to forget. Their conscience would not let them, for they knew there were others left behind.

Steve Kiba was one such man of conscience. He is willing to stand up and be counted, and at the 1992 Senate Select Committee Hearing on POW/MIA Affairs he did just that.

'I was born 5 February 1932 in Lundale, an impoverished mining community on Buffalo Creek in Logan County, West Virginia. My parents were immigrants from Hungary, and both worked hard to raise their eleven children. My early childhood was spent in various mining camps along the creek. In 1945 our family moved to Akron, Ohio. I graduated from Kenmore High School in 1950. On 31 July 1950 I enlisted in the air force and spent five and a half years serving my country. My primary duty was as a radio operator on a B-29.

On the night of 12 January 1953, while on a routine leaflet drop mission over North Korea, our "unarmed" B-29 was attacked and shot down. Our aircraft was definitely over North Korean territory, approximately forty miles south of the Yalu River.

During the Korean "Police Action" I was a radio operator on a B-29 in the 581st Air Resupply Squadron [581st Air Resupply and Communications Wing, tasked with unconventional and psychological warfare]. Colonel John K. Arnold was our wing commander. The crew members on our stripped-down, virtually unarmed B-29 were Captain Eugene Vaadi, aircraft commander; First Lieutenant Wallace Brown, pilot; First Lieutenant John Buck, bombardier; Captain Elmer Llewellyn, navigator; Second Lieutenant Henry Weese, radarman; Tech Sergeant Howard Brown, flight engineer; A/2C Daniel C. Schmidt, CFC gunner; A/2C Harry Benjamin, left scanner; A/2C John Thompson, right scanner; A/1C Alvin Hart, tail gunner; and A/1C Steve Kiba, radio operator.

Our home base was Clark Field, Philippines, but two of our aircraft were TDY [on tour of duty] to Yakota AFB, Japan, and were attached to

An unarmed B-29 Superfortress from the 581st Air Resupply and Communications Wing, similar to that being flown by Colonel Arnold and his crew when it was shot down on 12 January 1953. The crew were held prisoner by the Chinese until 1955.

the 91st Strategic Reconnaissance Squadron. Our job was to fly leaflet drop missions over North Korea. Our first mission was on 12 January 1953. Because it was our first mission we had three extra men on board: Colonel John Arnold, the wing commander; Major William Baumer, instructor pilot; and First Lieutenant Paul Van Voohris, instructor radar man and Weese's friend.

About 2245 hours we were attacked simultaneously by MiG-15s and radar-controlled ack-ack. Our B-29 sustained heavy damage: three engines were burning and the forward bomb-bay was engulfed in flames. Captain Vaadi gave the order to abandon the aircraft. We bailed out and were scattered all over the North Korean hillside.

By late afternoon on 13 January most of the crew and "extras" had been captured. After we were captured we were taken to an old stone jail-house. About 1700 hours a young Chinese interpreter boasted to me that they had now captured thirteen airmen from our B-29 – two last night as they touched the ground. I asked him how everyone was, because I knew that Llewellyn and Baumer had been injured. He told me that only two men were wounded and all the others were in good shape. I now knew that thirteen of the fourteen were at least alive. Of the eleven of us who returned home, none of us was captured the night of the attack. The two captured that night had to be Weese and Van Voohris.

About 1800 hours the Chinese put Benjamin and me in an American weapons carrier. Tech Sergeant Brown, First Lieutenant Brown and Captain Vaadi were already in the carrier. There were also twelve heavily armed guards accompanying us. The weapons carrier drove us to a small town and stopped at a large U-shaped building. We were taken from the weapons carrier one by one and into the building and put into separate rooms. For about two hours we were on display for the townspeople. At 2100 hours I was blindfolded, handcuffed and placed in leg irons and put in a truck with other crew members. The truck took us to some old wooden barracks somewhere in the North Korean countryside.

The next morning an English-speaking Chinese soldier came into my room to ask me a few questions. I enquired about the other crew members. He, too, told me that two crew members were captured as soon as they hit the ground. He gave me some information about the other crew members. For example, Tech Sergeant Brown played football. Schmidt was worried about his wife, Baumer and Llewellyn were wounded, but not to worry because they would be treated well, and Benjamin was always singing and was in the room below mine. He apologised for the quality of the meagre food, the frigid room and the absence of toilet articles. He said because of the war many things were scarce and difficult to get here in North Korea.

I was also questioned by a mean English-speaking Chinese soldier. On 16 January he asked me if I knew where I was. I told him I was in North

Korea. He got upset and screamed that I was in the People's Republic of China. I insisted that I was in North Korea. This went on for about two hours. Later that same afternoon the friendly soldier came to my room. We chatted for a while and he informed me that shortly I would be taking a long train ride and my living conditions would improve greatly. He said that where I was going would be much better than a POW camp. I asked him if I was being taken to China and if he was also coming. He said yes, I was going to China but he had to remain here in North Korea.

That evening several Chinese soldiers came to my room. They blindfolded me, handcuffed me and placed leg irons around my ankles. They carried me downstairs and put me into an American jeep. They took me to another large U-shaped building where we (two guards and I) stayed until almost midnight. Then we walked to the train station, got on a passenger car loaded with Chinese soldiers and headed north. You see, we were taken into Red China by force on a train.

We arrived in Mukden, Manchuria, about 1200 hours on 17 January. While in Mukden from 17 January to 1 February I was held in two different prisons: the Hotbox and the Peanut Palace. At the Peanut Palace I underwent horrendous interrogations which lasted anywhere from six to twenty-four hours a day. Here, too, the interrogators arrogantly bragged about how the brave, heroic People's Volunteers shot our plane out of the sky and how two of our crew were captured as soon as they reached the ground.

At 1100 hours on 1 February I was escorted to the train station by two heavily armed guards. On this trip the two guards and I had the entire passenger car to ourselves. We arrived in Peking about 0200 hours on 2 February. From the train station I was taken to a political prison on the outskirts of town. About 2100 hours on 4 February I was moved to another prison in the heart of Peking. We called this prison the "Hotel".

Here at the "Hotel" the interrogations resumed. A session would last anywhere from a few hours to over twenty-four hours. The interrogators would work in four- to six-hour shifts. Even though there was a stool in the room, most of the time the prisoner had to stand. If you were out of your cell and in an interrogation session when meals or drinking water were served, you just missed out. This happened often.

I was continually threatened with death – told that no one knew I was alive and that the US government had abandoned me. They kept saying they would never send me home. They kept pointing out that I was enduring pain and misery twenty-four hours a day for a pittance – a paltry two dollars, fifty cents per day or ten and a half cents per hour. You know, the Chinese interrogators were right about one thing: being a POW was not a nine-to-five job. A POW's fear, anxieties, pains, hunger and thirst knew no time limitations.

In the interrogation sessions on 7 March they accused our crew of spying because of the three extra men. They also accused us of working for the CIA. In almost every session after that they attempted to force us to confess to it.

About 2100 hours on 5 April I was moved to another prison, the Spider Web on the outskirts of Peking. It was here I saw the other Caucasians.

Towards the end of April I learned that Schmidt was in my cellblock. One of our guards tore holes in the paper screen that covered half my inside window. The holes were large enough for me to see anyone who was taken down the hall to the toilet. I tried to communicate with Schmidt by tapping code, coughing code and calling out my name. Schmidt would acknowledge by smiling and coughing. He couldn't do much more because the guard was watching him too closely.

Sometime in the early hours of 1 June I heard the Chinese move someone into our cellblock. Later that morning I heard an unfamiliar set of footsteps coming down the hall to go to the toilet. This newcomer was using crutches. I watched him through the holes in the screen as he went to and returned from the toilet from 1 June to 1 July. This new man was Caucasian, five feet nine inches tall, medium build, with fair complexion and a shaven head. As his hair grew back, it appeared to be dark brown or black. He wore the same type of clothes as Schmidt and I.

I tried to communicate with him by tapping code, coughing code and calling out my name and asking him his name. He was being watched too closely to answer me. I didn't see this man or Schmidt each and every time they came down the hall, because some of the guards would make me sit down on my board and they would stand in front of the holes in the screen.

After 1 July I didn't see the new man again. I did continue to hear and occasionally see Schmidt. About the time the new man moved in Schmidt was having trouble walking. He moved so slowly that by the time he reached my window the guards would make me sit down and one guard would stand in front of my window.

In May and June the political commissar must have really gotten concerned about my "incorrect" attitude and behaviour, for the number and length of the political indoctrination or "re-education" sessions were increased. I was subjected to hour after hour of lectures dealing with the birth and history of communism, communist ideology, communist goals and aspiration, communist guerrilla techniques to world domination. It was apparent that despite my vehement objections a fervent endeavour was being made to indoctrinate me. What really impressed and frightened me were the strong convictions and visible dedication of the lecturers to the ultimate party goals. They made no bones about it: their main goal was the eventual destruction of our free democratic society. All lecturers expressed the view that time was of no essence; it really didn't matter whether it took five, ten, fifty or even one hundred years.

About 1000 hours on 18 July I was moved to another cellblock. I was put in the last cell on the left – cell fifteen. I was there from 18 July to 4 August and saw numerous Caucasians.

My bedboard was sitting directly under the outside window. There was a picket fence-type thing that covered the bottom half of the window. The top half of the window, except for two panes, was covered with paper. They had evidently been broken and replaced, and the Chinese had forgotten to repaper them. The top half of the window was propped open. Sitting on the board I could look up and see outside into the court-yard. Three cellblocks connected to form this courtyard or patio. As I was looking at the patio I saw two men walking. They appeared to be Caucasians. One was built like our aircraft commander; he was even bald-headed. The other man looked enough like our pilot to be his brother. I was pretty sure these two men were white, but I wasn't positive because they were on the far side of the patio. They were out for about fifteen minutes. After they were taken in two other men were brought out. They, too, were kept on the other side of the patio. They moved and exercised like Caucasians. I watched them until they were taken back to their cells. Two others were then brought out. One seemed to have a crippled leg. He was using a crutch and a cane. I continued to watch them, and the longer I did the more convinced I became that they were white.

I had to be careful not to let the guards see what I was doing; if they thought I was watching the prisoners in the patio I would be moved to another cell or cellblock.

That afternoon during the siesta period I noticed another man walking on the patio. He was walking around the circle. As he approached my side of the patio I saw that it was John Thompson. After the siesta I kept my eye on the patio and saw a group of twelve Chinese prisoners. They puttered around in the flower gardens near the cellblocks and in the centre of the circle for a while and then walked for a while.

One morning, I think it was 21 July, I was sitting on the board and from time to time I would glance up at the window. I saw a man walking around the circle in the patio. He passed within six feet of my window. He was definitely white, of medium build, about five feet eleven inches tall, light (blond) hair, light complexion and was wearing black pants with a white patch and a white shirt with a black patch. Schmidt, Thompson, the other whites and I were also wearing the same type of clothes as this man. He was quite active and walked at a lively pace. He reminded me a little of Benjamin. I thought I knew who he was, but I wanted to watch him for a while and get a better look. About this time my door opened and the houseboy escorted me out to walk on another patio. When I returned to my cell the white man was just being taken in.

After the two-hour siesta I saw the bald-headed one and the slim one walking on the patio again. I watched. When my guard went towards the far end of the cellblock I stood up on the board and tried to get a better look at the two men. I saw that they were definitely white, but they were just a little too far away for me to identify. I watched these men for about the next two or three weeks. As he was being returned to his cell I got several good looks at the man who reminded me of Benjamin. I was pretty sure he was the extra radarman, Paul Van Voohris, who accompanied us on our ill-fated mission. Every time he was being taken in I would pound code on the wall with my cloth shoe to let him know who I was. I also called out my name as he neared my window, and I called his name. He would glance up and smile. He had to be careful too, because his guards watched very closely.

During this time I noticed that Thompson, Van Voohris and the Chinese prisoners were permitted to walk around the circle, but the other whites were kept on the far side of the patio. This led me to believe that they were not members of our crew.

On 4 August I was moved to another cellblock and put into a cell next to the toilet. On 12 August, my 212th day in Hell, I finally got to take a bath. The wooden tub was oval-shaped. It was half-full of lukewarm but dirty water. I was not allowed to use soap because others had to use the water after me, and I certainly was not the first to use it. The houseboy allowed me five minutes in the tub.

On 20 August I was moved into the fifth cell on the left side of the cellblock. Later I was escorted to the interrogation area and informed that I would be put with a crew member. I asked to be with Hart, Weese or Van Voohris. My request was denied. They re-read the prison rules to me and informed me that we would be getting more reading material – communist propaganda – that we must study.

That evening they moved Dan Schmidt into my cell, and other crew members were moved into the cellblock. John Buck and Wally Brown were in the first cell on the left side; Eugene Vaadi and Elmer Llewellyn were in the third cell; Howard Brown, Harry Benjamin and John Thompson were in the sixth cell. They also moved two men into the fourth cell on the right side.

After the bell rang for board time Schmidt hobbled over to the honey bucket. While he was there, the guard rolled up the flap on our inside window. He also rolled up the flaps on the windows of the other cells. On his way back to his board Schmidt looked out the flap and said that there were Americans in the cell across the hall.

I jumped up and rushed over to the window and took a look. I saw two white men. One was short, about five feet eight inches; the other was about five feet ten. Both were dressed the same as we were. Their hair was cut short just like that of the other Americans. Schmidt and I started talking and calling each other by name and raising our voices in hope of getting their attention. The guard rushed down the hall and told us to shut up and go to sleep. He rolled down our flaps and stood by our window until we both lay down.

The next morning the houseboy came into the cellblock and let us out to get our own wash water. The water barrel was at the upper end of the cellblock. On the way to the barrel I strained my ears to pick up the voices from the other cells. While at the barrel I heard Buck and Wally Brown. On the way back I heard Vaadi and Llewellyn. I also heard voices in English coming from the cell across the hall, but I couldn't identify them.

On 22 August we were given reading material. Schmidt and I heard the men in the cell across the hall reading in English. We attempted to contact the mystery cell by calling out our names and asking them who they were. We tried again the next day, but with no success. On 23 August Schmidt and I began chatting with Howard Brown, Benjamin and Thompson in the sixth cell. We would wait until the guard was at the upper end of the cellblock.

About 1100 hours on 24 August the guard told Schmidt and me that our inside window was dirty. He handed me a damp rag and ordered me to clean it. I climbed up on to the window ledge and started wiping the glass. I looked across the hall and noticed that the mystery cell door was wide open. I looked into the cell and saw that it was empty. The two mystery English-speaking Caucasians had been moved out – bedboards, honey bucket and all.

For the younger airmen the "re-education" sessions continued, and the political indoctrinators unceasingly harassed us with their foul propaganda and threats of violence and horrible consequences should we persist in harbouring our reactionary attitudes. Over and over they screamed that we would never leave the People's Republic of China, that no one knew we were alive, and that if they so desired they could kill us, torture us or keep us chained and caged for ever. Most of them delighted in telling us in detail their torture techniques. They also seemed to take special delight in taunting us with the threat of never going home and telling us that if our government and people really cared about us they would do something to secure our release.

Back in our cells we prayed for relief from our miserable existence and illegal, unjust detention. We kept hoping and praying to hear the droning of American bombers overhead and the cheerful shouts of friendly Marines rushing down the corridors of our cellblocks to throw back the steel bolts on our cell doors. But the bombers never came, and the steel bolts were never drawn.

Every night we lay on our hard boards and dreamed of the good life in the States. Our escape from the boring, tedious and painful reality was short-lived, for our sleep was very frequently shattered by terrible nightmares and morning always found us still caged and chained. The growing hunger pains, the incessant thirst, the various and numerous body aches, the fears, the frustration, the disillusionments were all working on our bodies and minds. The thought that no one knew we were alive and the thought that so few even cared kept invading our minds and slowly shaking our morale. Our morale steadily deteriorated, and we felt that our hopes of ever being released were rapidly diminishing. The vicious interrogators' threats of never allowing us to go home and of letting us rot away in our filthy cells were fast becoming a reality.

On 27 January 1954 we and the five airmen were taken from our respective cells and escorted to the shower building. While we were undressing the attendant had us stop and step into stalls while they brought in another man. Howard Brown and I were in one of the bath stalls and we watched as the stranger undressed. He was about five feet nine or ten, about 140 pounds and had brown hair and whiskers. He was white and appeared to be about fifty years old. His sides seemed to be caved in and he looked as if he really had endured a rough time. He was put into the bath stall next to the one in which Howard Brown and I were. As he entered the stall we tried to communicate with him, but we failed because the Chinese were watching him too closely. We were called out and allowed to finish undressing. We showered in water that was alternately ice cold and scalding hot. It was not very often that we had the opportunity to shower, so we did our best to take advantage of every drop.

On 10 March we were allowed to take another shower and we saw the old man again. We speculated that he might be one of the captured American fighter pilots mentioned in Hewellett Johnson's book or perhaps one of the newsmen being detained by the Reds.

On 27 March the five enlisted men were taken for another short walk. We were circling the patio when we heard a voice from behind the third window in Skid Row holler, "Damn if it ain't . . ." We stopped in our tracks and stared directly at the window and saw a white face and a hairy arm. The houseboy in Skid Row rushed into the cell and forced the man from the window and closed it. We later learned that it was Colonel Arnold.

On 18 May the nine of us were moved to the cellblock we called Skid Row. Before they moved us they moved Colonel Arnold to another cellblock. Ten days later we were moved back to Carnegie Hall and into the same cells we had just vacated. On going to the latrine we learned that our short sojourn in Skid Row was because the one-holer was being repaired. Also three natives were moved into the cellblock.

On 17 June we were taken by cells to the front office for another bull session. The interrogator we nicknamed "Bluebeard" told Schmidt and me that we were brought in so they could ask us if there was anything they could do to make our stay more bearable and comfortable. I told him they could send us home, especially since the war was over and there had been a prisoner exchange. He denied that the war was over and refused to discuss our being brought by force into Red China. He made it quite clear we were not prisoners of war but war criminals. He insisted that we had violated Red Chinese air space and suggested that unless we changed our attitudes and allowed ourselves to be re-educated we would be in the People's Republic of China for one helluva long time, regardless of whether or not the war was over.

We again enquired about the other crew members, but as usual we were advised to forget them and to worry only about ourselves. We asked to be put with the officers, but they flatly refused because the officers were bad and might corrupt our minds even more. I pointed out that many American soldiers and Marines were found in North Korea with their hands bound behind their backs and a huge gaping bloody hole in their heads. This accusation really unnerved Bluebeard and he seemed at a loss as to how to answer. After a brief pause he reminded us that the People's Republic of China followed a "lenient policy" towards the "many" American prisoners she was holding [the reader might recall that this was in June 1954, nine months after the last prisoners had supposedly returned in "Big Switch"].

Schmidt and I elaborated on what was wrong with the way they were treating us and suggested many changes and ways to improve the situation. But it seemed that any change or improvement hinged on our willingness to recognise and admit that we had committed a grave and serious crime against the People's Republic of China and our willingness to surrender our will and allow our minds to be cleansed of all the filthy, corrupt ideas which now permeated them. In our present state we were vicious enemies of the People's Republic and the Chinese people. According to Bluebeard our "only" hope of staying alive and of ever getting out of the People's Republic was to cooperate fully and unconditionally. Schmidt and I concurred that the Chinese could take their improved treatment and ram it. Consequently we noticed absolutely no improvement in our treatment or conditions.

On Saturday, 9 October each member of our crew was measured for a set of clothes. Late that afternoon we received a new set of blacks: cotton padded pants and jacket. Even though the Chinese denied that the war was over, we knew it was. We believed that we got the new clothes because they were going to release us. Our optimism was overflowing at this point. We expected to be taken to the train station anytime now. All through the next day we anticipated being taken from our cells to the train station. We waited, waited and waited, every minute dragging by, seeming like hours, but still no train ride.

Later that afternoon we were taken one by one to an interrogation

243

room where we were handed a piece of paper stating that our crew had violated Red Chinese air space and that we were to be tried and punished according to the laws of the People's Republic of China. Needless to say, we were all devastated. We were expecting to be released, but instead we were to appear in their kangaroo court to face charges of intruding into Red Chinese air space to carry out acts of espionage.

That evening nine members of our crew were transported to downtown Peking to the courthouse. Colonel Arnold and Major Baumer were brought to the courthouse in separate vehicles. Much false evidence was presented against us, including the false confessions signed under much duress on 27 July 1953. We were found guilty and returned to prison to await our sentencing.

On the afternoon of 23 November we were taken back to the Peking courthouse and the so-called judge called the court to order. The head judge read off the sentences ranging from ten years for Colonel Arnold, the "main culprit", to four years for the airmen, the "cannon fodder". Needless to say, we all felt crushed.

On 7 December the five airmen and four officers were moved to another cellblock near the shower building. The five airmen were moved into the large cell on the right, the four officers were put in the large cell on the left. About twenty minutes later Major Baumer was moved in with the officers. About 1700 hours Richard Fecteau was brought into the cellblock and put with the airmen. John Downey was put with the officers. The doors to the large cells were left unlocked and we could go from one cell to the other.

Downey and Fecteau were with us for three weeks and during this time we learned all about their deplorable situation. They were CIA agents and were shot down on 29 November 1952. They didn't know what happened to their two pilots. In many of their interrogations the Chinese tried to link them with us. Downey was accused of being the ringleader and in charge of both missions. He must really have been an extraordinary man to direct our mission from a prison cell deep in Red China. Downey and Fecteau were sentenced the day before we were. Downey got life and Fecteau got twenty years. [Both men had to wait until President Richard Nixon visited China in 1972 to gain their freedom.]

On the morning of 9 January 1955 we were given a haircut, shave and a new pair of dark blue padded pants and jacket. About 1400 hours we were escorted to a large open area near the administrative building. On the way to this area we were joined by Colonel Arnold, Downey and Fecteau. Upon arriving at the area we saw that there were many cameramen already there. We exercised for a while and then divided into sides and started a volleyball game. All this time the cameramen were busy taking movies and photos. We were able to exchange a few words with Downey, Fecteau and Colonel Arnold.

About 1900 hours we were all taken to a dining room and were served several Chinese dishes and some canned meat and fruit from packages from home. Although the Chinese food was good, it was the American food that delighted us. Throughout the entire meal photographs were being taken. After the meal they set up a ping-pong table and there were also small tables off to the side where we could write letters or play cards. On each small table there was a pan containing candy, apples, tangerines and cigarettes. Some of us sat and shot the bull; some played cards; others pretended to write letters. All the while the photographers were snapping pictures.

The next morning, 10 January, we discussed the party and the possibility of being freed. We all felt we had been deceived. Most of us were sorry and disgusted with ourselves for having allowed our pictures to be taken. We figured they would be used for propaganda. The Chinese would claim that the prints prove they are humane and lenient and treat their prisoners well. The thing that really upset us was that many people would be naive enough to believe it.

On 20 January our guard "Bugs" informed us that the Chinese government had invited our loved ones to visit us in Peking and that the US State Department had refused to let them come. The Chinese wanted us to write to our loved ones and encourage them to come. As we discussed the matter everything became clear. What the Chinese were after was a touching reunion at which they could release us into the custody of our loved ones. What ideal propaganda material such a scene would provide! Such a humanitarian move would accomplish three things: soften world opinion, efface any charges of barbaric and inhumane treatment we might register, and make our denials of border violation useless. Most of us agreed that we would rather rot in Red China than do anything which would devalue our denials and help the enemy. We wanted the whole world to know how rotten the communists were and that they shanghaied us and brought us into Red China by force and were holding us against our will. On 22 January we wrote home and urged our loved ones not to visit us in Red China under any circumstances. I wrote the return address as usual spelling peace with an "ie" instead of an "ea".

During the last week of the month we saw a white man on the patio. He was brought out about the same time every day. He appeared to be about fifty or so, wore glasses, had greyish hair and whiskers and was wearing the same coloured blue padded clothing as us. We also saw another man on the patio. He was tall, about six feet two or better, dark hair, crooked nose, and looked English. He was dressed in the same type of black padded clothing that we were given just before our trial. We continued to watch these two men. One day we succeeded in attracting the older man's attention; we called him Abuelo. He looked up at the window and smiled. Then he went through the motions of boxing. He was being guarded too closely to risk communicating with us.

We saw the two men quite often. Abuelo would look up at the window and smile every opportunity he had. We would stand on a bed board and wave to him and go through all kinds of contortions in sign language trying to tell him who we were. When he walked around the patio in a circle, and as he approached the window of our cell, we would talk louder to each other so that he could hear us. He would give an affirmative nod as he passed by the window. We tried the same on the other man, but always with the same result – nothing. He continued to walk with his chin on his chest and paid no attention to us. Occasionally we thought we saw a slight smile on his lips, but we were never sure we were getting through to him.

Later on Easter Sunday afternoon we saw Abuelo sitting under the tree directly across from the window of the cell next to our large cell. This small cell was used for storage. Thompson and I went into the small cell to get a better look and to try to talk to the old man. Schmidt watched for our guard and houseboy. We hissed to attract Abuelo's attention. He glanced up at the window and smiled. He told us he had been very sick. He said he was from New Zealand and was arrested in 1950. He was tried, found guilty and sentenced to one year by the People's Tribunal. He told us that his treatment was very poor.

At 1900 hours on Sunday, 31 July we were escorted across the prison to a building somewhere near the administration building. We waited outside and in about five minutes Colonel Arnold joined us. We were taken inside and we filed into a room in the same order as at the Peking courthouse. We remained standing in front of a desk behind which two Chinese officials were seated. One of them spoke; he told us that our case had been reviewed and that since the People's Republic of China is lenient towards those who have confessed their crimes they had decided to free us because of our good behaviour.

After they calmed us down they took us to the dining hall and served us a good Chinese dinner. From there we returned to the cellblock to pick up our belongings. Then we were taken to the train station and departed Peking at about 2330 hours. We stepped across the line into Hong Kong and into the most welcome arms of the British MPs at 1336 hours on 4 August 1955.

In Washington DC we were debriefed by both Air Force Intelligence and Civilian Intelligence. The sessions were conducted almost daily from 0800 to 1700 hours. They asked me hundreds of questions pertaining to our mission, our capture, our interrogations, our treatment at the hands of our captors, our three weeks with Downey and Fecteau and our seeing other Americans or allies, including Van Voohris. In these debriefing sessions I passed on the message Fecteau had given me concerning both Jehol and Samurai. [Jehol was the name of the town where the nine CIA trained Kuomintang agents were dropped two weeks prior to Downey and Fecteau's ill-fated mission on the night of 29 November 1952. Samurai was the code name assigned to their operation of training and inserting agents into Manchuria.] I was admonished to keep silent about this and about the other Caucasians I had seen. The other crewmen received the same warning. I was told that both Downey and Fecteau knew what they were getting into before they signed their contract and that the US government and the CIA would not recognise or even admit they were American citizens. As far as the US government and the CIA were concerned these two men did not exist. It's ironic: very few

The Arnold crew released by the Chinese in August 1955, two years after the end of the Korean War. Front to rear: *Major William Baumer, Captain Elmer Llewellyn, Captain Eugene Vaadi, 1st Lt Wallace Brown, 1st Lt John Buck, A/2C John Thompson, A/1C Steve Kiba (last man on the path). Two of the crew, 2nd Lt Henry Weese and 1st Lt Paul Van Voohris, both radarmen, were kept by the Chinese and never released.*

247

Americans knew about these unfortunate men, but the enemy knew every minute detail about them and their mission. And what's the big secret about the other Caucasians being detained?

These warnings greatly upset me. I liked and admired Downey and Fecteau. Weese and Hart were crew members and good friends. I didn't know Van Voorhis too well because he was an officer and I was an enlisted man, but I still considered him a friend. I was pretty certain that Hart was killed in his tailgun position when the MiGs attacked. I knew that both Weese and Van Voohris bailed out – crewmen in the rear of the aircraft saw them jump. I knew they were captured alive as soon as they touched the ground as numerous Chinese interpreters and inter- rogators boasted about it. I knew that Van Voohris was alive as of late July, early August 1953. I saw him.

It disturbed me to know there were still fellow Americans sitting in a Red Chinese political prison, their minds and bodies slowly but surely wasting away. It also disturbed me to find out that our own government was going to sit idly by and allow this to happen. It is a fact that Red China and North Korea did indeed hold American servicemen after the Korean conflict and it is a fact that the US government knew this and still abandoned these brave, loyal men to a life of never-ending misery and agony in a communist hell-hole somewhere in North Korea, Red China or the Soviet Union.

The American public, too, must share in the guilt for failing to voice their ire and disgust over this deplorable policy. Each and every American citizen owes it to our missing prisoners and to their families to join in a concerted effort to secure the release of the living and to obtain a full, accurate and complete accounting of the deceased. The patient, courageous MIA families have a right to know the truth about the fate of their loved ones. It is a disgrace, a blight on American history and a slap in the face of our founding fathers to send our young men off to war, risking life and limb, and then turn our backs on them if they are unfor- tunate enough to be captured and made prisoners of war.'

NINE

THE FORGOTTEN SOULS

WHERE DID ALL THE SABRE PILOTS GO?

During the Korean War a total of fifty-six F-86 aircraft were downed in aerial combat or by anti-aircraft artillery, and from these fifteen live pilots and one set of remains were repatriated. For the forty others the circumstances of loss indicate a high probability of death in nine cases. Of the remaining cases conditions were such that survival was possible. This missing in action rate of 55 per cent is unusually high when compared to the missing rates for pilots flying other types of aircraft. Is this entirely unexpected? The F-86 was a new type of aircraft and it is reasonable to expect that the Soviets would have wanted to obtain live pilots and an intact aircraft for intelligence purposes. If the Soviets wanted to defeat the F-86 they had to learn all they could about the aircraft and the manner in which it was flown.

Proof that Soviet intelligence was targeting F-86 pilots came from an unlikely source. Corporal Nick Flores was one of the Marines taken prisoner at Koto-ri in November 1950. He was one tough customer, resisting his captors at every opportunity and attempting to escape on three occasions. His last escape took place on 22 July 1952 from Camp 1 (Chongsong) and he was at liberty for ten days. Before he left, his fellow prisoners rallied round and gave him various articles of clothing that would help ensure his survival in the harsh terrain. He was given air force boots, overalls and a flight jacket with US Air Force on the front.

Flores originally led a dozen men out of the camp, but the majority decided to return due to sickness, wounds or fear. Flores and one other pressed on, but six days into their escape they agreed to split up and go their separate ways in order to increase the chance of one of them reaching friendly lines. Flores wanted to head westwards towards the coast in the hope of contacting the US Navy which was operating off shore near Sinuiju.

On the morning of 1 August the Marine's luck ran out and before he knew it he had walked into a camouflaged anti-aircraft position overlooking Sinuiju. The guns were manned by Caucasians wearing 'clean' uniforms and speaking Russian. One of them, presumably an officer, addressed Flores in English with 'You are the American pilot,' and ordered him bound and blindfolded. The Marine expected to be returned to his camp for punishment, but found himself bundled into a truck and driven across the twin bridges at Sinuiju to Antung in Manchuria. At Antung he was taken into a building where his escort officer turned him over to someone else, saying again in English, 'Here is the American F-86 pilot.' He then met a translater and an interrogator, who introduced himself as a Soviet colonel. In the background he heard the noise of several other people who appeared to be listening to the interrogation.

Over the next four hours Corporal Flores continued to insist that he was a Marine enlisted man and an escaped prisoner of war. However, his US Air Force uniform told another story and the Soviets clearly thought him to be an aviator. What he was unaware of at the time was that shortly before he stumbled upon the anti-aircraft site another American had been in that area. At 0920 hours Major Felix Asla, USAF, flying his F-86 in the vicinity of Sinuiju's twin bridges, was bounced by MiGs and was last seen spinning towards the south-east. Major Asla was never seen again, but at that time the Russians must have thought that Flores was the missing pilot.

The Russian interrogator insisted that Corporal Flores confess he was an F-86 pilot and demanded to know which squadron he flew with and the location of their airfield. He also repeatedly asked Flores about his knowledge of germ warfare, adding ominously that 'All the other pilots confessed' and he should as well. After four hours another person entered the room and spoke to the interrogator in Russian. The Soviet colonel was audibly distressed and halted the interrogation. Flores was taken to another room and a 'nurse' asked him if he needed any medical help. She asked several questions, posed as if he was a pilot, but then left the room when he insisted he was not.

After about eighteen hours, during which he was not physically mistreated or abused, the Marine was helped aboard another truck, still blindfolded. Once on the truck the blindfold was removed and he could see the earth-covered bunker in which he had been held. It was on a major airfield with rows of MiGs parked nearby. He was then driven back across the Yalu River and returned to Camp 1.

The treatment of Corporal Flores is significant in that it demonstrates that the Soviets had a special handling procedure for pilots, especially F-86 pilots. Captured pilots would be taken directly to a Soviet interrogation site, completely bypassing the normal prisoner-of-war camps. The pilots would not be mistreated, or at least not while there was a possibility of the interrogator gleaning the required intelligence by cooperation.

Regarding the fate of the missing F-86 pilots, a 26 August 1993 report on 'The Transfer of US Korean War POWs to the Soviet Union' compiled by the Joint Commission Support Branch, Research and Analysis Division of the DPMO came to the following conclusions:

'(1)   The Soviets had a programme of the highest priority to capture F-86 aircraft and pilots for technical exploitation.

(2)   The Soviet forces in North Korea had seventy teams whose mission was the recovery of US pilots. The Chinese turned pilots over to Soviet officers as a matter of policy.

(3)   Soviet policy was to establish a veil of deniability over the transfer of prisoners by taking them directly after capture to the Soviet Union. Such prisoners were never mixed with the general POW population in North Korean or Chinese hands.

(4)   There is no record of repatriated US POWs who were transported to the Soviet Union for technical exploitation and then repatriated.

(5)   The Soviet forces in Korea devised and executed a plan to force down at least one intact F-86.

(6)   Intact F-86 aircraft and at least one pilot were delivered to the Sukhoi and Mikoyan Design Bureaux for exploitation.

(7)   A number of POWs, notably including F-86 pilots, were transferred by air to the Soviet Union for exploitation of their technical knowledge.

(8)   The evidence suggests that the Soviets had a special interest in the MIAs shown on Table One [in the report] and specifically Captain Albert Tenney and First Lieutenant Robert Neimann. There is a good chance that Captain Tenney and his aircraft were transferred to the Soviet Union for exploitation.'

It is now believed that Captain Albert G. Tenney, USAFR, was captured alive and taken, together with his aircraft, to Moscow. Tenney's flight was making a high-speed descent over North Korea when it was attacked by enemy aircraft. The aircraft was seen to dive away from an enemy MiG fighter and execute evasive manoeuvres at an extremely low altitude. He was informed of his low altitude and was instructed to pull up. Immediately thereafter he levelled the wings of his F-86 which then struck the surface of the water in a low-angle high-speed glide approximately three miles offshore near the mouth of the Yalu River. Enemy aircraft forced the leader to leave the area and he did not see whether the aircraft sank into the water or not. When search aircraft returned to the scene later that day they could find no trace of the aircraft or pilot. In recent years information has been received from the Sukhoi and MiG Design Bureaux that at least two examples of the F-86 were sent to Moscow and one of these was full of sand. The pilot is believed to have accompanied the aircraft.

Other pilots had a good chance of surviving the loss of their plane, including Captain Robert H. Laier, USAF, who was declared missing in action on 18 June 1951. He was participating in a four-ship fighter sweep in the area of Sinuiju when he came under attack from enemy aircraft. When last seen his aircraft was seriously damaged, trailing smoke and in a steep dive at approximately 10,000 feet, thirty kilometres south-east of Sinuiju. An aerial search for his aircraft wreckage was unsuccessful. A subsequent unofficial Chinese propaganda broadcast supports a belief that he survived the shootdown and was captured.

First Lieutenant Laurence C. Layton, USAFR, was also declared missing in action, on 2 September 1951. A few minutes after arriving in the target area the flight engaged in combat with a number of enemy fighters. During the mêlée Layton's F-86 was hit. He radioed that he was going to try to reach the north-west coast of Korea and bail out. Another member of the flight accompanied Layton and observed him parachute from the damaged aircraft near the mouth of the Chongchon-Gang River, roughly six miles off the coast. Subsequent information reveals that Layton is believed to have been rescued by a large enemy powerboat.

First Lieutenant Charles W. Rhinehart, USAFR, was declared missing in action too, on 29 January 1952. During a combat mission over North Korea Rhinehart's F-86 experienced a flameout and all attempts to restart the engine were unsuccessful. At an altitude of 4,000 feet he was seen to successfully parachute from the plane and land in water off the mainland amid an area of numerous sand and mudflats some twenty-five miles south of Chongju, North Korea. A subsequent aerial search of the area failed to locate any trace of the pilot. He would have been an ideal candidate for MGB (later KGB) interrogation as he had studied aeronautical engineering at Iowa State College, had gone through USAF All-Weather Interceptor Aircrew Training and conversion training on the F-86-4 model, the newest variant of the Sabre at that time.

RETURN TO PYOKTONG

Private First Class Roger Dumas was taken prisoner while serving with the 24th Division on 4 November 1950. His brother Robert was also in the army and he was puzzled when he did not come home after the armistice was signed in 1953. For years the army told Robert that his brother's records had been lost in a fire and he could not possibly have been a POW in Korea. Eventually Robert painstakingly tracked down men who had been in Camp 5 with his brother. One of them told him that Roger was still alive at the end of the war, but on the day they were due to be exchanged he was pulled out of line and taken away. He was never seen again.

In 1982 Robert Dumas filed suit in the Federal Court to have his brother, who had been officially presumed dead in 1953, officially re-declared a prisoner of war. The judge eventually found for Dumas and ordered that, although the presumptive finding of death should remain in force, all army records should be changed to reflect the fact that PFC Roger Dumas was in fact a prisoner of war.

One of the men who testified that he had known Roger Dumas in the prisoner-of-war camp was Walter EnBom, a forward observer for an artillery brigade of the First Cavalry Division. Not only that, he had met Dumas twice. In 1955 EnBom re-enlisted, but in the US Air Force, and he was sent back to serve in South Korea. While on patrol along the demilitarised zone on 8 August 1956 EnBom and six other US troops were captured by the North Koreans. They were held for fifteen months, and during that time EnBom was returned to Pyoktong, a city on the Yalu River and the site where so many POWs were held during the war. There EnBom saw Roger Dumas again.

PFC Roger Dumas was being held in the Pyoktong jail and seemed to be physically well, but his mind was gone. He did not know his name or where he was, and he did not recognise EnBom. Not only that, there were between fifteen and twenty other American and British prisoners in the jail. They told him that they had not been repatriated at the end of the war.

Nowadays Walter EnBom keeps his mouth shut. He is so afraid of offending the US government and military that he now denies being in Korea, or being a prisoner of war, or of knowing Roger Dumas. In the meantime what has happened to the unfortunate souls being held in Pyoktong jail?

GHOSTS IN THE GULAG

While there is no doubt that the Russians made use of some of the United Nations prisoners of war for intelligence purposes – to turn them into spies for the Soviet Union, to pick their brains for technical information and to use others for medical experimentation – for others the gulag awaited. The vast network of labour camps stretching across Siberia held tens of millions of condemned souls. Most were Russian civilians or citizens of the Baltic countries annexed by Russia; some were German or Japanese prisoners from World War II; but among them were many foreigners.

Gleaning information from inside Russia during the early 1950s was no easy task. All communication and travel was controlled by the government and anyone who spoke out of turn was soon silenced. Some information did come out though, via refugees, smugglers, secret agents or diplomats friendly to the west. One of the collecting points of such information was the journalist Zygmunt Nagorski Jr, the general manager of the Foreign News Service, an organisation which specialised in gathering news from behind the Iron Curtain.

In May 1953 the journal *Esquire* published an article on 'Unreported GIs in Siberia' by Nagorski and the theme was that American soldiers captured by communist forces in Korea had been shipped to the Soviet Union to work in slave-labour camps, or to train as communist propaganda agents. The article read:

'We have almost forgotten about it by now, but a totally unexpected shock hit this nation on 15 November 1951. Morning newspaper headlines screamed the delayed news of a mass killing of American POWs by the Chinese and Korean communists. The report was by Colonel James M. Hanley, Judge Advocate General of the Eighth Army. It accused the enemy of slaughtering more than 2,500 captured American soldiers, and it gave details: names, dates and places.

General Ridgway, then our commander in Korea, was surprised to learn that Colonel Hanley's report had roused a fury of public opinion at home. To him it was an old story. In December 1950 he had sent to Washington a film which showed the recovered bodies of American prisoners shot in the back of the skull and buried with their hands still tied behind their backs. This murder of prisoners was not even a new communist tactic; during World War II several thousand Polish officers had been killed by the Russians in the Katyn Forest, and their bodies thrown into a mass grave. They, too, had been killed by bullets fired from behind; their hands, too, had been tied behind their backs.

In fact, by the time Colonel Hanley's report was issued the communists had changed their tactics. Up to April 1951 I received many reports indirectly from Korean and Chinese natives who had witnessed mass shootings of captured UN troops. Up to that time the Chinese and North Korean forces were harsh and brutal in their treatment of POWs. Then the orders, from Peiping [Peking] or from Moscow, changed. From that time onward GIs were treated as usable human material.

Our best information is that large numbers of Americans are now living in camps scattered in the various republics of Russia. The coordinating centre for these camps seems to be the city of Molotov. North-east of Molotov, in the area commonly known as north-western Siberia, Americans have been seen in at least six camps and other American POWs have been reported from camps situated on the Pacific coast of

Siberia, in Khabarovsk and in the towns of Chita and Omsk, both on the Trans-Siberian Railroad.

Molotov, formerly known as Perm, lies west of the Ural Mountains and has been an industrial centre since the early eighteenth century. The headquarters of the Soviet political police contains a large prison and American POWs have been kept there for periods of screening and interrogation.

South Korean prisoners were being sent to isolated camps in the Yakutsk Autonomous Soviet Republic. Many officers were being sentenced to fifteen to twenty-five years in labour camps.

All other UN prisoners are sent to camps located on the Chinese side of the Yalu River where they are interrogated by Chinese and Russian officers who speak perfect English. These officers conduct the first screening where American air force officers, artillerymen, tank special-ists and other technicians are separated from the rest and sent to special camps.

In June 1952 I heard descriptions, without names or locations, of two of the camps. At that time about 900 non-Korean POWs, mostly Americans and some British and Turks, were housed in the two camps. Each camp had about 450 men divided into units of fifty or sixty. The communists were trying their best to make their captives feel at ease. Food was decent, the daily routine was light and there was plenty of recreation. Books and magazines were available in English, French, Russian and German. Battle films, usually featuring villages and cities bombed by UN planes, were shown every night. Instruction in the Russian language was available to anyone who wanted it and short discussion sessions with camp political officers were held three or four times a day.

Various delegations visited the camps and tried to influence the opin-ions of the captives, including various peace committees, local schoolchildren, women's societies etc. The Yalu camps, however, play host to the GIs for only a few weeks. Then the political officers, who formerly led discussions on world events, now begin conducting daily interrogations and within a day or two they know which prisoners they want.

Most of the men are settled in ordinary POW camps in North Korea or China, but those suspected of anti-communism and those in whose remarks the officers see possibilities of conversion to the communist faith are turned over to the Russians. They are marked as dead on the official POW lists.

We know that last June, in the "Gajsk Camp" near Chermoz, about 200 Americans were used as forced labour. Every day a few men from each camp are taken to Molotov, where the Russians make further attempts to get them to cooperate. They never return to the camps they have left, but some probably wind up in Shivanda, a small place near Chita. This camp caters to a very few men who the communists consider worthy of special treatment. It is a luxurious undertaking with good food, clean accommodation and general conditions far above anything known by the average Russian. The selected few stay at the camp for a period of four to five weeks and then either graduate and receive an assignment or fail and return to the labour camps.

From Shivanda, the road is wide open to Moscow. Most of the few who take that road start their work by giving lectures on new American weapons, strategy, political trends and psychological warfare to select groups of Red Army officers. The others are used in various propaganda drives. Three American officers captured in Korea have made good-will visits to Warsaw, Sofia and Bucharest, bringing greetings to the peoples of Poland, Bulgaria and Romania from the American prisoners of war peace committee.'

Confirmation of these reports came from various sources. An army Combined Command for Reconnaissance Activities Korea memorandum of 24 February 1953 stated:

'The following information was received from Ministry of Foreign Affairs, Republic of Korea Government. Report originated from Nationalist Chinese Embassy. According to reliable information, the Communist Chinese Forces have transferred UN POWs to Russia in violation of the Geneva Conference. These POWs will be specially trained at Moscow for espionage work. POWs transferred to Moscow are grouped as follows: British 5, Americans 10, Canadians 3, and 50 more from various countries. Russia has established a Higher Informant Training Team at Uran in Siberia in October 1952. Five hundred persons are receiving training, one third of them women, Koreans, Filipinos, Burmese and American.'

CCRAK comments on the memorandum read:

'This office has received sporadic reports of POWs being moved to the USSR since the very inception of the hostilities in Korea. These reports came in great volume through the earlier months of the war, and then tapered off to a standstill in early 1951, being revived by a report from January of this year [1953]. It is definitely possible that such action is being taken as evidenced by past experience with Soviet authorities. All previous reports state POWs who are moved to the USSR are technical specialists who are employed in mines, factories etc. This is the first report that they are being used as espionage agents that is carried by this office.'

This may have been news to US Intelligence in February 1953, but it certainly was old hat by the time another year had passed and the repatriated prisoners of war had been debriefed. It was discovered that at least seventy-five of the returned US prisoners had agreed to spy on behalf of the communists. One British diplomat, George Blake, actually offered his services to his captors and became one of the most notorious spies who ever worked inside the British government. How many others were taken to Russia and persuaded to work for the KGB? British and American intelligence organisations must have a good idea, but of course they are not telling.

One person who did eventually let the cat out of the bag was Russian Premier Boris Yeltsin, who admitted in 1991 that Americans had been imprisoned in the Soviet Union during World War II and that others had been shot down during the Cold War. As a result of this Task Force Russia was formed to look into the allegations and to work with Russian researchers to ascertain the fates of these men. The Task Force would eventually be wound up after it became clear that the Russians were not telling the whole truth and were withholding vital information on American prisoners. The KGB were extremely reluctant to reveal any of the skeletons in their cupboards, but that did not stop some brave Russians from coming forward with information.

Lieutenant-General Yezerskiy stated that he had seen four to five Americans in Vorkuta, between 1954 and 1956. These individuals were at the time all in their early to mid-twenties. He said he thought they were all from the World War II period, but that they could have been from the Korean War.

In October 1992 Mikolai Dmitriyevich Kazersky contacted Task Force Russia and told them about an American he had met in one of the camps. Kazersky had been decorated twice in the Great Patriotic War, but had later been sentenced to twenty years' imprisonment. He was eventually released in the general amnesty following Stalin's death, but while in a camp called Zimka he met a US Korean War POW from California. The man said he was an American pilot shot down in North Korea, forced to land near Vladivostok. His radioman had also been in the camp, but had been moved elsewhere. The description of the pilot was a close match for Captain Ara Mooradian, who was reported missing in action on 23 October 1951.

A repatriated Japanese prisoner of war from Camp 21 at Khabarovsk reported a number of rumours about American POWs. He had heard from a camp guard that two Americans had been brought to Khabarovsk prison and were being investigated as spies. He had also heard from Soviet guards, prisoners and labourers in April and May 1953 that twelve or thirteen Americans, crew members of a military plane shot down by the Soviets, were in a Khabarovsk prison. Again he heard from prisoners in 1951 or early 1952 that an American fisherman, captured in the Gulf of Alaska, was brought to the Magadan region. Finally a guard on a Soviet prisoner train at No. 2 Station, Khabarovsk, had told him in about June 1952 that there was a prison camp in the USSR for Americans only.

In August 1993 Task Force Russia members interviewed Mr Boris Uibo in Estonia. He stated that in 1952 he served with an American Korean War POW in Camp 18, a close-hold camp for foreign prisoners near Potma in Mordova. The American's name was Gary or Harry and, according to Uibo, was definitely an American shot down in the Korean War. The two men worked together making wooden chess pieces. Uibo stated that there was a concerted effort by the Soviets to hide the fact that they were holding foreign prisoners.

In April 1993 Mr Povilas Markevicius of Vilnius, Lithuania, wrote to the Task Force to say that in the spring of 1952 he had met two American prisoners while imprisoned in Kemerovo Oblast. The Americans said they had been sentenced to twenty-five years' imprisonment. He described the one he had conversations with in poor Russian as about 170 to 173 centimetres tall, of swarthy complexion and with dark hair. The other American was taller with auburn hair. The main topic of conversation was always escape. One rainy and windy night in the spring the Americans actually did escape. Usually when escaped prisoners were caught their dead bodies were put in the middle of the square to threaten others. However, he did not see any dead bodies after this incident.

Although President Eisenhower knew full well that American prisoners were being kept by the Russians there was little he could do about it. One estimate at the time was that war with Russia would cause eight million casualties. Perhaps, when Stalin eventually died, the new Soviet leadership may have decided that the American prisoners were a liability and they may have ordered their elimination. On the other hand, they may not. The fact remains, though, that the Russians know a lot more than they are telling and the Americans and British are loath to push too hard to find out the awful truth.

THE CZECH MILITARY HOSPITAL

General Major Jan Sejna defected from Trieste to the United States in late February 1968. He was no ordinary army officer. Prior to his defection he was a member of the Czech Central Committee, which he had helped establish in 1956 and which is the top decision-making body, higher than the Politburo, in matters of defence, intelligence, counterintelligence, deception and internal security in the communist system. He was a member of the Main Political Administration that watches over the entire establishment and of its governing bureau. He was First

Secretary of the Party at the Ministry of Defence, Chief of Staff to the Minister of Defence and a member of the Ministers Kollegium. He was also a member of the military section of the Administrative Organs Department and was on a wide variety of government and party committees. Jan Sejna was therefore one of the seven or eight most knowledgeable individuals at the top of the Czech tree. He was personally responsible for monitoring many of the most sensitive operations and for disseminating Defence Council decisions and operational instructions. He was also the primary Ministry of Defence interface with the Soviet Union.

When such a personality begins to tell you about a military hospital that was built in North Korea specifically for experimenting on American prisoners of war, you sit up and listen. Soon, you believe.

The purpose of the hospital was to use the prisoners as guinea pigs to test a wide range of experimental mind-control and behaviour-modification drugs, to test biological and chemical warfare agents, to expose them to lethal and sub-lethal effects of atomic radiation and to determine how much physical and psychological stress the American soldiers could endure in contrast to the Asians, who were also among the guinea pigs. Another aim of the hospital was to give doctors experience in battlefield amputations. Yes, they would perform amputations on healthy prisoners just to give the doctors some practice. A crematorium was also built nearby to dispose of the body parts and the soldiers themselves when they were no longer required.

The exact location of the hospital is not known, but the author is sceptical about its location being in North Korea. To build such a facility inside North Korea would have been a decidedly risky proposition. It was very unlikely that the United Nations would fight their way back to the Yalu River again and thus uncover the hospital on the way, but one thing is sure, and that is that North Korea was bombed daily by the US Air Force and a few well-aimed bombs could have put paid to the facility. It may have been constructed underground, of course, but then again locating it inside the borders of China or the Soviet Union would have guaranteed its anonymity and security.

The hospital was designed for 200 'patients', although it was often overcrowded and at one time contained 600 patients. No patients were known to have left the hospital alive, except roughly a hundred who were still alive at the end of the war and who were shipped back to the Soviet Union through Czechoslovakia for more testing, apparently in four plane loads. They stopped in Prague and were given medical examinations before being sent to various experimental medical test facilities in the Soviet Union. This was done so that the Russians could deny that prisoners were sent from North Korea to the Soviet Union.

The existence of the hospital came to light through Dr Joseph D.

Douglass Jr of the DIA, who has extensively debriefed General Major Jan Sejna. Not only did Douglass's employers, the DIA, know about the hospital, but so did the Senate Select Committee for POW/MIA Affairs because Douglass sent a six-page memo to the committee chairman and vice-chairman in 1992. Instead of these bodies keeping the knowledge secret until it could be checked and verified, the DIA and CIA took action to discredit Sejna and sabotage efforts to learn more. The DIA asked the CIA to contact the Czech Intelligence Service, which was the worst possible thing they could have done. Not only did it alert the enemy to the 'leak' but it came at a time when the KGB was known to be active in finding sources and silencing them.

What put the DIA and CIA into a spin when the story of the hospital came to light in 1992? Possibly it was the fact that Jan Sejna had first told the CIA about the facility when he initially defected, in 1968. Not only that, he was not just talking about Americans from North Korea being used in experiments, but also American pilots taken prisoner in Vietnam during the 1960s and 1970s, shipped to the Soviet Union for similar experimentation. What should the DIA and CIA have been doing with the information? Surely they should have been covertly pursuing every lead in order to establish the fate of these poor men and to establish whether or not any were still alive – and if so, to plan their rescue.

In May 1956 Sejna was appointed Chief of Staff to the Minister of Defence. Not long afterwards General Major Kalashnik from the Soviet Main Political Administration came to Prague to discuss the importance of non-military weapons. Sejna was present at the meeting when Kalashnik discussed five important examples of such weapons: ideological offensive, which meant good deception and propaganda; good foreign policy designed to split the West; isolating the United States; economic and social chaos; and a new view about drugs and other chemicals that can affect the minds and behaviour of millions of people. Kalashnik's lecture was followed by a request for the Czechs to provide medical support for the experiments that were being run on American POWs in the Soviet Union.

The Czech response was prepared by Sejna, working with the Minister of Defence. The project was top secret and roughly fifteen Czech doctors and scientists were involved. They were sent initially to the Soviet Institute for Nuclear Medicine in Moscow, because their cover story was that they had gone to study the effects of nuclear war on soldiers. Their real mission, however, was to investigate the effects of chemical warfare agents and drugs, biological organisms and nuclear radiation on the captive GIs.

The results of the examinations were pored over annually. One item discussed was side-effects of the various drugs. These were irreversible, and where the prisoners were judged to be of no further value because of the side-effects, they were killed. Only a few were retained to see if the side-effects would eventually disappear and a few may have been placed in mental institutions for long-term observation.

As far as radiation was concerned the Soviets were searching for drugs which would enable soldiers to continue fighting even after having received lethal radiation exposures. Not only were captive GIs irradiated by radio isotopes and by the atomic reactor at the Institute for Nuclear Medicine in Moscow, but they were secured at spaced intervals along the ground in nuclear test ranges and subjected to the full force of actual atomic bomb explosions. As early as 1963 specialists within the US Atomic Energy Community knew that Soviet knowledge of the effects of high levels of radiation exposure on humans was greater than US knowledge.

In 1960 the Chief of the General Staff of the North Vietnamese Army visited Prague and Moscow looking for military assistance to fight the Americans. The Soviets agreed to supply weapons in return for a continued supply of prisoners of war with which to continue the medical experimentation. This was agreed and a new supply of guinea pigs was assured.

One interesting fact did emerge during the prisoner repatriations at the end of the Vietnam War in 1973: 586 American prisoners of war came home, most of them pilots or aircrew who would have suffered a wide range of injuries as they left their stricken planes to parachute to the ground. Not one amputee came home. Were such operations carried out at special military hospitals that may also have been conducting medical experiments?

THE ROMANIAN ENGINEER

In 1979 Mr Surban Oprica, a Romanian engineer, was sent to North Korea to help build a television factory. It was the first factory of its kind in North Korea and it was to be built not far from Pyongyang. He worked six days a week and on Sundays his North Korean hosts would take the guest workers on cultural trips to museums. One day in 1980 they went to the Museum of International Friendship, a six-storey temple-like building containing thousands of gifts given to Kim Il Sung by foreign dignitaries. Inside the museum, he said, he saw parts of American soldiers: limbs, hands, heads etc. They were preserved in some sort of liquid – perhaps formaldehyde. Other American items such as uniforms and flags were also on display.

During an earlier day-trip in early November 1979 he had seen something else which prompted him to volunteer to appear before the Senate hearings on prisoners of war and missing in action. There were fifteen or twenty Romanians on the bus that day. During the journey they saw a camp and fields where cabbage was growing. As they passed by Oprica saw 'a person with a European face, with blue eyes, very close to the bus. And I was very shocked. And everybody on the bus was shocked. And I was looking behind him and I saw seven or ten people with Caucasian faces. And behind them I saw more people working in the camp.' What Surban Oprica believed he saw that day was American prisoners of war working in the fields twenty-six years after the end of the Korean War.

THE STONEY BEACH REPORT

Other reports have come out of North Korea in recent years. On 31 December 1991 the commander of the US 501st Military Intelligence Brigade in Seoul sent a two-page information report to the Joint Chiefs of Staff in Washington DC. The subject was United Nations POW/MIA sightings in North Korea. A copy of the heavily censored report was sent to the author, and it read:

'This is a Stoney Beach Report. It provides information on the appearance of former American, British and Italian prisoners of war in the Democratic People's Republic of Korea. (DPRK). [Two lines censored.] Among the films [censored] played in is a fifteen-part series called "The Nameless Heroes", which was filmed from about 1978 to 1983. The series is about the heroic efforts of DPRK espionage agents to defeat the aggressive US invaders during the Korean War from 1950 to 1953. According to the source, the parts of the United Nations forces were played by US, British and Italian POWs. [Next three paragraphs censored.] Source is a DPRK defector who was repatriated back to the DPRK [censored].'

The report seems to suggest that the defector was perhaps an actor who also took part in the films. Maybe he was a North Korean plant, following a script written by his masters in Pyongyang. If the defector was indeed seeking asylum and he was sent back to North Korea, his fate can be imagined. How genuine is the report, and why was the defector sent back whence he came? Disturbingly, the last line of the report contains a warning that the report is classified confidential – not releasable to foreign nationals. Does that include British and Italian intelligence agencies? Surely they would like to know if any of their missing prisoners of war had turned up thirty years after the end of hostilities.

THE SEARCH FOR REMAINS

One of the items in the armistice agreement concerned the right for graves registration teams to enter North Korea to recover the remains of UN soldiers, both from established cemeteries and the battlefield. In the event the teams were not allowed into North Korea. The North Koreans would do the work themselves, and in 1954, during Operation 'Glory', they returned some thousands of sets of remains. However, the searching had been haphazard and most of the remains were un-identified. A total of 854 unknown remains are now interred in the National Memorial Cemetery of the Pacific in Hawaii, known as 'The Punchbowl'.

Between 1954 and 1990 there was no progress whatsoever in persuading the North Koreans to return remains of UN servicemen lost in the conflict. Then in 1990 and 1991 the Democratic People's Republic of Korea unilaterally recovered and turned over sixteen sets of remains to Senator Robert Smith and Representative G. V. 'Sonny' Montgomery. In 1992 another thirty sets of remains were repatriated through United Nations Command.

Following the signing of a UNC–North Korean People's Army agree-ment on remains repatriation, seventeen more sets were returned in July 1993, 131 in December 1993 and fourteen more in September 1994, making a total of 162. All the remains were sent to the army Central Identification Laboratory in Hawaii (CILHI) where they are under-going analysis for possible identification. So far only seven of the 208 remains have been identified due to the inexperienced recovery tech-niques of the KPA. Their procedures resulted in remains commingling and mismatched identification media, making identification problem-atic. At the time this book went to print, DNA samples were being gathered from family members to try to aid the identification process. Any British family members who have relatives missing in Korea are invited to contact the author for further information.

In 1994 DPRK's president, Kim Il Sung, unexpectedly accepted former president Jimmy Carter's proposal to permit joint recovery oper-ations. Progress was slowed by the North Korean demand for four million dollars in compensation for returning the 162 remains in 1993 and 1994. Eventually the US government agreed to pay 'reasonable' costs and two million dollars was agreed in May 1996.

The initial discussions with North Korean representatives focused on three areas: investigations into reported sightings of alleged Americans living in North Korea; access to North Korean military archives and museums to recover data about Americans held as POWs during the war; and setting a schedule for resuming joint excavations to recover American remains buried in North Korean cemeteries and other sites.

The talks in May 1996 ended with an agreement focused only on joint excavations.

Two months later a recovery team went into North Korea in search of remains. Three sites were to be investigated over a twenty-day period in Unsan County in north-west North Korea, where heavy fighting took place between the American 8th Cavalry and Chinese forces. At one location they were taken by local villagers to an overgrown foxhole and discovered the remains of Army Corporal Lawrence J. LeBoeuf. His comrades later recalled that he was hit when their unit was overrun in November 1950 and presumably died of his wounds. The fact that he was identified suggests that he was still wearing his dog-tags or carrying other identification. Victims of atrocities or death marches usually had these things taken away by their executioners, to make future identification difficult.

Deputy Assistant Secretary of Defense for POW/MIA Affairs James W. Wold was quoted as saying, 'There are more than 8,100 American servicemen missing in action from the Korean War. We expect to find at least 3,500 of them, but until we get there we really don't have a good feel for what those numbers might be.' At the moment the recovery teams are prohibited from visiting the sites of former prison camps and the areas covered by the various death marches. There is clearly a long way to go yet.

At least six Americans defected to North Korea in the 1960s, 1970s and 1980s, and at least four are still alive and living in North Korea. Permission to interview them has so far been refused.

At the current time North Korea, one of the world's last bastions of communism, is facing severe food shortages and malnutrition due to problems caused by the tightly controlled, centralised systems used by the police state. Severe flooding has also contributed to widespread famine, although the North Korean military forces do not seem to have been affected by these problems. They have the world's fourth largest army with 1.2 million troops and half of these are stationed along the demilitarised zone. Their arsenal includes chemical and biological weapons and long-range missiles, and they are working hard to acquire nuclear capability. Fifty years have passed since the beginning of that tragic war and the peninsula still has a long way to go to find lasting peace.

HOME AFTER FORTY-FIVE YEARS

Thus read the newspaper headlines on 16 December 1998. Two South Koreans listed as missing in action in the Korean War had escaped from communist North Korea after more than forty years in captivity. Park

Dong Il (seventy-one) and Kim Bok Ki (seventy-seven) flew home from a 'third country', believed to be China, where they had been hiding since their escape early last year. The two men were taken prisoner by Chinese troops during the closing stages of the war in 1953 and handed over to the North Koreans. They spent several years in a prisoner-of-war camp near the North Korean capital of Pyongyang and were then forced to work in a coal mine in the north of the country. Their escape route was probably across the frozen Tumen River, the same route taken earlier last year by Chang Mu Hwan, one of only three other South Korean POWs to escape the northern coal mines. South Korea claims that more than 20,000 of their POWs remain unaccounted for, of whom 130 are still believed to be alive.

And so the story continues. The armistice has held for almost fifty years, but true peace is a long way off yet. If the current joint recovery operations continue in North Korea a steady stream of remains are guaranteed, although the identification process needs drastic improvement. This book has detailed many of the war crimes and atrocities that took place between 1950 and 1953, but so far we have only written half the story. It is certain that American, British, South Korean and other Allied troops were still alive and in Chinese, North Korean and Russian hands at the end of the war. The majority are probably long dead, buried outside Siberian labour camps or in secret KGB research facilities. Perhaps one or two aged troopers are still working in far-away paddyfields in China or North Korea, having long ago given up all hope of seeing their country or loved ones again. We may never know. Perhaps one day the dusty KGB files in Moscow will give us the answers, but by then it will be too late. Too late for a rescue mission to succeed, too late for ransoms to be paid and too late for negotiations to bring the survivors home. In recent years the Soviet Union has been given billions of dollars in aid; did anyone think to add a clause to the agreement that the KGB files on foreign prisoners be opened at the same time? How many lost souls were condemned to sit in cold, dark cells dreaming of the sound of helicopters overhead and the pounding of Marines' boots in the corridor outside? The men fought as best they could, and when they became prisoners of war their governments turned their backs and abandoned them. That is the greatest atrocity of them all.

APPENDIX ONE

British Prisoners of War – Totals
From *The British Part in the Korean War Vol. II* by Anthony Farrar-Hockley.

	RN	RM	Army	RAF	Total
Repatriated	4	18*	955	1	978
Known to have died as a POW	–	9†	62	–	71
Presumed to have died as a POW	–	1	9	–	11
Total identified as having been taken prisoner					1,060

* Not including Condron, who opted to remain behind.
† Includes members of the Royal Navy – for example, sick berth attendants serving with the Royal Marines.

Notes
(1) Those 'known to have died as prisoners' were identified as such by repatriated POWs.
(2) Those 'presumed to have died' were identified as having been alive when captured, but who were neither declared thereafter by the communist side or known of by other UN prisoners of war.

Appendix Two

Prisoners of War Exchanged during Operations 'Little Switch' and 'Big Switch'
From page 484 of Farrar-Hockley, op. cit.

National origin	Little Switch	Big Switch	Total
United States	149	3,597	3,746
Republic of Korea	471	7,862	8,321
British Commonwealth			
Australia	5	21	26
Canada	2	30	32
New Zealand	–	1	1
South Africa	1	8	9
United Kingdom	32	946	978
Belgium	–	1	1
Colombia	6	22	28
France	–	12	12
Greece	1	2	3
Netherlands	1	2	3
Philippines	1	40	41
Turkey	15	229	244
Total United Nations	684	12,773	13,457
North Korea	5,640	70,183	75,823
China	1,030	5,640	6,670
Total Communist forces	6,670	75,823	82,493

Notes

(1) North Korean totals include 9,350 civilians interned, including twenty-three children. Of the remaining prisoners of war, 491 were women.

(2) Chinese prisoners included one woman.

(3) Canadian figures do not include Sqdn Ldr A.R. MacKenzie, who was held in China until 5 December 1954 when he was released through Hong Kong.

(4) A total of 22,604 North Korean and Chinese prisoners held by the United Nations opted initially not to be repatriated. Of these, 188 North Koreans and 440 Chinese decided to return to their own side. Fifteen and twenty-three respectively died while still under Indian custodial control; twelve and seventy-four elected to settle in India. Finally, 7,604 North Koreans and 14,235 Chinese elected to return to UN control, the Koreans ultimately passing to the Republic of Korea, the Chinese to the Kuomintang in Taiwan.

(5) Among the UN prisoners in the communist camps, 359 held by the communists declined repatriation (335 ROK, twenty-three US, one UK). After discussions within the custodial system, 325 Koreans, twenty-one Americans and one Briton elected to stay with the communist side, though the latter returned home later. Of the balance, two Koreans elected to go to India, eight Koreans and two Americans returned to the United Nations side.

APPENDIX THREE

British Army Personnel Killed or Presumed to have Died with no Recorded Burial Location

Number	Rank	Name	Unit	Date of Death
(a)	(b)	(c)	(d)	(e)
7013974	Cpl	ADAIR W	RUR	03.01.51
	Lieut	ADAMS-ACTON L S, MC	RNF	16.07.53
	Lieut	ALEXANDER C G	8th King's RIH	03.01.51
22583039	Fus	ALLEN G F	R Fus	25.11.52
22370578	Pte	ALLUM S A W	Gloster	23.04.51
	Major	ANGIER P A	Gloster	23.04.51
21011606	Pte	APTER L G	KOSB	04.11.51
22443865	Pte	ARMOUR W	KOSB	04.05.52
4344850	Pte	ARNO H	E Yorks	03.01.51
19040867	Spr	BALDWIN R A	RE	25.04.51
21125643	Pte	BAILEY H	R Leics	17.10.50
22530139	L/Cpl	BALLS D A	Gloster	23.04.51
14405268	Pte	BARBER D N	Gloster	25.04.51
13021614	Pte	BARCLAY F T	Gloster	24.04.51
14437187	Fus	BASTABLE L	RNF	03.05.51
21015246	Cpl	BISHOP L J	Gloster	23/24.04.51
22331783	Fus	BLOORE T E	RNF	25.04.51
22274867	Pte	BOATMAN P S	A & SH	23.09.50
22187748	Pte	BOTTEN R	Middx	27.10.50
14453219	Pte	BOWL V T	Gloster	03.07.51
22525626	Rfn	BRANNAN T	RUR	25.04.51
22539087	Fus	BROADWAY S D	RNF	25.04.51
3711805	Rfn	BROWN D, MM	RUR	25.04.51
22499550	L/Cpl	BROUGHTON C	King's	21.04.53
22420069	Pte	BUCKLEY D H	R Leics	05.11.51
6290618	Rfn	BUNBY M B	RUR	27.07.51
22356516	Pte	BURNHAM H	R Leics	05.11.51
14466141	Rfn	BUSTARD J C	RUR	15.01.51
4454278	Rfn	BUTCHER J	RUR	22.02.51
	Lieut	CABRAL H C	Gloster	27.11.51
5049612	Pte	CAIN J	Gloster	24.04.51
22525876	Fus	CANNON J W	RNF	03.01.51
22774275	L/Cpl	CARWOOD R D	DLI	22.11.52

Number	Rank	Name	Unit	Date of Death
(a)	(b)	(c)	(d)	(e)
22220588	Fus	CASPER T H	RNF	06.10.51
14191554	Gnr	CAWOOD G	RA	04/05.01.51
22447341	Pte	CHAMBERLAIN R	R Leics	05.11.51
71440	Pte	CHITTY N F	Gloster	25.04.51
14122252	Rfn	CLARKE C D	RUR	25.04.51
4041595	Pte	CLARKE C	Gloster	26.04.51
22421043	Pte	CLAYTON J	R Leics	05.11.51
22332701	Pte	CLUTTERBUCK F M	Gloster	26.04.51
22198188	Pte	COLLIER C H	Middx	27.10.50
7942522	Sgt	COLLINGS E R	8 Hussars	03.01.51
22249526	Tpr	COLLISON J	8th King's RIH	04.01.51
22530176	Pte	COOK R B	Gloster	23.04.51
22348454	Pte	CORNISH D A	Gloster	24.04.51
21127508	Rfn	CRAIG D	RUR	25.06.51
14478109	Pte	CRELLIN R	KOSB	04.11.51
14403670	Gnr	CURTISS T L	RA	04/05.01.51
14190507	Cpl	DAVIDSON W	RUR	01.06.51
22492807	Pte	DELLOW P J	Black Watch	19.11.52
6290154	Pte	DIX W E	Gloster	24.04.51
4468299	Pte	DONALDSON W J	Gloster	09.06.51
22422620	Pte	DOWIE T M	KOSB	04.11.51
	Lieut	DUNLOP V A	King's	25.04.51
22432734	Fus	DUTTON P	RNF	06.10.51
14456901	Pte	EDMUND W A M	KOSB	04.11.51
22459535	Pte	EDMUNDS J	Welch	21.07.52
4272098	Fus	EKE A	RNF	23.04.51
5049608	Pte	ETHERINGTON P J	Gloster	25.04.51
14189817	L/Cpl	FIELDING A	A & SH	23.09.50
22346580	Pte	FLUCK D G	Gloster	13.06.51
22377075	Pte	FOSTER D M	KOSB	04.11.51
5583656	Rfn	FOSTER M	RUR	03.01.51
	2/Lt	GAEL B S	Gloster	17.06.51
22289532	Pte	GALLOP B G	Gloster	01.08.51
3857481	Rfn	GARNER H W	RUR	04.01.51
6977940	Sgt	GAW D	RUR	25.04.51
1427414	Gnr	GIBSON T F	RA	23.04.51
22096764	Pte	GILDING R A	Gloster	25.04.51
22539421	Cpl	GILLELAND B J	King's	24.06.53
	Capt	GLEN C H	DWR	29.05.53
22233422	Rfn	GOULDSBOROUGH C	RUR	25.04.51
19035231	Pte	GRAY C G	Gloster	23.06.51
22348472	Pte	GRAY R T	Gloster	29.06.51
4758377	Gnr	GRAYSTON N	RA	04/05.01.51
22287002	Pte	GUDGE K G	Gloster	24.04.51
22433517	Pte	HALDANE T	KOSB	04.11.51
22559889	Sgt	HALL E M	Int Corps	31.03.52
22522209	Pte	HARRIS G H	Gloster	05.06.51
22273326	Pte	HARRISON W E	Gloster	01.05.51

Number	Rank	Name	Unit	Date of Death
(a)	(b)	(c)	(d)	(e)
893476	Gnr	HARRISON R	RA	04/05.01.51
22231688	Spr	HARVEY R	RE	01.05.51
3598814	Rfn	HEELEY S	RUR	04.01.51
14447894	Rfn	HILL B N	RUR	06.01.51
5989281	Pte	HILL Y N	Gloster	25.04.51
22530111	Pte	HILTON F B	Gloster	26.04.51
22420640	Pte	HOBBS A E	KOSB	04.11.51
	Capt	HOLMAN W M, MBE	RA	03.01.51
22341335	Pte	HONE P D	Gloster	24.04.51
3598090	Rfn	HOWARTH H	RUR	07.09.51
5570070	Pte	HUGHES R W	Gloster	25.04.51
22488586	Pte	HYDE F C	Black Watch	19.11.52
22304253	Pte	JONES D G E	Gloster	25.04.51
5123706	L/Cpl	KAIN J	RNF	25.04.51
14190918	Sgt	KAVANAGH L	RUR	04.09.51
14187325	Rfn	KENNEDY T	RUR	03/04.01.51
22267354	Fus	KENYON F	RNF	05.11.51
22295024	Cpl	KERR J F	KOSB	04.11.51
6846356	Rfn	KERR J J	RUR	19.07.51
14470871	Pte	KINNE R	A & SH	17.10.50
22462423	Pte	KIRK W	Black Watch	06.07.52
14474759	Fus	LANGLEY D	RNF	25.04.51
22666363	L/Cpl	LAVENDER R A	R Fus	28.06.53
22189576	L/Cpl	LEE G L S	Gloster	25.09.51
1609936	Fus	LEONARD C G	RNF	06.10.51
22247826	Cpl	LEVETT J S	8th Hussars	18.08.51
	2/Lt	LOCK J M	RAOC	09.11.50
14465525	Rfn	LYONS E B	RUR	--.08.51
22249497	Pte	MADGWICK E G	Gloster	01.05.51
19033341	Rfn	MAHER D	RUR	28.09.51
22144108	Pte	MAILE A D	Middx	20.07.51
7014112	Rfn	MARTIN R	RUR	22.04.51
2066117	Cpl	MAYCOCK P J	Gloster	25.04.51
7014124	Rfn	McCRACKEN R J	RUR	04.01.51
3599032	Rfn	McCURRIE P	RUR	26.02.51
13111735	Pte	McDONNELL P J	Acc	04.01.51
14455197	Pte	McHALE C	A & SH	04.11.51
14190414	Pte	McHARDY C	A & SH	21.10.50
22417209	Pte	McKAY T G	KOSB	04.11.51
22417269	Pte	McKENDRICK R	KOSB	04/05.11.51
22422589	Pte	McLACHLAN J C L	KOSB	04.11.51
	Lieut	McMILLAN-SCOTT A H F	KOSB	04.11.51
7043191	Rfn	McWILLIAMS W	RUR	12.04.51
22366609	Pte	MEIKLE D	KOSB	04.11.51
14467055	L/Cpl	MEW D D	Gloster	21.09.51
21071500	Pte	MILLS C	W Yorks	07.07.51
22511786	Rfn	MONTGOMERY S	RUR	23.04.51
1609997	Pte	MORLEY J	Gloster	24/25.04.51

Number	Rank	Name	Unit	Date of Death
(a)	(b)	(c)	(d)	(e)
4448675	WOII (CSM)	MORRIS J	KOSB	04/05.11.51
22184326	Pte	MORRISS E C	Gloster	25.04.51
14470966	Pte	MORTON R F	KOSB	05.11.51
22219421	Rfn	MULLAN S B	RUR	25.04.51
6983997	Rfn	MURRAY J W	RUR	04.01.51
22525638	Fus	MURRAY K C	RNF	25.04.51
14473932	Cpl	MUSGRAVE R F	KOSB	04.11.51
14462575	Sgt	NORTHLY D	Gloster	22.04.51
7013525	Sgt	NUGENT F	RUR	18.04.51
22461469	Pte	O'GARA M	R Leics	05.11.51
22580314	Pte	O'NEILL P	King's	13.04.53
14189156	Pte	PAGE D O	Middx	27.10.50
22530239	Pte	PEARCE A K	Gloster	25.04.51
22457096	Pte	PENNINGTON F	R Leics	05.11.51
14459082	Pte	PENROSE M C W J	Gloster	01.06.51
22463590	Pte	PERFECT R M	R Norfolk	24.07.52
5107891	Sgt	PHILLIPS A, MM	R Warwick	05.11.51
19090813	Pte	PHILPOTT W	R Sussex	01.05.52
6979710	Rfn	PORTER J	RUR	25.04.51
5110764	Cpl	POSSEE W D	Gloster	26.04.51
22366067	Pte	PRICE J D	KSLI	17.11.51
	Lieut	PROBYN D F P C	8th King's RI Hussars	08.02.51
22493860	Fus	PRYOR A R	R Fus	01.12.52
	Lieut	RADCLIFFE E L W	DLI	16.04.53
6979786	Rfn	REIDY M	RUR	02.08.51
22273903	Spr	RENNIE R A	RE	25.04.51
3856991	Rfn	RIDING G	RUR	25.04.51
	2/Lt	ROBERTS W K	Leics	05.11.51
22380289	Pte	RODGER J H	KOSB	05.11.51
22525246	Fus	ROOMES E	RNF	03.01.51
410466	2/Lt	RUDGE G D	Cheshire	25.04.51
22137489	Gnr	RUSSELL A W	RA	25.04.51
	Lieut	SANDER G	Middx	30.10.50
5885232	Pte	SHELTON F W	Gloster	01.08.51
22198632	Pte	SHEPPARD A J	Gloster	26.04.51
14421345	Cpl	SHORT J E	Gloster	24.04.51
22341319	Pte	SKOINES J B	Gloster	24.04.51
22370442	Pte	SMITH D	A & SH	04.11.51
5437816	L/Cpl	SMITH R A	RUR	18.07.51
22232031	Pte	SMITH W	RAOC	19.11.52
22586750	Fus	SNARE J M	R Fus	25.11.52
11410044	Gnr	SNELL G A	RA	23.09.51
	2/Lt	ST CLAIR-MORFORD P A	KSLI	07.02.52
22392194	Pte	STEPHENS M L	KSLI	18.11.51
	Major	STEPHENSON P B, MBE	King's	01.12.52
22432744	Pte	SUGDEN R	R Leics	05.11.51
3856975	Rfn	SUTTON W	RUR	11.03.51

Number	Rank	Name	Unit	Date of Death
(a)	(b)	(c)	(d)	(e)
1469820	Pte	SYNNOTT W F	Gloster	24.04.51
22411038	Pte	SYRON J R	R Leics	05.11.51
949846	Gnr	TAPLIN L G	RA	03.01.51
5569912	L/Cpl	TAYLOR I J	Gloster	24.04.51
22314975	Fus	TAYLOR J	RNF	25.04.51
22574004	Cpl	THOMPSON J H	DWR	20.05.53
19034856	Cpl	THURLOW G M	DWR	29.05.53
14417408	Rfn	TICE A E	RUR	28.05.51
22447332	Pte	TOPPING H S	R Leics	05.11.51
22530194	Pte	TUCKER H F E	Gloster	23.04.51
14186737	Rfn	TWEEDIE J	RUR	25.04.51
22522457	Pte	WALKER D	W Yorks	19.11.51
	Capt	WASHBROOK R F	RA	21.11.51
	2/Lt	WATERS T E, GC	W Yorks	01.06.51
22229890	Pte	WEBSTER J C	RAMC	23.04.51
1429896	Fus	WELLMAN W C	RNF	25.04.51
22360963	Pte	WELLS D	KSLI	17.11.51
22504484	Fus	WHATLEY N O	R FUS	25.11.52
22249692	Pte	WHITMORE L	R Warwick	17.11.51
1439092	Rfn	WILCOX W	RUR	04.01.51
22584567	Cpl	WILLIAMS J R	R Fus	10.11.52
22368876	Fus	WILLIAMSON A	RNF	06.10.51
22459565	Pte	WILLICOMBE K J	Welch	03.08.52
22329595	Pte	WINTER D W	Gloster	24.04.51
5672255	Rfn	WOODHOUSE W J	RUR	04.01.51
	2/Lt	WORMALD J	R Norfolk	30.05.52
22406521	Pte	WRIGHT J	KOSB	04/05.11.51
14470458	Gnr	WRIGHT L	RA	03.01.51
22787802	Pte	WRIGHT T W	DWR	29.05.53
22540417	Spr	WYLIE C L	RE	25.04.51

Number	Rank	Name	Unit	Date of Death	Remarks
(a)	(b)	(c)	(d)	(e)	
22207636	Gnr	BARWICK R J	RA	08.07.50	Buried at sea
7265169	Pte	COLEMAN C B	RAMC	02.10.50	Lost overboard
19039541	Sgt	FINCH B	Middx	09.07.50	Buried at sea
22602797	Spr	HURST A C	RE	31.07.53	Missing, believed drowned
14191203	Gnr	JENSON K	RA	08.07.50	Buried at sea
1931911	Cpl	LONG S G	Middx	09.07.50	Buried at sea
14184609	Cpl	MASKELL A H	R Sussex	31.01.53	Buried at sea
880249	Sgt	MERSH F T	RA	08.07.50	Buried at sea

Appendix Four

Declassified Reports and Correspondence

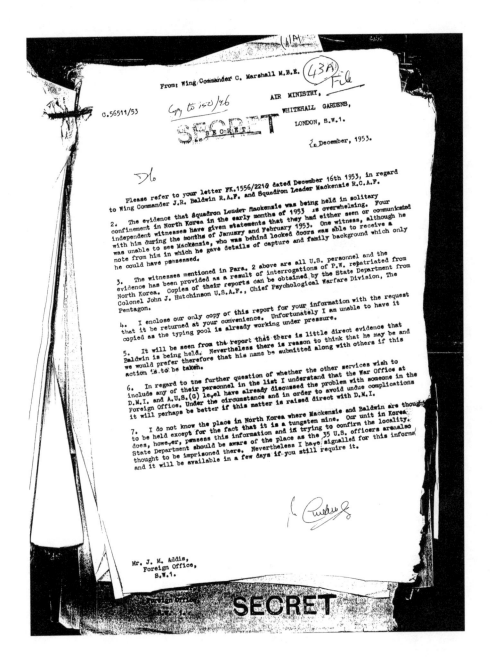

From: Wing Commander C. Marshall M.B.E.

AIR MINISTRY,
WHITEHALL GARDENS,
LONDON, S.W.1.

C.56511/53

SECRET

2ª December, 1953.

Please refer to your letter FK.1556/221@ dated December 16th 1953, in regard to Wing Commander J.R. Baldwin R.A.F. and Squadron Leader Mackenzie R.C.A.F.

2. The evidence that Squadron Leader Mackenzie was being held in solitary confinement in North Korea in the early months of 1953 is overwhelming. Four independent witnesses have given statements that they had either seen or communicated with him during the months of January and February 1953. One witness, although he was unable to see Mackenzie, who was behind locked doors was able to receive a note from him in which he gave details of capture and family background which only he could have possessed.

3. The witnesses mentioned in Para. 2 above are all U.S. personnel and the evidence has been provided as a result of interrogations of P.W. repatriated from North Korea. Copies of their reports can be obtained by the State Department from Colonel John J. Hutchinson U.S.A.F., Chief Psychological Warfare Division, The Pentagon.

4. I enclose our only copy of this report for your information with the request that it be returned at your convenience. Unfortunately I am unable to have it copied as the typing pool is already working under pressure.

5. It will be seen from the report that there is little direct evidence that Baldwin is being held. Nevertheless there is reason to think that he may be and we would prefer therefore that his name be submitted along with others if this action is to be taken.

6. In regard to the further question of whether the other services wish to include any of their personnel in the list I understand that the War Office at D.M.I. and A.U.S.(G) level have already discussed the problem with someone in the Foreign Office. Under the circumstance and in order to avoid undue complications it will perhaps be better if this matter is raised direct with D.M.I.

7. I do not know the place in North Korea where Mackenzie and Baldwin are thought to be held except for the fact that it is a tungsten mine. Our unit in Korea does, however, possess this information and is trying to confirm the locality. State Department should be aware of the place as the 35 U.S. officers are also thought to be imprisoned there. Nevertheless I have signalled for this information and it will be available in a few days if you still require it.

Mr. J. M. Addis,
Foreign Office,
S.W.1.

SECRET

1. *Secret British Air Ministry letter to the Foreign Office sent three months after the end of the prisoner exchanges in Korea. The letter discusses British Wing Commander J R Baldwin and Canadian Squadron Leader A Mackenzie being held in a Tungsten Mine with 35 American officers. Mackenzie was released by the Chinese two years later. The others never came home.*

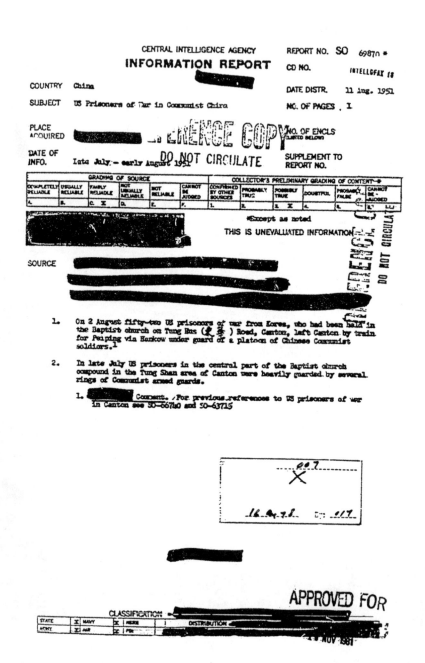

CENTRAL INTELLIGENCE AGENCY

INFORMATION REPORT

REPORT NO. SO 69870 *

CD NO. INTELLOFAX 18

COUNTRY China

DATE DISTR. 11 Aug. 1951

SUBJECT US Prisoners of War in Communist China

NO. OF PAGES 1

PLACE ACQUIRED

DATE OF INFO. late July - early August 1951

SUPPLEMENT TO REPORT NO.

*Except as noted

THIS IS UNEVALUATED INFORMATION

SOURCE

1. On 2 August fifty-two US prisoners of war from Korea, who had been held in the Baptist church on Tung Hua (東華) Road, Canton, left Canton by train for Peiping via Hankow under guard of a platoon of Chinese Communist soldiers.1

2. In late July US prisoners in the central part of the Baptist church compound in the Tung Shan area of Canton were heavily guarded by several rings of Communist armed guards.

   1. Comment. For previous references to US prisoners of war in Canton see SO-56740 and SO-63715

2. Declassified CIA report number SO69870 dated 11 August 1951 reporting the movement of 52 US prisoners of war by train from Canton to Peiping (Peking) under guard. None of them returned home.

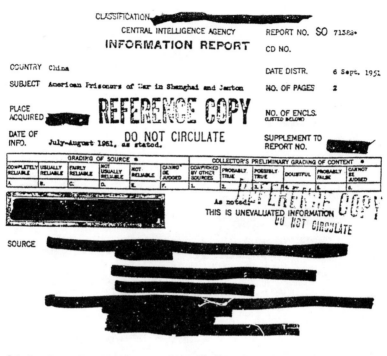

CENTRAL INTELLIGENCE AGENCY

INFORMATION REPORT

CLASSIFICATION

REPORT NO. SO 71388

CD NO.

COUNTRY China

SUBJECT American Prisoners of War in Shanghai and Canton

PLACE ACQUIRED

DATE OF INFO. July–August 1951, as stated.

DATE DISTR. 6 Sept. 1951

NO. OF PAGES 2

NO. OF ENCLS. (LISTED BELOW)

SUPPLEMENT TO REPORT NO.

THIS IS UNEVALUATED INFORMATION

SOURCE

B-6 1. Names of more American prisoners of war at the camp on Yuyuen Road, Shanghai are the following:

Fa-hsing (發興): Major, adviser to 30 Regiment, 9 Division.

K'o-lin-ssu (柯林斯): Air liaison officer, Chinese division (sic).

Pei-k'o (貝克): Captain, 29 Regiment.

Shih-lai-te (世萊得): Major.

Ta-erh-ti (大尔弟): Air Force Lieutenant.

The date of this information is 15 August 1951.

B-3 2. As of mid-July about 60 American prisoners of war were being held in the former villa of CH'EN Chi-t'ang at Plum Blossom Village in Canton. They were given two meals daily of the same food Chinese Communist soldiers receive and were being given daily political and ideological training. Their guards were drawn from the garrison regiment of 15 Army Group Command Headquarters.

F-6 3. The Chinese Communist 4 Field Army under the command of LIN Piao has selected a group of United Nations prisoners of war who can speak Mandarin or Cantonese and sent them to Canton. About 126 such prisoners have arrived in Canton, including 13 Americans, 8 British, and 105 South Koreans. More than 40 were in the first group of arrivals, and the remainder came later in another group. The American and British prisoners are confined in the former USIS office in Shameen, Canton. They are restricted to the building, but are receiving

CLASSIFICATION

Document No. 009
No Change in Class.
☐ Declassified
Class. Changed To: TS S C
Auth.: HR 70
Date: Aug 24 By: 015

3. Declassified CIA report number SO71388 dated 6 September 1951 reporting the discovery of 60 American prisoners of war at Plum Blossom Village in Canton, China. Item one lists the names of five American prisoners of war in Shanghai, including a Captain from the 29th Infantry Regiment. None of them came home.

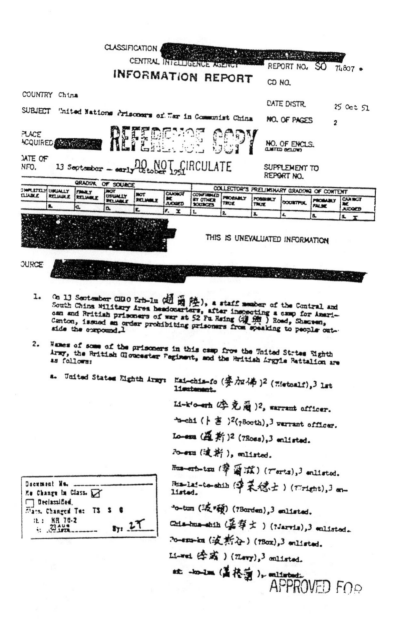

4. *Declassified CIA report number SO74807 dated 25 October 1951. Item one states that local people have been forbidden to talk to American and British prisoners of war held in a compound at 52 Fu Hsing Road, Shanghai. Item two lists the names of some of the British and American prisoners held in the camp including 1st Lt Metcalf, Warrant Officer Booth and enlisted men Ross, Wright, Jarvis and Borden. None of whom came home.*

By ~~Boylan~~ NARA, Date 11/20/85

FOREIGN SERVICE DESPATCH

DO NO~~T~~ ~~TY E~~ IN THIS SPACE

6/1,95a.241/3-20

FROM   AMCONGEN, Hong Kong

1716
DISP. NO.

TO   THE DEPARTMENT OF STATE, WASHINGTON.

March 23, 1954

REF

SUBJECT: American POWs Reported en route to Siberia

A recently arrived Greek refugee from Manchuria has reported seeing several hundred American prisoners of war being transferred from Chinese trains to Russian trains at Manchouli near the border of Manchuria and Siberia. The POWs were seen late in 1951 and in the spring of 1952 by the informant and a Russian friend of his. The informant was interrogated on two occasions by the Assistant Air Liaison Officer and the Consulate General agrees with his evaluation of the information as probably true and the source as of unknown reliability. The full text of the initial Air Liaison Office report follows:

First report dated March 16, 1954, from Air Liaison Office, Hong Kong, to USAF, Washington, C2.

"This office has interviewed refugee source who states that he observed hundreds of prisoners of war in American uniforms being sent into Siberia in late 1951 and 1952. Observations were made at Manchouli (Lupin), 49°50'-117°30' Manchuria Road Map, AMSL 201 First Edition, on USSR-Manchurian border. Source observed POWs on railway station platform loading into trains for movement into Siberia. In railway restaurant source closely observed three POWs who were under guard and were conversing in English. POWs wore sleeve insignia which indicated POWs were Air Force noncommissioned officers. Source states that there were a great number of Negroes among POWs shipments and also states that at no time later wore any POWs observed returning from Siberia. Source does not wish to be identified for fear of reprisals against friends in Manchuria, however is willing to cooperate in answering further questions and will be available Hong Kong for questioning for the next four days."

Upon receipt of this information, USAF, Washington, requested elaboration of the following points:

1. Description of uniforms or clothing worn by POWs including ornaments.
2. Physical condition of POWs.

~~DNForman/RDYoder/jme~~   ~~SECRET~~

INFORMATION COPY

5. *Declassified Secret despatch from US Embassy Hong Kong to State Department in Washington, DC, concerning a refugee report of a train load of US prisoners of war seen at Manchouli on the USSR-Manchurian border in late 1951. The evaluation of the report was 'probably true'. The men were heading for Siberia and two more train loads would follow them.*

No. 947

The Embassy of the United States of America
presents its compliments to the Ministry of Foreign
Affairs of the Union of Soviet Socialist Republics
and has the honor to request the Ministry's assistance in the following matter.

The United States Government has recently received reports which support earlier indications
that American prisoners of war who had seen action
in Korea have been transported to the Union of Soviet
Socialist Republics and that they are now in Soviet
custody. The United States Government desires to
receive urgently all information available to the
Soviet Government concerning these American personnel
and to arrange their repatriation at the earliest
possible time.

American Embassy,
Moscow. April 5. 1954.

6. *5 April 1954 note from the American Ambassador in Moscow to the Soviet Ministry of
Foreign Affairs requesting information on reports of US prisoners of war in Soviet custody. The
Soviets denied holding the men. The note was declassified in 1986, 32 years after it was sent.*

BIBLIOGRAPHY

Books;

Anderson, Ellery. *Banner over Pusan*. Pub Evans Bros 1960.

Appleman, Roy. *Disaster in Korea*. Pub Texam A&M University Press 1989.

Davies, Sam. *In Spite of Dungeons*. Pub Hodder & Stoughton. 1954.

Farrar-Hockley, Anthony. *The British Part in the Korean War Vol 1 and 2*. Pub HMSO 1990.

Farrar-Hockley, Anthony. *The Edge of the Sword*. Pub Frederick Muller 1955.

Holles, Robert. *Now Thrive the Armourers*. Pub George Harrap 1952.

Hoyt, Edwin. *The Pusan Perimeter*. Pub Stein and Day 1984.

Jolidon, Laurence. *Last Seen Alive*. Pub Inkslinger Press 1995.

Kestner, Franklin. *To the Last Man*. Pub Westernlore Press 1991.

Kinne, Derek. *The Wooden Boxes*. Pub Frederick Muller 1955.

Large, Lofty. *Soldier Against the Odds*. Pub Mainstream 1999.

O'Kane, Henry. *O'Kanes Korea*. Pub privately South Lodge, Honiley CV8 1NP.

Zellers, Larry. *In Enemy Hands*. Pub University Press of Kentucky 1991.

Thinking Soldiers – by men who fought in Korea. New World Press, Peking. January 1955.

Documents;

Report by Henry Cabot Lodge, Jr to UN General Assembly 26 November 1953 ref A/2563 on '*Question of atrocities committed by the North Korean and Chinese Communist Forces against United Nations prisoners of war in Korea*'.

Booklet '*Treatment of British prisoners of war in Korea*'. Ministry of Defence 1955. 41 pages. Written testimony of Steve Kiba submitted to Senate Select Committee on PoW-MIA Affairs for 11-10-92 hearing.

Extract of Interim Historical Report, Korea War Crimes Division, Judge Advocate Section, cumulative to 30 June 1953. Pentagon library ref DS920.8.U58 c.3.

Pamphlet No 30-101 '*Communist interrogation, indoctrination, and exploitation of prisoners of war*' by Department of the Army. May 1956.

INDEX

Page reference in bold type denotes photograph.
Page reference in italic type denotes map.